THE TARGET BOOK

D1614685

Bromley Libraries

30128 80008 764 8

THE
TARGET
BOOK

The History of the Target Doctor Who Books
David J Howe with Tim Neal

First published in England in 2007 by

Telos Publishing Ltd

61 Elgar Avenue, Tolworth, Surrey, KT5 9JP, England

www.telos.co.uk

Telos Publishing Ltd values feedback. Please e-mail us with any comments you may have about this book to: feedback@telos.co.uk

Previously published in a different form in *Doctor Who Magazine* Issues 291, 293, 295, 297, 299 and 301

ISBN: 978-1-84583-021-2 (softcover)

ISBN: 978-1-84583-023-6 (hardcover)

Text © 2000, 2001, 2007 David J Howe, Tim Neal

Foreword © 2007 Terrance Dicks

All illustrations and sketches are the copyright of the individual artists.

Bromley Public Libraries	
DEL	
30128 80008 764 8	
Askews	14-Nov-2008
070.509421 COL	£19.99

The moral rights of the authors have been asserted.

Int ... layout by Arnold T Blumberg

www.atbpublishing.com

Printed in India

2 3 4 5 6 7 8 9 10 11 12 13 14 15

British Library Cataloguing in Publication Data.

A catalogue record for this book is available from the British Library.

This book is sold subject to the condition that it shall not by way of trade or otherwise, be lent, resold, hired out or otherwise circulated without the publisher's prior written consent in any form of binding or cover other than that in which it is published and without a similar condition including this condition being imposed on the subsequent purchaser.

DEDICATION

Dedicated to the memory of Richard Henwood who died on 28 May 2003.

ACKNOWLEDGEMENTS

FIRST OF ALL, MY THANKS TO GARY GILLATT AT *DOCTOR Who Magazine* for commissioning the series of articles that form the backbone to this book. All the pieces have been revisited, revised and expanded from their original appearance in the *Magazine*.

I'd like to thank Chris Achilleos (www.chrisachilleos.co.uk), Peter Brookes, Jeff Cummins (www.jeffcummins.com), Peter Darvill-Evans, Terrance Dicks, Val Edwards, Brenda Gardner, Elizabeth Godfray, Richard Henwood, Barry Letts, Tony Masero, David McAllister, Brian Miles, Alister Pearson, Nigel Robinson, Dom Rodi, Andrew Skilleter (www.andrewskilleter.com) and Bob Tanner, all of whom provided help and shared their memories of their involvement in the *Doctor Who* Target book range with me.

Some quotes from Richard Henwood are taken from an article written by him for the *Doctor Who* Appreciation Society magazine *Tardis* and are used by kind permission of the author. Book and publication information is extracted from *Howe's Transcendental Toybox: The Unauthorised Guide to Doctor Who Collectibles* by David J Howe and Arnold T Blumberg. Some references are from Tim Neal's comprehensive *On Target* website at www.targetbooks.info.

With thanks to Virgin Publishing and BBC Worldwide for research assistance.

Additional thanks for this edition go to, first and foremost, Tim Neal for his support and assistance with every aspect of this book. His website at www.targetbooks.info continues to be the definitive resource. Also thanks to Julian Knott, Russell Cooke, Tony Clark, Roy Knipe, Marcus Hearn, Glen McCoy, Gary Russell, Bill Donohoe (www.billdonohoe.com), Colin Howard (www.colinhowardartwork.com), Pete Wallbank (www.petewallbank.org.uk), Ian Burgess, Steve Kyte, Derek Handley and Mark Bentham.

David J Howe

CONTENTS

FOREWORD 8

INTRODUCTION 11

PART ONE: THE TERROR BEGINS 13

PART TWO: TAKEOVER.. 25

PART THREE: JOURNEY INTO PERIL 41

PART FOUR: PRISONERS OF SUCCESS............... 59

PART FIVE: THE FINAL BATTLE 81

PART SIX: COUNTDOWN TO DOOM................... 109

CODA 135

APPENDIX A: OTHER TARGET RANGES.......... 138

APPENDIX B: THE DOCTOR WHO LIBRARY ... 144

APPENDIX C: OFF TARGET 148

APPENDIX D: COVERS FOR THE TELEVISED STORIES... 154

INDEX 166

FOREWORD

AVID AND TIM'S EXCELLENT BOOK BROUGHT BACK many memories of Target days – besides telling me a lot I'd forgotten or never known. Much of what I feel, or felt, about the series, you'll find in the text. However …

What strikes me most in retrospect is the amazing casualness with which it all began. This tall, thin, beaky-nosed enthusiastic character called Richard Henwood turned up in the office demanding more *Who* books. Despite several years' steady employment as *Who* script editor, I was still a freelance at heart – never turn down the chance of a job! Despite a total lack of qualification – I'd written scripts for radio and television, but never any books – I volunteered.

We decided on 'Spearhead from Space' as the first of my novelisations.

'Don't like that title,' said Richard loftily. 'Change it to *Doctor Who and the Auton Invasion*.'

This shows how unimportant the books were at first. It was all very small beer – a minor part of a minor children's list by a minor publisher. Titles were changed arbitrarily, the books appeared in any old order. Later all this was to change as the books became steady best-sellers. In time, the *Who* novelisations swallowed Target Books, and the publishers as well. By the time W H Allen had taken over the list, and was itself up for sale, it was widely acknowledged that the company's main, if not only, asset, was the *Doctor Who* list.

When I eventually left *Doctor Who*, the novelisations were my lifeline. They provided what every freelance needs – a steady stream of work. With a wife, three children and the mortgage on a big old ruin in Hampstead, I needed it more than most.

For a few golden years, everything was wonderful. I was still writing most of the books, and large cheques seemed to arrive by every post. Later, as I tell in the book, the tax bills arrived … Still, it was a great time while it lasted.

There was another fringe benefit. Editors, particularly *Who* editors, seem to have short life-spans – in the job, that is. They move on. With any luck, when they move, they want you to write for them.

'You don't lose an editor,' I always used to say. 'You gain a publisher!'

First was Richard Henwood himself. I'd already done a series for him called *The Mounties* – Richard's idea. 'What children want is good old-fashioned adventure!' he insisted, though I had my doubts. Still the books sold reasonably well – even in Canada. Richard's move to Blackie meant more work for me. More successful than *The Mounties* was a series about crime-solving kids, *The Baker Street Irregulars*, and a series of supernatural stories.

The most important of these wandering editors was Brenda Gardener, who was to set up her own publishing company, Piccadilly Press, now very successful after early struggles. Over the years, I must have written as many books for Brenda as I had *Who* novelisations – maybe more.

Gradually things changed on *Who*. More and more writers wanted to novelise their own scripts.

THE FACE OF EVIL
based on a DOCTOR WHO adventure first broadcast in 1977

TERRANCE DICKS

WARRIORS OF THE DEEP
based on a DOCTOR WHO adventure first broadcast in 1984

TERRANCE DICKS

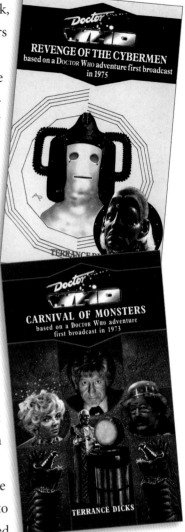

REVENGE OF THE CYBERMEN
based on a DOCTOR WHO adventure first broadcast in 1975

CARNIVAL OF MONSTERS
based on a DOCTOR WHO adventure first broadcast in 1973

TERRANCE DICKS

My standard approach had always been, 'I do all the work, and you get half the money.' A shrewder generation of writers realised they could do all the work and get all the money.

Eventually the show came off the air and every novelisable script had been novelised. Enter Virgin and Peter Darvill-Evans with the original *Who* novels. I wrote *Exodus*, one of the first of these, and a handful of others over the years.

It always tickled me to think of Peter toiling away in Ladbrook Grove on *Who* and Victorian pornography – the firm's only two profitable lines. Were we going to get more sex in *Who*? Or possibly, more *Who* in the pornography?

'What's all that wheezing and groaning coming from the bedroom?'

It was all a long time ago, and everyone knows what's happening today. *Who* is back with a bang, and there seem to be more *Who* books than ever on the market. Many of them, and many of the scripts of the show itself, are written by people who grew up reading my *Who* novelisations at their mother's knee. Some of them have been kind enough to tell me so.

I was surprised and pleased to be asked to write one myself, *Made of Steel* in the Quick Reads series. I can claim to have introduced Martha Jones to the public, since she appeared in the book before the new series started. It was nice to still be a small part of the legend.

Who has always been a large part of my life. I always used to say it was like a relay race, you staggered on for a while and then passed on the baton. I'm happy to let a talented new generation carry it now.

One of the most amazing features of the continuing *Who* phenomenon is the extraordinary degree of interest in every aspect of the show.

This excellent book gives an accurate and detailed account of an important – and hitherto neglected – part of *Doctor Who* history. It was certainly important to me, and judging by the many fans who've told me how much Target *Who* books meant to them in their younger days, important to fandom as a whole.

I heartily recommend it, and hope readers enjoy it as much as I did.

Terrance Dicks
London, April 2007

INTRODUCTION

ARGET BOOKS. TWO WORDS THAT ENCAPSULATE
a wealth of meaning and emotion – especially to *Doctor Who* fans. Maybe you are transported back to childhood days spent enjoying memorable *Doctor Who* adventures; possibly discovering for the first time that there were stories before Jon Pertwee took over as the Doctor. Perhaps the words spark off memories of finding battered paperbacks in jumble sales, or the desperate hunt to locate that elusive copy of *The Wheel in Space*. Maybe the term is as synonymous with *Doctor Who* as the title music and the TARDIS.

There cannot be many fans of the series who are not aware of the range of novelisations released between 1973 and 1994 by assorted publishers, and yet despite this great familiarity, not a great deal is known about the background to the range: how it all came about; how the books developed and grew into one of the major publishing success stories of the '80s; and how the Target name was eventually allowed to die.

This book is an attempt to redress that balance. For many viewers, the novelisations

LEIGHTON BUZZARD
BOOK CENTRE
66 NORTH STREET

BOOKS FOR EVERYONE
Angling to Zen   Agatha to Xaviera
Featuring a wide range of
Penguins, Puffins and Pelicans

Celebrity opening
16th SEPTEMBER by
TOM BAKER
Doctor Who
who will be pleased to sign copies of the
Doctor Who books from 10.30 am onwards

Rush & Warwick, Beaudesart, Leighton Buzzard

were their first opportunity to relive old adventures – this was ten years before the advent of *Doctor Who* on commercially available video – and in many cases, were among the first books they read. Almost all the writers and editors currently working on *Doctor Who Magazine*, the BBC's range of original novelisations, and Big Finish's series of original *Doctor Who* adventures on audio, grew up on the works of Terrance Dicks, Malcolm Hulke, Barry Letts, Brian Hayles *et al.*

The novelisations hold an important place in *Doctor Who* history as a range of merchandise that, along with *Doctor Who Magazine* (started in 1979) and the BBC Videos (started in 1983), outlasted the classic show that spawned them. They were the forerunners of all the original novels that appeared through the '90s, and provided immense enjoyment for a generation that eagerly awaited each successive title. There were 153 different novelisations issued with the Target logo on their spine, over 800 individual printings and re-printings, and over 13 million copies in print by 17 March 1994, when a reprint of *Doctor Who – The Talons of Weng-Chiang* became the last book to be issued under the Target imprint.

This is their story.

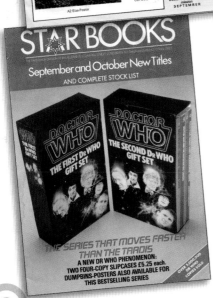

PART ONE: THE TERROR BEGINS

1

14 GLOUCESTER ROAD IN SOUTH KENSINGTON, LONDON is an unimposing sight. A modest shop-fronted mews property on a busy street in one of the more upmarket areas of the capital. This was in 1972 home to the Universal-Tandem publishing company. The building housed a small studio and a kitchen as well as offices, and the art department was located in a converted garage next door. Universal-Tandem was not large, and was run by an entrepreneur by the name of Ralph Stokes. Stokes employed approximately nine staff to handle everything, and the company specialised in publishing mass market paperback fiction and non-fiction.

The company had been formed in the early '60s. Stokes had been working at Four Square Books and, when that company began to go into decline, started talking to a man named Anthony Gibbs, who was at the time running a publishing house called Anthony Gibbs and Phillips, which operated from a back room at 33 Beauchamp Place. Stokes joined forces with Gibbs to start a new imprint for Anthony Gibbs and Phillips and asked a similarly disillusioned friend from Four Square Books, Brian Miles, if he would run the sales side. Stokes, Gibbs and Miles founded the Tandem imprint (so named because they intended to publish hardback and paperback editions simultaneously: in tandem) in 1964, and the Allan Wingate name was used for their hardback library editions. Allan Wingate had been a publishing house that went bankrupt after the War. Paul Hamlyn, who started out selling book remainder stock from a barrow in Charing Cross Road, bought the Wingate stock and the name, and when Gibbs started Anthony Gibbs and Phillips, he bought the Allan Wingate name from Paul Hamlyn for a penny.

Although all the elements were in place, the company was struggling due to a

TOP: 14 Gloucester Road, original premises for the Universal Tandem Publishing Company. BOTTOM: Ralph Stokes.

TERRANCE DICKS

'I see the task of the novelisation as reproducing the effect of watching the TV show in the reader's head. Sometimes, with no budgetary restrictions, you can even improve on it.'

Terrance Dicks, DWB, March 1989

Terrance Dicks is by far the most prolific of the *Doctor Who* authors, both within and beyond the range, with over 220 books published. Born in East Ham, London, in 1935, he was educated at the local grammar school and went on to read English at Downing College, Cambridge. After national service, he got a job as an advertising copywriter. This lasted for five years, during which time he started writing radio scripts as a sideline. Eventually he switched to full-time freelance writing, first on plays and comedy series for radio and then in television on programmes including *The Avengers* and *Crossroads*.

He began working on *Doctor Who* in the late 1960s. He script-edited the show for part of the 1969 season and for the whole of the Jon Pertwee era (1970-1974), and then contributed several scripts for the show thereafter.

Aside from *Doctor Who*, Dicks also served as script editor on *Moonbase 3* (1973) and the BBC's classic serials, all alongside producer Barry Letts. He took over as producer on the latter serials before they were cancelled by the BBC in 1988. He also contributed a script to *Space: 1999* ('The Lambda Factor', 1976).

He was approached by Target editor Richard Henwood in 1973 to novelise some of the *Doctor Who* serials he was then overseeing. This led to a 17 year stream of *Doctor Who* titles for Target and started Dicks on the road as an author. Alongside his 64 novelisations, Dicks wrote several non-fiction titles for the range: *The Making of Doctor Who* (1976 – updated from the book he had helped Malcolm Hulke write in 1972), two volumes of *The Doctor Who Monster Book* (1975 and 1977), *The Doctor Who Dinosaur Book* (1976), *The Adventures of K9 and Other Mechanical Creatures* and *Terry Nation's Dalek* ▶

lack of money, so, in an attempt to raise funds, Stokes flew to New York in the late '60s and eventually made contact with the Universal Publishing and Distributing Company Inc. That was a successful publisher of sports magazines, but also ran a paperback imprint called Award Books, and an imprint called Softcover Library under which had been published a large number of soft porn titles. At Stokes'

Nick Carter's novels were very popular in the early seventies.

request, the Tandem imprint was bought by Universal, and the UK subsidiary was thereafter called Universal-Tandem Publishers. Gibbs remained with Anthony Gibbs and Phillips, while Stokes and Miles joined the new subsidiary, which was still based at Beauchamp Place. There were immediate benefits for the new company: financial support from America and the ability to distribute the Universal Award titles in the UK, with selected key titles repackaged: for example a range of Nick Carter thrillers, and some of the Softcover Library books, all of which sold very well indeed. Things went so well that eventually Universal-Tandem was able to move from Beauchamp Place to larger premises at 14 Gloucester Road.

Universal-Tandem's book covers were almost exclusively handled by a freelance designer, Brian Boyle. When the company moved to Gloucester Road, there was by coincidence a large empty garage next door, and Boyle offered to rent this and convert it into an art studio with his own money, meaning that he would be on hand to work with the company in the future. This arrangement worked well, and Boyle played an active part in advising on, designing and supplying the covers for Universal-Tandem.

By 1972, the company was doing so well that Stokes and Miles wanted to expand further. As the main imprint, Tandem, was already stretched with the books in hand, the obvious solution in order to publish more was to start a new imprint. 'We were minnows at that time,' remembered Brian Miles. 'Names like Pan, Penguin and Corgi were very powerful, so we had to do things that were far more astute and clever and looking for the main chance. For example, when Lord Longford was associated with Granada publishing, he stopped them putting out Xaviera Hollander's *Happy Hooker* books. So we picked them up for next to nothing and they did really well for us.'

An area of publishing that seemed attractive to Stokes and Miles was children's books. 'I was aware that there was a market for children's publishing,' explained

The Happy Hooker by Xaviera Hollander.

Miles, 'especially as I was already doing business with Scholastic Publications, who specialised in that area. They would take copies of books we published as they could sell them to the wider state school market. The chap I dealt with there was an editor called Richard Henwood, and so having decided to start our own children's list, I rang Scholastic with the intention of seeing if Richard would be interested in coming to work for us. They told me that he had left the company, but gave me his home number. I rang Richard at home and put the proposition to him to come and put our list together. I think he was really pleased.'

'I was hired to that end and with a relatively open chequebook,' recalls Richard. 'I wasn't completely sure that there was room for another imprint within the children's paperback market. I needn't have worried.'

Henwood describes Universal-Tandem as: 'Small, friendly, unorthodox, with a dash of eccentricity that came from Ralph, who was an Aquarian, as I recall. I augmented it upon arrival and quickly grew to like and respect my new boss immensely. He was an "old-style" publisher, and the profession, now massively corporatised, is much the poorer in spirit without his ilk.'

Thirty-nine year old Henwood's role was to work with Miles to put together a new children's imprint for the company. Unfortunately, at that time, Universal in America was on a downward trend, and promised funding to set up the list was not forthcoming. Henwood therefore found himself in the position of having to do everything himself. 'We were on our own, and for the time being I would have to do without a secretarial assistant. I would have to do everything myself – reading, selection, negotiation, contracts, editing and production – everything, indeed, except publicity and sales. I could think of no comparable editor in children's book publishing with such a job specification.'

Henwood was given an office in the basement of 14 Gloucester Road, and from there he planned how best to launch the new list. From the start it was an uphill struggle. Books published in a paperback imprint originate from two sources: works commissioned from scratch; and paperback rights to existing hardbacks. To this end, Richard contacted some authors regarding ideas for the range and got some original material underway, and also started visiting children's hardback publishers to see what there might be in the way of material to buy paperback rights to.

'What was I after? Selling lots of good books that youngsters wanted to read and not what the children's book literati thought they *ought* to read,' explains Henwood when asked about his hopes for the range. 'An old historical conflict this, that has come down through the centuries from the 1500s. I was hitting for an age group of 4-15 years with the "core-centre" of the list pitched at 11-14-year-olds. I also wanted

Special (both 1979). He has also written two *Doctor Who* stage plays and several spin-off video scripts and audio plays.

When Virgin Publishing started their range of original *Doctor Who* novels, Dicks contributed *Timewyrm: Exodus* (1991), *Blood Harvest* (1994) and *Shakedown* (1995), and he continued writing original *Doctor Who* fiction for BBC Books with *The Eight Doctors* (1996), *Catastrophea* (1998), *Players* (1999), *Endgame* (2000), *Warmonger* (2002), *Deadly Reunion* (with Barry Letts – 2003), *World Game* (2005) and the novella *Made of Steel* (2007).

Dicks' original fiction for children began with two series of books for Target. First was *The Mounties* trilogy in 1976 (*The Great March West*, *Massacre in the Hills* and *War Drums of the Black Foot*), then came the *Star Quest* trilogy (*Spacejack*, *Roboworld* and *Terrorsaur!*).

In 1978, Dicks began a series of ten adventure books featuring *The Baker Street Irregulars* – Dan, Jeff, Liz and Mickey – late-20th century kids who battled criminals with the wit and ingenuity of Sherlock Holmes. The series ran from *The Missing Masterpiece* (1978) to *The Criminal Computer* (1987). All were published in hardback by Blackie & Son Ltd, and were commissioned by Richard Henwood, who had moved to Blackie from Target. Blackie also published Dicks' series of six inter-connected contemporary horror novels for children: *Cry Vampire!* (1981), *Marvin's Monster* (1982), *Wereboy!* (1982), *Demon of the Dark* (1983), *War of the Witches* (1983) and *The Ghosts of Gallows Cross* (1984).

Following this, Dicks began a long and successful association with Piccadilly Press. Initially this involved books for very young readers, including the adventures of *T R Bear* (a walking, talking teddy bear), *Sally Ann* (a determined ragdoll), *Goliath* (a golden retriever), *Harvey* (a St Bernard) and *Magnificent Max* (a talking black and white cat). These were followed by the series *Jonathan's Ghost* (four books, 1988-91), *The MacMagics* (three books, 1990-91), and *Chronicles of a Computer Game Addict* (four books, 1994-98).

These ranges for younger readers were followed by books for a teenage audience: the *Changing Universe* series (three titles, 1998-2000) and the *Second Sight* series (four titles, 2000-02). He also wrote the 12 book *The Unexplained* series, concerning British teenager Matthew Stirling, who embarks with his father Professor James Stirling on a range of adventures investigating paranormal goings-on.

Alongside these series and one-off works of fiction for pre-school to ▶

teenage readers, Dicks has written several non-fiction titles, including *Europe United* (1991), *A Riot of Writers* (1992), *Uproar in the House* (1993) and *A Right Royal History* (1994).

Dicks continues to write and to contribute to the ever-increasing universe of *Doctor Who*. He is married to Elsa, with three sons, Stephen, Jonathan and Oliver.

VWOORP!

'...a strange wheezing and groaning filled the air...'

Terrance Dicks, 1974
Doctor Who and the Auton Invasion

VWOORP!

DAVID WHITAKER

David Whitaker was born in Knebworth in 1928. He started his career in the theatre, writing, acting and directing for a wide range of companies, including the York Repertory Group. There, one of his plays, *A Choice of Partners*, was seen by a member of the BBC Script Department and he was commissioned to adapt it for television. On the strength of this, in 1957, Donald Wilson invited him to join the Department's staff. For the next few years, Whitaker's work covered plays, situation comedies, light entertainment features and spectaculars, musical biographies – the most notable being *Hello Ragtime* – and series such as *Compact* and *Garry Halliday*.

He was the first story editor on *Doctor Who* in 1963-1964. He also contributed several stories of his own: 'Inside the Spaceship' (1964), 'The Rescue' (1965), 'The Crusade' (1965), 'The Power of the Daleks' (1966), 'The Evil of the Daleks' (1967), 'The Enemy of the World' (1967/8), 'The Wheel in Space' (1968) and 'The Ambassadors of Death' (1970). In addition, he wrote the stage play *The Curse of the Daleks* (1965) and stories for the first *Dr Who Annual* (1965).

Whitaker's other TV work included scripts for *Undermind* ('The New Dimension', 'Test for the Future', 1965), *Mr Rose* ('The Fifth Estate', 'The Missing Chapter', 1968), *Public Eye* ('If This ▶

cover designs that hooked the attention, and titles that instantly communicated the guts of the book's content: something constantly given insufficient importance to in those days by many children's book editors, who hadn't had the advantage of the mail-order experience and training I'd received at Scholastic. An example: I bought from a company called World's Work the paperback rights to a book by Gordon Douglas Griffiths about a kitten that got lost on Dartmoor. They had published it with what I recall to have been an ineffective title and an indifferent cover.

Abandoned! by Gordon Douglas Griffiths.

Notwithstanding, it was runner-up for the 1973 Whitbread Literary Award (children's book division). I had a hell's-own game persuading the editor at World's Work to allow me to change the title. (It was to their benefit, since we would sell more copies and they would gain a greater royalty.) Reluctantly and sniffily, they gave me permission; the book was published by us in 1974 with the title *Abandoned!* and a photograph on the cover of a lonely-looking black kitten sitting on grass and backed by ferns. (Heaven knows where the art director got hold of *that* photo.) It sold like hot cakes, not least to Scholastic, who bought an entire print-run for distribution.'

The name of this new list was to be 'Target', an idea originated by Brian Miles. 'At that time,' Miles recalls, 'and probably still today, any imprint logo had to be good. I remember driving into work via Chiswick House roundabout and thinking that I wanted alliteration in the names. Tandem and … Target! That's when it came to me. The symbol was already there … Target Books said so much about what we were trying to do … it was perfect. So I suggested this to Ralph and to Brian Boyle and they loved it too. It was a perfect logo. We had badges made, posters … it really worked well.'

Despite the enthusiasm of everyone at Universal-Tandem, Henwood encountered a mixed reception when talking about his plans for the new list with other children's publishers. 'Jane Hollowood – who had created the Pan Piccolo list a year or so before – reckoned there was still room for another imprint, but hardback editors were sniffy, since Universal-Tandem was a small stable with not the greatest of reputations for high quality books. To break into the

Badjelly the Witch by Spike Milligan.

DOCTOR WHO
by DAVID WHITAKER
Based on the
B.B.C. television serial
by TERRY NATION

in an exciting
adventure with
the Daleks

market, they had to have someone, I suppose like me, who knew many of the hardback people and stood some chance of fighting his corner against the likes of Kaye Webb at Puffin, who, I discovered, was routinely given first option on any paperback edition of a new hardback novel. With an open chequebook, I gleefully snatched *Badjelly the Witch*, a new children's book by Spike Milligan, from her grasp. She was furious. Almost overnight, advances on paperback rights shot up as a consequence. But undoubtedly, what guaranteed the success of Target was the *Doctor Who* acquisition right at its heart. Definitely a publishing scoop of the first order that, retrospectively, I feel very lucky and privileged to have had come my way.'

It was when visiting the offices of publishers Frederick Muller in Tottenham Court Road that Henwood first discovered the *Doctor Who* titles. 'I was ushered into the boardroom by the rights manager, and arranged on the table were some 20 books. One swift glance told me that I was almost certainly wasting my time, but my eyes strayed back to a trio of tired looking hardbacks in the centre. "*Doctor Who…*" I mused aloud to myself. "Oh, I don't know …" The fact is (I'm ashamed to say) that, back then, I didn't. As a matter of deliberate choice, we had no television at home, and I had seen only a few minutes of the odd episode of *Doctor Who* in someone else's house. However, I said, "I'll take an option on that trio, if I may."

'"They didn't sell very well into the libraries when we published them in 1964," said the rights manager, "… but Armada paperbacked one as an experiment. It's out of print now."

'Back at Gloucester Road, I showed my morning's "catch" to Brian Miles. Without hesitation, he exclaimed "*Doctor Who* … They'll sell!"

DOCTOR WHO AND THE ZARBI
by BILL STRUTTON
Based on the successful B.B.C. television serial

is Lucky, I'd Rather Be Jonah', 1968), *The Gold Robbers* (1969), *Paul Temple* ('The Victim', 1970) and *Elephant Boy* (1973), amongst others.

Whitaker met actress June Barry in 1962 and the couple were married in 1963. He married again in 1978 in Sydney, Australia.

David Whitaker died on 4 February 1980. At the time, he was working on a novelisation of his *Doctor Who* story 'The Enemy of the World'.

'His face was old and lined, yet somehow alert and vital at the same time. His eyes seemed to blaze with a fierce intelligence, and a commanding beak of a nose gave his features an arrogant, aristocratic air.'

Terrance Dicks, 1981
Doctor Who and an Unearthly Child

DOCTOR WHO AND THE CRUSADERS
by DAVID WHITAKER

Based on the successful B.B.C. television serial

The original Frederick Muller hardback editions of the first three Target *Doctor Who* releases.

WHAT'S IN A NAME...?

Originally the Target range established itself by buying up book titles that already existed and selling them to as wide a children's market as possible. Sometimes this would mean changing the original title of a book to something more dynamic and appealing. Early examples included Margaret Greaves' *The Grandmother Stone*, which, under Target, became *The Stone of Terror*, John Rowland's *Railway Pioneer*, which became *Rocket to Fame*, and Ruth M Arthur's *After Candlemas*, which became *Candlemas Mystery*.

The *Doctor Who* range was not immune to such enhancement, particularly if the onscreen story title was felt to lack sufficient excitement. The following is a list of those books that had a different title from the story as originally seen on screen.

Story Title	Book Title
'Spearhead from Space'	*Doctor Who and the Auton Invasion*
'Doctor Who and the Silurians'	*Doctor Who and the Cave-Monsters*
'Colony in Space'	*Doctor Who and the Doomsday Weapon*
'The Moonbase'	*Doctor Who and the Cybermen*
'Robot'	*Doctor Who and the Giant Robot*
'Invasion of the Dinosaurs'	*Doctor Who and the Dinosaur Invasion*
'Terror of the Zygons'	*Doctor Who and the Loch Ness Monster*[1]
'Frontier in Space'	*Doctor Who and the Space War*

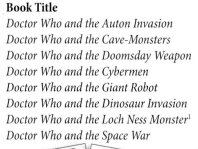

1 This was originally advertised as *Doctor Who Meets the Loch Ness Monster*

Terrance Dicks was script editor on *Doctor Who* when contacted about novelising some of the stories.

'I expressed some lingering doubt, which in retrospect I realise had more to do with lack of personal enthusiasm for sci-fi literature than what should have been uppermost on my mind – *Doctor Who*'s marketing potential.

'"Tell you what I'll do," said Brian. "If you don't trust my judgement, I'll telephone round the reps this evening." Their replies were quite unanimous – a sure-fire winner!'

Realising that this *Doctor Who* range could be far bigger than the three titles he had bought the paperback rights on, Henwood contacted the BBC to discuss options on publishing further titles. In a letter dated 3 November 1972, he set out his intentions, requesting: first option to novelise all *Doctor Who* scripts; access to photographs from the stories in question; and permission to re-illustrate the first three William Hartnell titles with likenesses of Jon Pertwee's Doctor. This final idea was later dropped: by the time the BBC received the cover roughs from the publishers on 10 January 1973, Hartnell's face was that depicted.

Henwood initially wanted to publish a further three or six

paperbacks, depending in part upon the success of the initial three re-issues. Brian Miles recalls that they were all happy with what Richard wanted to do. 'To hit the market with any force or impact, you had to publish three or six titles in one go. So we were all very enthusiastic about the *Doctor Who* titles, and the initial launch was very successful, with those three books as the centrepiece.'

Henwood was put in touch with the *Doctor Who* production office and spoke both to producer Barry Letts and to script editor Terrance Dicks. 'By the end of 1972, *Doctor Who*'s ratings on television were increasing steadily,' says Barry Letts. 'When Richard Henwood found that the rights to the *Doctor Who* books were available, he felt like he'd discovered a real treasure. He came to us asking about doing more books, and I was all for the idea. Anything that increased the profile of the show was bound to be a good thing.'

Terrance Dicks was enthusiastic about the idea of novelising the scripts – he had previously written to Frederick Muller and suggested the same thing, but had received no reply to his letter – and offered his services as author. 'When Richard came to us at the *Doctor Who* office and said that he wanted to do more books, asking us who would write them, my immediate response was "I will!" because I'd always wanted to do a book. It was a golden opportunity and a way into book writing … which it certainly proved to be.

'Richard asked which one I wanted to do, and after some discussion I chose "Spearhead from Space" as they wanted something fairly current. "Oh, I don't like that title," said Richard. "What's it about?" So it was renamed *The Auton Invasion*, the first of the new range. They used to change the titles like that, and nobody really cared in those days. It was all done in a very casual higgledy-piggledy way … *The Auton Invasion* was the first book of any kind I'd written, and I worked very hard on it. I remember I was late delivering it by about a week, which is quite serious in television terms. I took it around to the publishers myself and handed it in. I didn't hear for ages after that, and thought that perhaps they hated it, or that the range had been stopped or something. When I eventually phoned up to ask what was happening, Richard said, "It's gone to the printers! Now which one are you going to do next?"'

Dicks has always seen the books as more than just spin-offs. 'Each book is written as a self contained unit,' he explained to a journalist in the late '70s, ' and is capable of standing on its own without the television series. The turning of a script into a book is not as easy as it might sound. Certainly all the dialogue is available, but one has to make the transition between the media and convey all that is taken care of by visual image on the screen purely by the written word.'

As well as writing the books, 38-year-old Dicks ended up working as a kind of unofficial editor to the range. He would choose the titles to be done and have first option on writing them. To reduce his workload, he recruited other contributors from amongst the original scriptwriters he was working with at the BBC, including

BILL STRUTTON

'There were fewer problems involved with an adaption from existing scripts than there were starting a novel from scratch, of course. The story was there, and so was the dialogue. All I did was fill in the descriptions.'
Bill Strutton, Doctor Who Magazine *(number 158), March 1990*

William Harold Strutton was born on 23 February 1923 on Yorke's Peninsula in South Australia. He was the last of nine children. He went to Adelaide University before joining the Australian army at the outbreak of the Second World War. He fought in the Middle East and Greece, being captured by the Germans in Crete in 1941. He was imprisoned in Stalag VII, where he learnt to speak German, Spanish and French. At the end of the war, he was repatriated to Bicester in the UK and became a journalist.

His first novel, a detective story called *A Jury of Angels*, was published in 1957. This was followed by *A Glut of Virgins* (1973). He also wrote two non-fiction accounts of the Second World War: *The Secret Invaders* (aka *The Beachhead Spies*, 1958, with Michael Pearson,) and *Island of Terrible Friends* (aka *Commando Force 133*,1961).

Moving into television, Strutton contributed scripts to *Ivanhoe* (seven episodes, 1958-59), *Top Secret* ('The Inca Dove', 'After the Fair', 1961), *The Avengers* ('Toy Trap', 1961), *Echo Four-Two* ('The Dummies', 'The Kite Dropper', 1961), *The Saint* ('Iris', 'The Rough Diamonds', 1963), *R3* ('On the Spike', 1964), *The Man in Room 17* ('The Bequest', 1965), *The Protectors* ('Freedom!', 'The Reluctant Thief', 1964), *Undermind* ('Song of Death', 1965), *Strange Report* ('Grenade: What Price Change?', 1969) and *Paul Temple* (three episodes, 1970), among others. In total, he wrote over 200 teleplays.

His single *Doctor Who* contribution came with 1965's 'The Web Planet', which he novelised for publishers Frederick Muller the same year. The novelisation was reissued as part of the launch of Target books in 1973.

Following a heart attack in 1978, he retired to his Elizabethan house in Surrey and then moved to Palafrugell in Spain.

Strutton died on 23 November 2003.

CHRIS ACHILLEOS

'Patrick Troughton was the easiest to draw, because there is a lot of character to latch onto in his face.' *Chris Achilleos,* Doctor Who Magazine *114, July 1986*

Christos Achilléos, the artist chosen to launch the Target *Doctor Who* range, was born in Cyprus in 1947. He moved to England with his family in 1960. He trained as an artist at Hornsey College of Art. His first cover work was for Brian Boyle at Tandem books. He provided covers and illustrations for books ranging from westerns to martial arts to science fiction, including the *Dollar* Western series and Edgar Rice Burroughs' *Pellucidar* series.

He went on to produce 28 *Doctor Who* novelisation covers, plus the covers for both of the *Doctor Who Monster Books* and Target's *The Making of Doctor Who*. He also produced the internal illustrations for four of the early books. Five of his covers were released as *Doctor Who Portfolio No 1* in 1986. He produced further original *Doctor Who* artwork in 1983 when David Howe from the Doctor Who Appreciation Society commissioned him to create a poster and cover for a special magazine on the anniversary story, 'The Five Doctors', and in 2005/6 when he painted pieces featuring the ninth and tenth Doctors.

He has supplied fantasy artwork for many publishers, including the covers for the mid 1980s reissues of the original James Blish *Star Trek* adaptations, John Norman's *Gor* series, Richard Kirk's *Raven* series and novels by Michael Moorcock, Piers Anthony and Anne McCaffrey. A commission for *Men Only* magazine saw him move into more 'glamorous' illustrations and develop his acclaimed 'Amazonian women' style of artwork. He contributed costume and character design ideas to the films *Heavy Metal* (1981), *Willow* (1988) and *King Arthur* (2004).

A lot of his artwork has been collected together in book form: *Beauty and the Beast* (1978), *Sirens* (1986) (both ▶

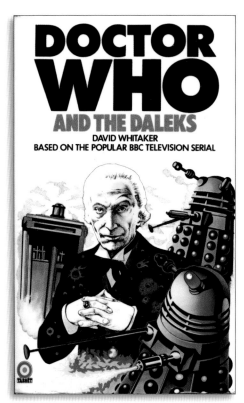

Malcolm Hulke and Brian Hayles.

'For a time, there was a handful of us doing them,' explains Dicks. 'At that time, I was still script editing the show for the BBC, so it helped. But over a period of time, the others dropped away. This was mainly because the books weren't paying very much money – not in television terms anyway – and eventually when I decided to leave *Doctor Who* along with Barry and Jon, I was back in the freelance market and this was a steady stream of work for me.'

Henwood and Dicks wanted to concentrate to start with on stories featuring the then current third Doctor, and the initial schedule of titles was to be 'Spearhead from Space' and 'Doctor Who and the Silurians' in December 1973, 'The Ambassadors of Death' and 'Terror of the Autons' in March 1974 and 'The Claws of Axos' and 'Colony in Space' in May 1974. Dicks had recommended excluding 'Inferno' and 'The Mind of Evil', both scripts by Don Houghton. It was thought that once the novelisations were up and running, then previous Doctors' stories could also be covered.

A contract was drawn up between the Universal-Tandem Book Publishing Company and the BBC allowing the former to publish *Doctor Who* paperbacks with separate provision for hardbacks. After brief negotiation, a royalty of two-and-a-half per cent of the cover price was agreed to be paid to the BBC for each copy sold.

The final, revised, choice of stories for the initial tranche of new novelisations was 'Spearhead From Space' (novelised as *Doctor Who and the Auton Invasion*), 'Doctor Who and the Silurians' (*Doctor Who and the Cave Monsters*), 'Day of the Daleks', 'Colony in Space' (*Doctor Who and the Doomsday Weapon*), 'The Dæmons' and 'The Sea Devils'. All the titles were prefixed with 'Doctor Who and' but for convenience in this text, this has been generally omitted. These had all been commissioned by July 1973 for publication at the rate of one every two months starting in January 1974. Henwood contracted Terrance Dicks to handle Robert Holmes's 'Spearhead from Space' and Louis Marks's 'Day of the Daleks', Malcolm Hulke to write up his own scripts and Barry Letts to novelise 'The Daemons', which the producer had co-written for television with Robert Sloman under the name Guy Leopold.

As well as producing *Doctor Who* on television and contributing to the range of books, Barry Letts took on the responsibility for approving all the material being produced for the range on behalf of the BBC. This was mainly the cover images. 'I was always pleased with the covers,' says Letts, 'but I always disliked the internal illustrations. I actively fought against them, but the publishers liked them. I remember that there was one illustration in *The Dæmons* that was simply all wrong: it was of the scene in the barrow where the Doctor and Jo confront Bok the gargoyle, just before the Doctor sings the Venusian lullaby to scare it away. As the artist had originally drawn the picture, all the shadows were going the wrong ways, and the illumination was all wrong … I wasn't happy, and I said so at a meeting with Richard Henwood and the artist. So they re-did that picture.'

Letts recalls that originally the publishers had wanted to use photographs on the covers. 'We looked into this and found that there were photographs available, but when we asked Jon Pertwee about it, although he was very pleased, he asked the further question: "How much?". Unfortunately the publishers were not prepared to pay to use Jon's image in photographs, and he wouldn't agree to them doing it with no payment. They therefore decided to use artwork instead, as there was no payment due on artwork.'

The artist chosen to handle the all-important covers for the new *Doctor Who* books was a young 24 year old Cypriot called Christos Achilleos. After leaving college in the early '70s, Achilleos had ended up working for Brian Boyle on some of the Universal-Tandem covers. He eventually moved on and went to work for an agency that handled freelance artists. Boyle remembered him in 1972 when Stokes and Miles were discussing the *Doctor Who* covers, and got back in touch.

'One day I got this call from Brian Boyle,' Achilleos recalled. 'He said that

of which contain examples of his *Doctor Who* artwork), *Medusa* (1988) and *Amazona* (2004).

After a difficult period in the 1980s, the 1990s saw success and greater international acclaim for Achilleos through the burgeoning trading card market. He has moved on to consolidate and co-ordinate his lifelong archive of artwork, continuing to promote his back catalogue and to produce original works for companies like BBC Worldwide.

'…like, yet not quite like, the trumpeting of a thousand mad elephants…'
Malcolm Hulke, 1974
Doctor Who and the Doomsday Weapon

AUTHORS' RANKING

Although Terrance Dicks was the undisputed king of the *Doctor Who* novelisation with 64 titles to his name, the hierarchy from there on down is much more hotly disputed.

1st	Terrance Dicks (64)	
2nd	Ian Marter (9)[1]	
3rd	Malcolm Hulke (7)	
4th	Gerry Davis (5)[2]	
	John Peel (5)[3]	
5th	Pip and Jane Baker (4)	
	Nigel Robinson (4)	
	Eric Saward (4)[4]	

And with three titles each to their name, came: Christopher H Bidmead, Ian Stuart Black, Donald Cotton, Terence Dudley[5], Peter Grimwade, Philip Hinchcliffe, John Lucarotti and Philip Martin[6].

1 One completed by Nigel Robinson
2 One with Alison Bingeman
3 Counting his two 'The Daleks' Master Plan' volumes separately
4 Including his novelisation of radio serial 'Slipback'
5 Including his novelisation of spin-off 'K9 and Company'
6 Including his novelisation of unmade script 'Mission to Magnus'

Brian Hayles, one of the initial tranche of authors contracted by Target to novelise their television scripts.

Covers for three of Target's other releases in 1973. The cover for *The Story of the Loch Ness Monster* is also by Chris Achilleos.

Universal-Tandem were doing three *Doctor Who* books, and would I like to do the covers? They wanted to have something like the ones that Frank Bellamy had done for the *Radio Times*; in fact it turned out that they had already asked Frank if he would do them but he had turned them down, so they asked if I would do them in that style.

'At first I had just the three to do, and I didn't know whether they intended to continue the series or not. After that, there was quite a long gap of about six to 12 months, and then they asked if I would do another one. That was *The Cave Monsters*. They just asked me for them one at a time at first; they didn't tell me that it would end up as one a month!'

Achilleos was provided with photographs courtesy of the BBC via Terrance Dicks, and created his covers using a style similar to that of Frank Bellamy. 'Generally when you illustrate a book,' he recalled, 'you get a copy of it and either it's a reprint, in which case you can have a look at what the other fellow's done, or if it's new, you just read through a manuscript quickly looking for something visually exciting, maybe an actual scene in the book. But the cover is more than just an illustration of a particular bit in the book, it has to be a graphic interpretation of it. The cover of a book is what sells it.

'As far as designing the *Doctor Who* covers was concerned, it was left entirely up to me. The art director would tell me which one was next, and I just gave him the finished product, which was how I got away with so much.

'I have had some arguments over some of the covers that I've done though.

The launch of the Target range on 15 May 1973. Pictured are, L to R: Ralph Stokes (Managing Director); Arnold E Abramson (chairman); an intruder from Skaro; Brian Miles (sales director); Carola Edmond (editor); and Richard Henwood (editor-Target books).

When I did *The Zarbi* – which was actually the first one that I completed – and first heard the basic plot, I thought, great, I can do these fantastic giant ants! But the BBC disagreed; they insisted that the Zarbi should look like those that had appeared in the TV series. So I had to change it. I also wanted to change the Daleks a bit, make some of them different. There must be all sorts of Daleks – different ranks with different functions – so that's why the ones on the cover of *Doctor Who and the Daleks* don't look the same as the TV versions.'

For the initial three covers, Achilleos painted images that would become synonymous with *Doctor Who* in the mid to late '70s. Following the style of Frank Bellamy, each cover featured a black-and-white-stippled portrait of the Doctor surrounded by two key elements from the story, along with numerous stars, planets and comets to provide visual interest. The books also retained the internal illustrations that had been used in the Muller hardback editions (by Arnold Schwartzman for *The Daleks*; John Wood for *The Zarbi* and Henry Fox for *The Crusaders*).

The launch of the new Target Books range took place on Tuesday 15 May 1973 at the Cadogan Hotel in Belgravia, the official publication date having been 13 days earlier on 2 May. These events were carefully scheduled as Henwood attached great numerological importance to dates: 2 May was his birthday, and the number 15 has, in Henwood's words, 'fortunate vibrations attached to it'. Twelve books had been chosen to launch the list: *Doctor Who and the Daleks* (David Whitaker); *Doctor Who and the Zarbi* (Bill Strutton); *Doctor Who and the Crusaders* (David Whitaker); *The Nightmare Rally* (Pierre Castex), a film tie-in with the Disney production *Diamonds on Wheels*; *The Loner* (Ester Wier), an adventure story set in the North featuring grizzly bears; *Wings of Glory* (Graeme Cook) a non-fiction history of aerial warfare; *Fishing* (J H Elliott), non-fiction advice for young anglers; *Investigating UFOs* (Larry Kettelkamp), another non–fiction title; *Small Creatures in My Back Garden* (Christopher Reynolds), nature study non-fiction; *The Pond on My Window Sill* (Christopher Reynolds), more nature study non-fiction; *Ice King* (Ernestine N Byrd), another story of the frozen North, this time featuring polar bears; and *Helen Keller's Teacher* (Mickie Davidson), a novel based on the real-life story of a deaf, dumb and blind girl who is brought life, hope and fame by her teacher.

When the three *Doctor Who* titles were originally written, they were never intended to be a part of an ongoing book series. In fact, David Whitaker's adaptation of Terry Nation's scripts for the first Dalek adventure took great liberties with the source material. Whitaker realised that he had to write a self-contained novel that could exist without reference to the TV series, and so developed an alternative introduction. Scientist Ian Chesterton comes across a traffic accident on a foggy Barnes Common. A car has been involved in a smash with an army lorry, killing the driver. Ian meets history teacher Barbara Wright on the road; she is hurt, but together they go to look

TOP: The first Target catalogue. BOTTOM: Malcolm Hulke, author of several of the novelisations.

VWOORP!

'...grinding, mechanical, un-natural...'

Brian Hayles, 1975

Doctor Who and the Curse of Peladon

VWOORP!

TARGET BOOKS OCT./NOV. '73

TARGET

TOP: A counter display for Target books. BOTTOM: Cover for the second Target catalogue.

for her student Susan, whom she was driving home. They find a strange key that hung around Susan's neck and meet a mysterious stranger with a box of everlasting matches …

Bill Strutton's *The Zarbi* is a far more faithful recreation of its respective TV story, its six chapters even corresponding to the six televised episodes. Whitaker's *The Crusaders* was also a far more standard novelisation, but benefited from Whitaker being able to expand on several of the characters and historical situations that had been, out of necessity, sidelined in the TV version.

Despite the books' undoubted long term success, critical acclaim was not forthcoming when they were originally published. *The Crusaders* attracted negative comment from the *Times Literary Supplement*, which in 1966 described it as: 'An undistinguished historical story … neither helped nor hindered by the intrusion of the ubiquitous Doctor and his young companions … A rather silly book.' This view was revised by the *TLS* in 1974, when the same title was described as being 'rather more sophisticated; the history is soundly researched, the sadism distinctly kinky.' In general, however, the *TLS* was unimpressed by the reissues: 'In expert adapting hands, good written fiction can make satisfactory television material. The converse is seldom true. By the time it has undergone translation into book form, the excellent ham of *Doctor Who* is more than a little off … Children who come to these books to renew past pleasures may find that the thrills have lost their urgency.'

Despite this dismissive critical reception, and confirming the enthusiasm from Brian Miles and the sales reps, the *Doctor Who* titles were an enormous success. All three titles quickly sold out of their initial printings – estimated to have been around 20,000 copies each – and, according to the Target catalogues for the time, were reprinted in October/November 1973 and again in January/February 1974. The crowning glory was the appearance of *The Daleks* at sixth place in W H Smith's top ten books on 20 July 1973. Henwood recalls that the launch of the Target range was the proudest moment in his publishing career, and that 'everybody who was anybody' in children's publishing came along: including editors from rival lists and *The Times*'s fastidious children's books editor, who felt that the *Doctor Who* books in particular would succeed and, it seemed, even grudgingly wished them luck.

Doctor Who in print was back up and running after a break of some six years. The inclusion of these highly successful titles in the launch of the Target list was to have far reaching consequences, not least that Universal-Tandem was thriving and attracting much interest, especially from other publishers, some of whom were looking to expand their companies by absorbing others …

PART TWO: TAKEOVER

IN 1973, RICHARD HENWOOD GAINED SOME WELCOME assistance on the Target list when he was joined by Elizabeth Godfray, a 22 year old university graduate. According to Henwood, Managing Director Ralph Stokes immediately backed his choice of Elizabeth as his first secretarial assistant, 'principally because he liked the "funny hat" she wore at her interview. He was like that. Very instinctive.'

Godfray admits that much of the job involved just keeping an eye on things, as Henwood already had the forthcoming titles commissioned. 'I was PA and secretary for Richard,' she explains, 'and I also worked with the art director, Brian Boyle, and really just kept an eye on everything. I also did a lot of copy editing and desk editing of the books as they came in. They hardly needed anything doing to them as the writers were so good. Richard and I were situated in the basement at 14 Gloucester Road doing the children's publishing, and it was all very nice, even if we never saw the sun!'

The first original novels were published in January 1974. Terrance Dicks' *The Auton Invasion* and Malcolm Hulke's *The Cave Monsters* were, like the first three titles, not met with critical acclaim, at least as far as *The Times Literary Supplement* was concerned: 'William Mayne once said that fantasy is just a tool of the trade, and the same remark applies to the best of science

'First came a rather scruffy little man in baggy chequered trousers and an ill-fitting frock coat, which he wore with a wide-collared white shirt and a straggly bow tie. His deeply lined face, wise, gentle and funny all at once, was surmounted by a mop of untidy black hair.'

Terrance Dicks, 1990
Doctor Who–The Space Pirates

Terrance Dicks, Richard Henwood, Barry Letts and Elizabeth Godfray in February 2001.

MALCOLM HULKE

'An adaptor has to take some liberties, and I make no apology.'
Malcolm Hulke, from the introduction to his book Crossroads: A New Beginning

Malcolm Hulke did not begin writing professionally until he was in his thirties. Throughout the 1960s he wrote for a range of adventure series and soap operas. He co-created and wrote (with Eric Paice) the science-fiction serials *Target Luna* (1960), *Pathfinders in Space* (1960), *Pathfinders to Mars* (1961) and *Pathfinders to Venus* (1961). He also provided scripts for *The Avengers* (1962-69, several with Terrance Dicks), *GS5* (1964), *The Protectors* (1964), *Danger Man* (1965) and *Gideon's Way* (1966).

Hulke's first contribution to *Doctor Who* was 'The Faceless Ones' (co-written with David Ellis) in 1967. This was followed by 1969's epic 'The War Games' (co-written with Dicks), which led onto a steady run of adventures for Jon Pertwee's Doctor in the early '70s. He wrote Target novelisations of all his stories (with the exception of 'The Faceless Ones') and also one of Robert Sloman's ('The Green Death').

Before he began writing the novelisations, he wrote, with Dicks, *The Making of Doctor Who* (1972) for Pan Books. It contained imaginative first person retellings of the Doctor's adventures from various 'official' perspectives. The book was later rewritten and updated by Dicks for the Target range.

Alongside his *Doctor Who* novelisations, Hulke was also busy in the mid-'70s novelising stories from the long-running soap opera *Crossroads*. These books were *A New Beginning* (1974), *A Warm Breeze* (1975), *Something Old, Something New* (1976) and *A Time for Living* (1976). In 1977, he wrote *The Siege*, the first in a series of children's books under the overall title *Roger Moore and the Crime Fighters*.

Non-fiction included *Cassell's Parliamentary Dictionary* (1975), *The Encyclopedia of Alternative* ▶

fiction: when it ceases to be that, SF can be tedious for the unaddicted,' wrote an unknown reviewer on 5 July 1974. The reviewer went on to say that the two new titles 'are strictly for addicts. They are books designed to hold the attention by putting the "goodies" in danger on nearly every page; no time is wasted on such irrelevancies as characterisation, description, or realistic dialogue. Nor is there any attempt to explain how any of the electronic hardware actually works. No Daleks, either, to liven up the proceedings by eradicating everyone in sight. The illustrations are dreadful: it's all done better on television.'

This seems to miss the point that the books are novelisations; and it can be argued that they were never intended to be appreciated for their literary merit anyway, and that the views of the tens of thousands of happy readers were far more important. Margery Fisher, distinguished editor of the children's book journal *Growing Point*, and who also contributed to *The Times Literary Supplement*, was rather more positive. '... I do recommend the two *Doctor Who* stories [*The Auton Invasion* and *The Cave Monsters*] ... [The *Doctor Who* television series] really *is* good popular entertainment, with the written

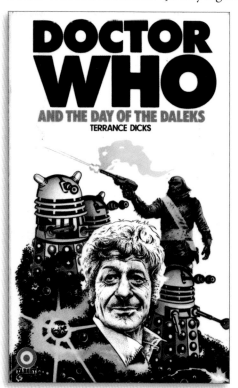

word coming out top beyond any doubt.' Perhaps more important, especially considering the ultimate longevity of the range, were the views of readers who were also fans of the television series. The publication of these two original novelisations was covered by teenage fan Keith Miller in the newsletter of the *Doctor Who* Fan Club – which was being run with the support of the *Doctor Who* office at the BBC.

Miller was very positive about the titles. 'I liked the prologue where the Doctor in his guise as Pat Troughton is banished to Earth. I think this interpretation of the TV series "Spearhead from Space" was very good

indeed … The highlight of the book, I think, was near the ending and its climax where the Autons smashed through the shop windows to occupy London. The invasion itself was taken into more detail in the book, with details of how even the government reacted. This is one advantage the book has over the TV series.' Miller also enjoyed the way that Malcolm Hulke related some of the events in *The Cave Monsters* through the eyes of one of the reptile characters – unnamed on television. 'In my opinion, Chapter 8, "Into an Alien World" was the best, with it being written from Morka's point of view … The story was average, which was hardly surprising as the TV series was run of the mill too, but the ending was good with the Doctor's disapproval of the caves being blown up.'

By the time Richard Henwood left Universal-Tandem in May 1974, and moved to Thomas Nelson as Editorial Director of their Children's Books division, he had 18 *Doctor Who* titles either already published or at various stages in the process. Henwood recalled that going to Thomas Nelson was like 'walking into the first harsh, cold winds of corporate publishing. I was immediately appointed to some four committees! It was all bureaucratic, hateful. Universal-Tandem was at the very opposite extreme: somewhat amateurish, laid-back, fun and above all *human*. There's little of that in publishing these days. I was lucky to be there.'

Henwood's successor as editor of the Target range was Michael Glover. Glover had actually taken over from Henwood when the latter left Scholastic Publishing to join Universal-Tandem, and now succeeded him at Universal-Tandem as well. Glover recognised the strength of the *Doctor Who* titles, and made plans to release even more. Given that all the *Doctor Who* titles had quickly sold out of

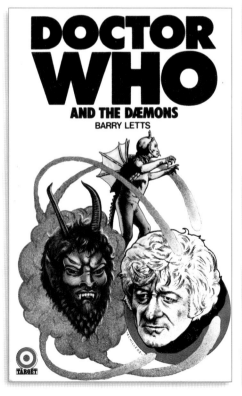

Medicine and Self-Help (1978) and the seminal reference work *Writing for Television in the '70s* (1974), which included contributions from Barry Letts, Robert Holmes, Terrance Dicks and Peter Ling.

Hulke died on 6 July 1979.

PETER BROOKES

'Chris Achilleos was far better suited to it than I was.'
Peter Brookes, interviewed by David Howe

Peter Brookes was born in Liverpool on 28 September 1943. In 1966, after a brief spell with the RAF, he began a three year course at the Central School of Arts and Crafts in London, during which time he had his first illustration published, on the cover of *New Society* (1968).

He rarely struggled to find work during the 1970s. He approached listings magazine *Radio Times* and was commissioned to provide black and white illustrations to accompany programme listings. These included illustrations for the 1974 season of *Doctor Who*. Also in 1974 he produced his first of many covers for the magazine. He also provided a regeneration sequence illustration for the *Radio Times* special publication to mark *Doctor Who*'s tenth anniversary.

He worked for a short time as political cartoonist for the *New Statesman*. Then Target's art editor Brian Boyle, a visiting lecturer at the Central School of Arts and Crafts, asked him to paint a short run of covers for four *Doctor Who* releases in 1975. In 1976, Brookes returned to the Central School as a lecturer. From 1979 to 1990, he then lectured at the Royal College of Art.

He continued to provide occasional covers and illustrations for *Radio Times* up until 1988. He was the principal cover artist (with Nick Garland) for the *Spectator* magazine from 1986 to 1998. He has also produced covers, cartoons and artwork for the likes of *Marie Claire*, *Cosmopolitan* and *Time* magazines. In 2003, he produced a set of five illustrations for use by the Royal Mail on a set of stamps marking the fiftieth anniversary of the discovery of the structure of DNA.

Brookes has been political cartoonist at *The Times* since 1992 and has won the Cartoon Art Trust's award for Political Cartoonist of the Year on three separate occasions. Various collections of his *The Times* cartoons have been published.

their initial print runs and had been reprinted several times, this was a sound, and fairly straightforward, decision to make.

Elizabeth Godfray recalls that Glover was very different from Henwood. 'Michael and Richard were totally different people. Richard was a real gentleman, an eccentric in his own way. He had very singular views on all sorts of things, but quite charming. Totally committed to the job and the books and no question of it. Michael was perhaps less commercial. He was a more literary person. Very clever. It's not surprising he didn't stay very long as he was always destined for greater things. I guess he learned a lot in that short time at Target, and he worked very hard.

'When Richard left, I remember Michael complaining vociferously about the offices in the basement at Gloucester Road, and we were moved out to somewhere near South Kensington underground station. I recall we were constantly trekking back and forth to the Gloucester Road offices. I'm sure that's because Michael didn't want to work in the basement offices but also because the Target range had grown too big for those premises.'

Capitalising on the winning formula established for the first three books, artist Chris Achilleos was asked to provide covers for the new titles, and this eventually stretched into a run of nine paintings. 'As it took me at least a week to do each one, it was taking up too much of my time,' he recalled. 'I didn't have time to do the other commissions that were coming in, so I told them that I wanted to stop doing them.'

In order to try and spread the load a little, Brian Boyle turned to an artist named Peter Brookes, who, like Achilleos, had previously worked with Boyle on Universal-Tandem titles in the early '70s. Brookes completed four covers for the range: *The Giant Robot*, *The Terror of the Autons*, *The Green Death* and *The Planet of the Spiders*. 'I was working on several covers for Brian,' explained Brookes, who moved on to become a political cartoonist for *The Times*. 'These were a part of a series of commissions, and I did them as they came in.'

Brookes believes that he may have been asked to do the *Doctor Who* covers because he had also been working for the BBC's listings magazine, *Radio Times*, and had completed several small pieces of *Doctor Who* artwork for them – to accompany the programme listings for the eleventh season – as well as a colour illustration for the 1973 *Radio Times Doctor Who* Special magazine, a two-page spread showing the first three Doctors 'regenerating' into each other.

'I have never been all that interested in science fiction and fantasy,' says Brookes, 'and I rather suspect that I asked not to be given any more *Doctor Who* work after those four covers. Chris Achilleos was far better suited to it than I was. As far as I recall, the covers were done in a pseudo-Frank Bellamy style, but aside from that, I was pretty much left alone: Brian would have asked me in the first place because he knew I would come up with something suitable without needing lots of hand-holding and explanations.'

Brookes also began a short-lived trend for additional artwork on the back cover. These additional colour illustrations depicted a 'snapshot' from the story. All four of the Brookes-covered novelisations featured these illustrations. They were also provided by Achilleos for *The Three Doctors* and *The Tenth Planet*.

All the cover artwork was sent to the BBC for approval, and generally they were passed without comment. The last of Brookes' commissions, *Planet of the Spiders*, was the only one of his covers to receive an adverse comment back. Philip Hinchcliffe, who had taken over producing *Doctor Who* from Barry Letts during 1974, commented when he saw the rough sketch on 1 May 1975 that the likeness of Tom Baker in a small sequence of 'regeneration' images at the bottom of the cover image was very poor. As a result, a photograph was supplied and the artwork amended accordingly. Hinchcliffe was also

Six of the early run of Target novelisations featured artwork on the back cover. Down the left hand side is art by Peter Brookes from *Doctor Who and the Giant Robot*, *Doctor Who and the Terror of the Autons* and *Doctor Who and the Green Death*. Down the right hand side is art by Peter Brookes for *Doctor Who and the Planet of the Spiders*, and by Chris Achilleos for *Doctor Who – The Three Doctors* and *Doctor Who and the Tenth Planet*.

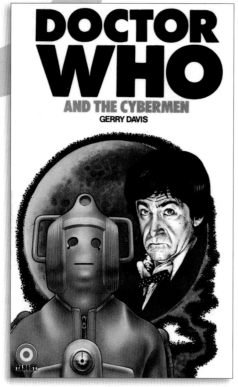

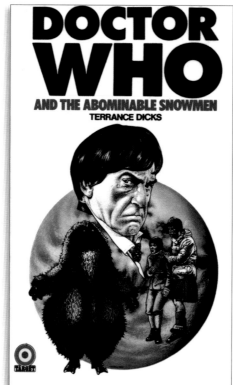

'He was an odd-looking fellow, this Scientific Adviser, tall and thin and beaky-nosed with an old/young face and a mane of prematurely white hair. He dressed oddly too, in ruffled shirt and elegant velvet smoking jacket, the ensemble completed by a long, flowing cape.'

Terrance Dicks, 1984
Doctor Who–Inferno

Cover for the third Target catalogue.

concerned at the use of older Doctors on the covers when Tom Baker was *the* Doctor on television. This led to the book covers tending to feature an image of the Doctor only when it was a Tom Baker story; stories from earlier eras of the show featured aspects other than the lead character. With the publication of *The Giant Robot*, the design of the covers was changed to include an adaptation of the television show's diamond logo, rather than the black block capital logo that had been used previously. This was simply to tie the books more closely to the TV series, and, with the BBC's ratings for the show continuing to rise, was seen to be a sensible move. An initial idea to feature the Doctor's face within the final 'O' of the *Doctor Who* logo was dropped however after only one book.

The books released through 1974 and 1975 were mainly third Doctor stories. After the initial two new novelisations in January 1974, the other titles were: *The Day of the Daleks* (Terrance Dicks); *The Doomsday Weapon* ['Colony in Space'] (Malcolm Hulke); *The Dæmons* (Barry Letts); *The Sea-Devils* (Malcolm Hulke); *The Abominable Snowmen* (Terrance Dicks); *The Curse of Peladon* (Brian Hayles); *The Cybermen* ['The Moonbase'] (Gerry Davis); *The Giant Robot* ['Robot'] (Terrance Dicks); *The Terror of the Autons* (Terrance Dicks); *The Green Death* (Malcolm Hulke); *The Planet of the Spiders* (Terrance Dicks); and *Doctor Who – The Three Doctors* (Terrance Dicks).

Reaction to these titles from Keith Miller was, on the whole, favourable, with certain of them being positively raved about: 'Wow! What a superb version of "Colony in Space" … It was good the way that Malcolm kept referring back to life on Earth, the terrible conditions, the way you had to pay to get sunshine, how every inch of the ground had been built upon and so on … Good touch when Ashe remembered

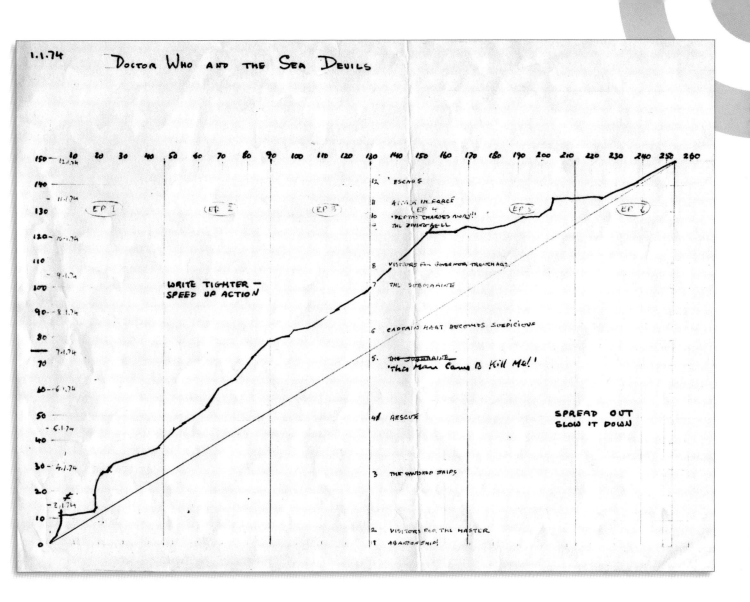

1.1.74

DOCTOR WHO AND THE SEA DEVILS

WRITE TIGHTER — SPEED UP ACTION

SPREAD OUT SLOW IT DOWN

12 ESCAPE
11 ATTACK IN FORCE
10 'DEPTH CHARGES AWAY!!'
9   THE DIVING BELL
8   VISITORS FOR GOVERNOR TRENCHARD
7   THE SUBMARINE
6   CAPTAIN HART BECOMES SUSPICIOUS
5   THE SUBMARINE
    'THIS MAN CAME TO KILL ME!'
4   RESCUE
3   THE MANNED SHIPS
2   VISITORS FOR THE MASTER
1   ABANDON SHIP!

EP 1   EP 2   EP 3   EP 4   EP 5   EP 6

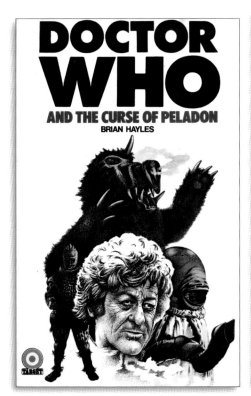

TOP: When writing his novelisations, Malcolm Hulke would draw up a chart to aid him in the writing process. Reproduced here is his chart for the writing of *Doctor Who and the Sea Devils*. The vertical axis to the left shows the number of pages in the book from 0 to 150. Across the chart, it is split into six blocks, each corresponding to an episode of the television script. Up the middle can be seen the chapters in the book, with titles marked in (note that chapter 5 was originally called 'The Submarine' before this title was used for chapter 7 instead). The straight diagonal line therefore shows the ideal book. The upper triangle represents 'write tighter - speed up action' while the lower triangle is 'spread out, slow it down'. The darker irregular diagonal line was the path that Hulke took when writing the novel. The peaks and troughs of the writing can be seen, with the exciting, fast paced sequences rising quicker than the more paced scenes. It is, however, unclear what the horizontal axis at the top represents. It is not time as each episode was 25 minutes in duration and this shows each episode as containing 45 'units'.

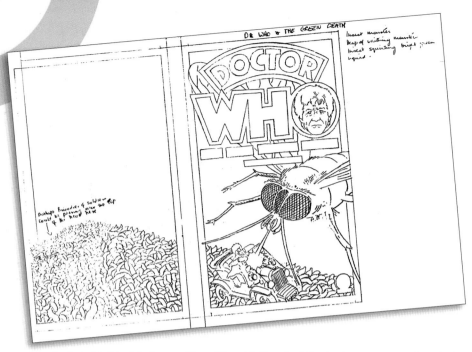

Peter Brookes' original sketch for the cover of *Doctor Who and the Green Death*. Note that there was an assumption at the time that the cover art would extend onto the back cover (ultimately a separate piece of art was commissioned for the back) and that the Doctor's face would appear over the 'O' of 'Who' on the front cover as with the published cover for *Doctor Who and the Giant Robot*. The text on the back cover says: 'Perhaps Brigadier or soldiers could be peering over the top of the heap here.' The text alongside the front cover reads: 'Insect monster. Heap of writhing maggots. Insect squirting bright green liquid'.

BARRY LETTS

'(I regret doing only one novelisation) for a number of reasons. Firstly I thoroughly enjoyed it, and secondly I could have done with the money!'

Barry Letts, Doctor Who Magazine *(number 337), December 2003*

Barry Letts was born in Loughborough in 1925 and was originally an actor. He performed in repertory in York and worked for a local radio station in Leeds. He appeared in a number of British films and TV series throughout the 1950s and 1960s.

He took up directing in 1967 and worked on *Z-Cars* and *The Newcomers* as well as *Doctor Who* ('The Enemy of the World', 1967). He was producer of the show for the Jon Pertwee era from 1970 to 1974 and also directed and co-wrote some of the serials, including 'The Dæmons' (1971), which he later novelised for the Target range.

His script editor throughout that ▶

"the terrifying creatures space travellers had found over the centuries – Monoids, Drahvins … Daleks." … All in all I think it is the best original Target have brought out so far.'; 'At last! A Pat Troughton adventure [*The Abominable Snowmen*]. The cover was superb (apart from the beady little green eyes on the Yeti) which was to match the story inside.'; '[*The Curse of Peladon*] is very well written by Brian Hayles … One thing that was never in the series, mainly because it was so hard to do, was Alpha Centauri's colour change every time he/she/it got confused or frightened … Next to *The Doomsday Weapon* this is one of my favourite Target originals.'; 'As [*The Giant Robot*] follows the TV prog word for word, this review is a waste of time … But I think the [cover] illustration [will] take some time to get used to. [It] lacks the finesse of Achilleos, and yet somehow reflects what the programme is today. The drawing of Sarah is terrible!'; and, finally, 'Yeauch! Wot an 'orrible cover [*The Terror of the Autons*]. Come back Chris Achilleos. All is forgiven …'.

After Brookes' run of four covers, Achilleos did indeed return, and completed a further 16 covers, his final contribution to the range being the May 1977 release *The Ark In Space*.

In the year following the launch of the Target list, Universal-Tandem found itself doing better and better. This growth, and the generally positive view that the publishing industry had of the company, meant that it was seen as a potentially lucrative acquisition by others. There was also another element to consider: as the fortunes of Universal-Tandem in the UK grew, so those of the parent company, the Universal Publishing and Distribution Corporation in New York, started to slide.

Brian Miles, Universal-Tandem's Sales Director, remembers the situation well: 'Tandem was growing in this country with our own lists, as well as the lists we were importing from America and elsewhere – we hit a small crest with books from Olympia Press, for example. We were also handling distribution for various other smaller companies. We were bombing along, and doing very well. But as we were going up, the Americans were going down.

'Robert and Arnold Abramson in America saw their empire dissolve. Their magazine sales were falling, their paperback side (the Softcover Library and Award Books) was dismal. They didn't have the right editorial strength, they wouldn't invest any money, they were going for the quick fix all the time. They were on their way out.

'What made it worse, was that every month they drew from Tandem in the UK a £10,000 management fee … and when they came over here, they always stayed at the Savoy and we picked up the bill. They were draining money from us as fast as we could make it.'

The scene was set for another company to take centre stage.

In 1975, Howard and Wyndham were a successful 'glamour' publishers. They had acquired W H Allen in 1971, and that publishing imprint dated back to the 18th Century. W H Allen had started publishing *belles-lettres*, works about the Middle and Far East and dictionaries of Islamic and Oriental languages, and it was only after the Second World War that the business changed to that of more popular titles. Before 1973, the company had only published hardback books, but in that year it moved into the mass market paperback field. The Star imprint was created and started publishing in 1974. Recent titles had included a biography of Eric Morcambe and Ernie Wise – at that time, Britain's top television comedians – and they were working their way through numerous other showbiz people. Ralph Fields, the Chairman of Howard and Wyndham, was also running several London

time was Terrance Dicks. Together, the pair created the short-lived BBC science fiction show *Moonbase 3* (1973).

After producing *Doctor Who*, Letts returned to directing (including 'The Android Invasion' for *Doctor Who*, 1975). He then became producer on the BBC's Sunday classic serials. Productions included *Rebecca of Sunnybrook Farm* (1978), *The History of Mr Polly* (1980), *The Hound of the Baskervilles* (1982), *Beau Geste* (1983), *The Invisible Man* (1984), and *Sense and Sensibility* (1985).

Letts returned to *Doctor Who* in 1980 when he was appointed Executive Producer to oversee new producer John Nathan-Turner for Season 18.

He wrote two *Doctor Who* radio serials in the 1990s and adapted these for Virgin (*The Paradise of Death*, 1994; *The Ghosts of N-Space*, 1995). He collaborated with Terrance Dicks on the *Doctor Who* novel *Deadly Reunion* (2003), published to coincide with the show's fortieth anniversary, and single-handedly wrote *Island of Death* (2005) for the same range.

He has also written two radio plays based on *Blake's 7* (1998), and contributed a script to the Big Finish *Sarah Jane Smith* range on audio (2003).

Peter Brookes' original sketch for the cover of *Doctor Who and the Terror of the Autons*. The writing on the back is: 'This "claw" to be on front.' The text against the front cover is: 'Nestene monster-planning black background. Dr Who jumping out of UNIT jeep in foreground'.

ABOVE: Cover for Marvel Comics' *The Fantastic Four* issue 49, illustrated by Jack Kirby and published in April 1966. Comparison of the hands of Galactus on the comic cover and Omega on the cover for *Doctor Who–The Three Doctors* suggests a definite influence on the creation of the *Doctor Who* cover.

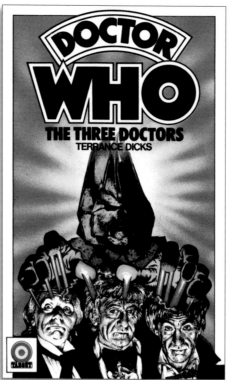

BELOW: Peter Brookes' sketch for the cover of *Doctor Who and the Planet of the Spiders*. An amendment requested by Philip Hinchcliffe, then producer of *Doctor Who* on television, was for the regeneration sequence to be re-drawn to make Tom Baker more recognisable.

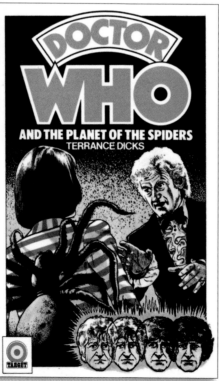

theatres. 'They were doing very well on many fronts,' frowned Miles. 'However, they'd launched a paperback imprint of their own called Star Books, which wasn't doing well. They could see that we were doing well and they took us. It wasn't said to me directly, but I think the Abramsons – Arnold, Bob his brother and Arnold's son Peter – decided to get out of publishing altogether. Someone – and I forget his name now – earned a 'finders' fee for bringing Howard and Wyndham and Universal-Tandem together. The takeover came about because the New York parent company wanted to capitalise on their investment.'

Howard and Wyndham made a take-over of the Allan Wingate hardback list, and the Tandem and Target paperback lists by acquiring all the share capital in the company for £100,000 in early April 1975. A contemporary report in the *Bookseller* explained that their intention was to maintain the editorial policies and staffs of both the Tandem and Star imprints as separate entities, and Ralph Stokes was offered a place on the board of W H Allen. Meanwhile, a new company called Tandem Publishing Ltd was created to handle the combined paperback publishing side.

From July 1976, however, the publisher was listed as Wyndham Publications Ltd, and the list combined the Star imprint with Tandem and Target, and a new imprint, Warner, created to market titles originally published in America in the UK. Managing director was Henry Kitchen, while Piers Dudgeon and Ralph Stokes looked after the editorial teams of the new company. From a financial perspective, the takeover was made to bolster the parent company's paperback backlist and turnover.

Although the *Doctor Who* schedule was largely unaffected by the behind the scenes changes, the people from Universal-Tandem felt very aggrieved. 'I

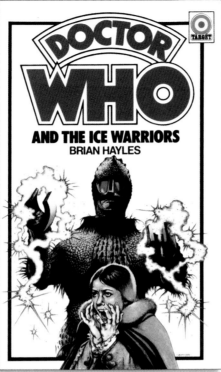

left in May 1976,' said Miles. 'I was so sick of publishing, having seen what Howard and Wyndham were doing, that I decided to move away from it entirely, and I went to work for my brother who was supplying first aid products to industry.' Miles eventually returned to publishing and later took great pleasure as Sales Director in seeing Grandreams publishing house go from virtually nothing to a multi-million

BELOW: The original entrance to 123 King Street–in between a Starburger and a Cancer Care shop on a busy high street.

LEFT: The building at 44 Hill Street in Mayfair. RIGHT: The adventures of Agaton Sax by Nils-Olof Franzén and illustrated by Quentin Blake. An early success for the Target range.

ARTISTS' RANKING

Although the sixth Doctor would no doubt disapprove, there is more than one way to skin a cat when it comes to ranking the Target novelisation artists in terms of how prolific they were. We've gone with total number of original pieces of artwork used on any *Doctor Who* Target paperback novel, and have indicated the number of 'first run' uses versus use on a reprint.

1st	Alister Pearson – 87 (26/61)[1]	
2nd	Andrew Skilleter – 45 (34/11)	
3rd	Chris Achilleos – 28 (28/0)[2]	
4th	David McAllister – 12 (12/0)	
5th	Jeff Cummins – 10 (6/4)[3]	
	Tony Masero – 10 (10/0)	
7th	John Geary – 6 (4/2)	
	Roy Knipe – 6 (6/0)	
9th	Peter Brookes – 4 (4/0)	
	Bill Donohoe – 4 (3/1)[4]	
	Mike Little – 4 (4/0)	
	Nick Spender – 4 (4/0)	
13th	Steve Kyte – 3 (3/0)	
	Alun Hood – 3 (0/3)	
15th	Tony Clark – 2 (2/0)	

There were also ten first-run Target novelisations that used photographs ▶

pound company. Miles still harbours a lot of ill feeling regarding the takeover. 'Tandem was literally destroyed overnight. Everyone involved in the success of the earlier company left or was sacked. Ralph Stokes, whose place on the W H Allen board was a myth – he was given an office and then ignored totally – also left; Carola Edmond, who was a super editor at Tandem, moved on; and a lot of the sales people also jumped ship. All as a result of the Howard and Wyndham take over. We had been moved to stinking rotten offices in King Street by Hammersmith Broadway … It was a dreadful time for everyone.'

The King Street offices were not ideal: entered through an insignificant doorway and up a narrow flight of stairs they comprised a cramped set of rooms above shops in one of London's most traffic congested areas. However this move was to be only temporary, as during 1977, those in King Street were moved to join the rest of W H Allen at 44 Hill Street in upmarket Mayfair – a large and elegant building with a cavernous lobby, marble floors and more space than ever before.

The impact on the *Doctor Who* titles from the Howard and Wyndham takeover was negligible – largely consisting of including the new publishers' details inside the books – and the Target imprint remained as it was. Another decision that seems to have been made by the new company was to recommence a simultaneous library hardback release of the *Doctor Who* books. This had been done by Universal-Tandem for the first five titles, but had then been stopped. The hardbacks were restarted at the end of 1975 with *The Planet of the Spiders*, and these were again issued under the Allan Wingate imprint.

When Michael Glover left the company early in 1976, he was succeeded as editor of the Target list by Elizabeth Godfray. 'The path had been well mapped out for me,' she remembered. 'Richard and Mike were the main editors, in all fairness. I just carried on what they had been doing in terms of sequels and whatever. I was never in the same league as either of those two. All the contacts had been made, there were certain titles in the range that were going to carry on, not just *Doctor Who* but *Agaton Sax*, Terrance Dicks' *Mounties* series, and so forth. I wasn't there as editor for very long, and I recall that all the titles had been decided.'

Godfray oversaw the books from January 1975 until she left in January 1977 to work at Hamlyn publishing: a far bigger organisation. 'After a few months of just me doing this, it became very hard work,' she explained. 'We were publishing four or more books a month, with all the associated problems. It all became too much, and that's why I decided to move on. It had been hard work when we had an editor and an assistant, but when there was just an editor … Also, you ended up having to do everything yourself: design the cover, write the blurbs that appeared on the covers, liaise with authors, copy edit, commission, sort out contracts … It was a lot of work.

'It was, however, a brilliant grounding experience working at Tandem; I learned so much about every aspect of publishing while I was there. The takeover by W H Allen wasn't too bad to begin with. At first everyone kept their jobs. We moved offices to 123 King Street in Hammersmith, and Universal-Tandem was allowed to continue as it had done. Later on W H Allen moved to 44 Hill Street in Mayfair which was very much posher.'

on their covers. These included *Doctor Who – Time-Flight* by Peter Grimwade and *Doctor Who – Terminus* by John Lydecker, which were the only two books in the range never to have painted covers.

1 Pearson also painted the covers for several Target *Doctor Who* non-fiction releases.
2 Achilleos also painted the covers for the two *Doctor Who Monster Books* and *The Making of Doctor Who*, published by Target.
3 Cummins also painted some of the covers for the *Doctor Who Discovers…* range, published by Target.
4 Donohoe also painted the cover for *The Programme Guide* and a cover for *Doctor Who and the Curse of Peladon* that was used only on the hardback release (see page 67).

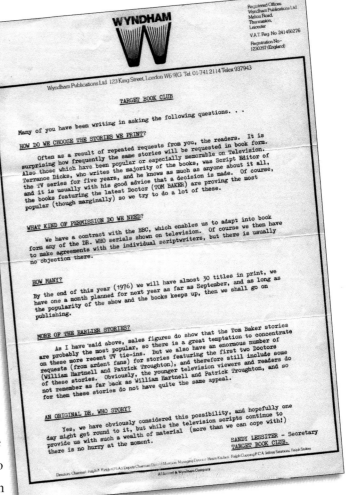

An early sheet from the Target Book Club answering readers' questions.

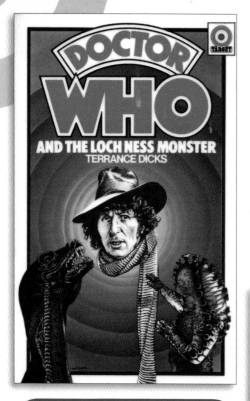

The range of Target books had proved so successful that during 1976 a book club was set up and run by the publishers to deal with inquiries and to promote the Target range more effectively. Godfray recalls that this was probably as a direct result of the correspondence that they received to do with the *Doctor Who* novels, and Henwood feels that it may also have been an attempt to rival the Puffin Book Club, which itself had been set up to rival Scholastic's similar club. The Target Book Club was administered by Sandy Lessiter, who responded to questions from readers and also mailed out advance schedules of books, catalogues and cover proofs. Also very popular were the Target badges – small, metal pin-badges of the colourful imprint logo. The club was eventually closed down during 1977.

The novelisations published through 1976 were: *The Tenth Planet* (Gerry Davis), *The Dinosaur Invasion* ['Invasion of the Dinosaurs'] and *The Space War* ['Frontier in Space'] (both by Malcolm Hulke), *The Ice Warriors* (Brian Hayles), and *The Loch Ness Monster* ['Terror of the Zygons'], *The Revenge of the Cybermen*, *The Genesis of the Daleks*, *The Web of Fear*, *The Planet of the Daleks* and *The Pyramids of Mars* (all by Terrance Dicks). All the covers were by Chris Achilleos.

In 1976, Keith Miller's *Doctor Who* Fan Club was superseded by the newly-formed *Doctor Who* Appreciation Society, and their magazine *Tardis* featured some reviews of the books written by society President Jan Vincent-Rudzki: 'On the whole [*The Tenth Planet*] is well written and keeps to the script closely. However the writer, Gerry Davis, seems to have had a brainstorm while writing parts of it … "Why?", you all ask (I hope) did Gerry Davis change the end, and the other parts of the book? They didn't improve the story in any way, and in some cases

GERRY DAVIS

'My favourites are *The Tomb of the Cybermen* and *The Highlanders*, which I was able to get some humour into. I found with Troughton's character that you could put a lot of jokes, games and surprises in and still maintain the suspense.'

Gerry Davis, DWB (number 59), October 1988

Gerry Davis became a BBC story editor in 1965 at the invitation of Head of Serials Donald Wilson, who had been impressed by a course he had written on TV scriptwriting. He had previously been a newspaper reporter, a merchant seaman and a writer for the Canadian Broadcasting Corporation, and had studied opera and worked as a cinema translator in Italy.

Davis served as script editor on *Doctor Who* from 'The Celestial Toymaker' (1966) to 'The Evil of the Daleks' (1967), overseeing the transformation of the first Doctor into the second. His first story for *Doctor Who* was 'The Highlanders' (co-credited to ▶

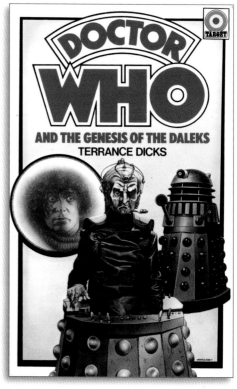

harmed it.'; 'The characters [in *The Web of Fear*] were very well brought out, and as each one was killed off it was almost like losing a friend … I would say the book is almost as good as the TV original, so I thoroughly recommend it.'

Miller meanwhile began publishing a fanzine called *Doctor Who Digest*. His comments on the 1976 batch of books were mostly favourable, however Terrance Dicks was starting to receive some adverse comment regarding an alleged lack of depth of writing in his work: 'I didn't exactly give the TV serial ["Revenge of the Cybermen"] a rave review, but strangely enough, I found the book better. I say strangely enough because it was written in Mr Dicks' traditional script-to-book-and-never-mind-the-detail style.'; 'When I heard that Terry Dicks was doing [*The Genesis of the Daleks*] I groaned inwardly because I could imagine 140 pages of dialogue and no detail, but I was proved wrong … On the whole, I thought the book was quite good, faithful to the TV series and Mr Dicks' attempt at detail was noted.'; 'The major boo-boo of [*The Space War*] was the ending where Mr Hulke had the Doctor enter the TARDIS perfectly healthy, where, as all of us Whoeys know, the Master shot the Doctor and he fell into the TARDIS desperately ill. Summing up, I'm afraid I had to force myself to finish the book, and felt no sense of satisfaction when I did.'; 'I thought [*The Pyramids of Mars*] was a very good interpretation of the TV story … The added prologue at the beginning of the book was a brilliant touch on the part of Mr Dicks, which set more detail into the story, and the history of Horus and Sutekh was quite fascinating. Terry seems to be getting better at slight detail as this chapter showed, but still there were long periods when he lapsed into script-to-book.'

Terrance Dicks had left the BBC in 1974 to concentrate on freelance writing, with the Target *Doctor Who* novelisations as a steady stream of work. Despite the fact that he was no longer script editor of *Doctor Who* on television, he was still normally given first refusal on the novels: 'It was all very unplanned and spontaneous,' he explained, 'both in terms of my doing them and then the other people dropping out. I never made any attempt to get my hands on it all, but it just ended up with my doing them all. The other writers found it all very hard work. Script writers don't like writing books; they find it a lot harder than writing for television. And it's lonely. And the money is peanuts compared with television. A lot of them just didn't want to be bothered with the books in the early days. I used to explain to them that I did all the work and they got half the money – that was the way it was split. It wasn't until later on that the script writers realised that they could do all the work and get *all* the money.'

Once Elizabeth Godfray left W H Allen at the start of 1977, no replacement editor for the Target list was appointed until May 1978, when Brenda Gardner joined, but as an interim measure Fanny Torrance, Managing Editor at W H Allen, looked after the range. In general terms, things were running smoothly: new titles for each year were suggested and initially administered by Terrance Dicks, with one or two

Elwyn Jones, who actually did little or no work on the scripts). He then teamed up with Dr Kit Pedler to create the Cybermen. He adapted a number of stories that he had worked on, as both writer and script editor, for publication by Target between 1975 and 1986.

Also in the 1960s, Davis worked on the soap operas *Coronation Street*, *199 Park Lane* and *United!*. In the late 1960s, he and Kit Pedler teamed up with producer Terence Dudley to create the science-gone-bad show *Doomwatch* (broadcast from 1970 to 1972). He wrote three novels with Pedler that expanded on some of their *Doomwatch* ideas: *Mutant 59: The Plastic-Eater* (1971), *Brainrack* (1974) and *The Dynostar Menace* (1975).

Working largely in the United States from the mid-1970s on, Davis contributed to the film *The Final Countdown* and TV shows such as *The Bionic Woman*, *Vegas* and *Captain Power and the Soldiers of the Future*.

He contributed 'Revenge of the Cybermen' to Tom Baker's first season as the Doctor, and in the 1980s suggested another *Doctor Who* storyline, 'Genesis of the Cybermen', to script editor Eric Saward, but the latter was not produced. When the BBC stopped making *Doctor Who* in 1989, Davis teamed up with Terry Nation and approached the BBC with an unsuccessful bid to relaunch the show.

Davis died on 31 August 1991, aged 64.

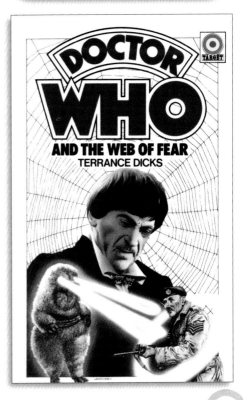

BRIAN HAYLES

Brian Hayles was born in Portsmouth on 7 March 1931. He trained as a sculptor and taught art in Canada for some years before becoming a full-time writer for television and radio.

He contributed television scripts to *Suspense* ('Last Race, Ginger Gentlemen', 1963), *Out of the Unknown* ('1+1 = 1.5', 1969; 'Deathday', 1971), *Doomwatch* ('The Iron Doctor', 1971; 'Hair Trigger', 1972) and *The Regiment* ('Setting In', 1973) amongst others. He also wrote the original serials *Legend of Death* (1965) and *The Moon Stallion* (1978), as well as the screenplays for the films *Nothing but the Night* (1972), *Warlords of Atlantis* (1978) and *Arabian Adventure* (1979).

He wrote six *Doctor Who* adventures between 1966 and 1974, two of which he adapted for Target.

As well as scriptwriting for the long-running BBC Radio 4 soap *The Archers*, Hayles also wrote a novel based on life between the World Wars in its fictional village of Ambridge. *Spring at Brookfield* was published in 1975 by Allan Wingate.

His adaptation of his BBC television script *The Moon Stallion* was published in 1978. The serial starred Sarah Sutton, who was featured on the book cover, and mixed Arthurian legend with blind Victorian teenage girls and warlocks.

His novel *Goldhawk* was published posthumously in 1979. The book told the fictional story of a criminal mastermind up against a CID officer in a diamond heist at Heathrow.

Hayles died on 30 October 1978.

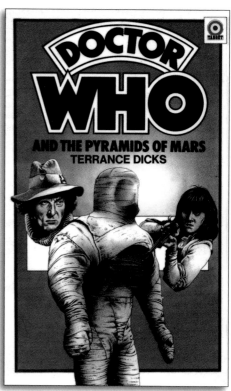

being written by other writers, and sales were very healthy indeed. Contemporary reports from 1978 indicate that collective sales of the first 35 titles (up to *The Mutants* published in September 1977) were topping two and a quarter million copies.

Tom Baker at a Target signing event circa 1977.

PART THREE: JOURNEY INTO PERIL

BRENDA GARDNER JOINED W H ALLEN IN MAY 1978 to look after the Target range. 'I had been working at Penguin for seven years as an assistant editor,' explained Gardner, 'and this was to be my first experience as a commissioning editor. I answered an ad in *The Bookseller* and went for an interview. I'm convinced they hired me because I said I could work on both paperback and hardback …'

Gardner was brought in, she recalls, primarily to look after the *Doctor Who* list, although there were other titles around. 'There were a few other children's books, and I was supposed to be doing some picture books and some children's fiction, as well as *Doctor Who*, which was certainly their biggest asset. The range had the most titles and made the most money. It really was successful. The bulk of my work was supposed to be commissioning new books and building the list up, and the *Doctor Who* list was more of a caretaking job – it wasn't a hard thing to do. Manuscripts came in, we copy-edited them, and then published them. It was very straightforward.

'I'd never experienced anything like *Doctor Who* before. It was very successful. We had several children who would phone up for news, and we had to send information out to various people and fans … There was a lot of interest. I even went along

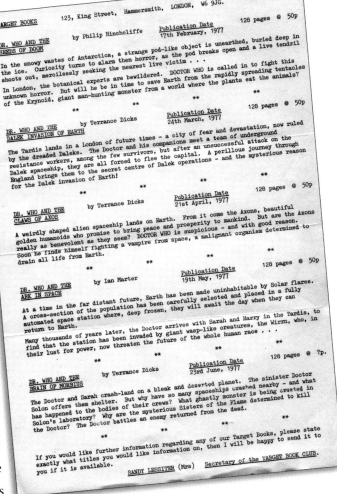

A Target Book Club promotional sheet giving news about forthcoming titles.

Two of the regular Target authors from this period: actor Ian Marter, and *Doctor Who* producer Philip Hinchcliffe.

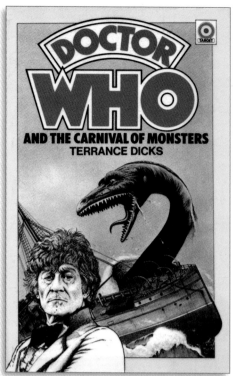

to some of the conventions – not as a guest or anything, but just to see what was going on.

'I always saw the books as being children's books, and for me it was a children's series. I was surprised when I met some of the fans and realised that they were a lot older and that the show had a much wider cult basis than I had previously thought. We didn't really think of it as a cult in those days, however.'

The publishers were more than happy for Dicks to provide most of the titles, as Gardner recalls. 'There wasn't any pressure to bring in new authors, but at around that time the series saw an increase in popularity, and we were talking about how we could use that: how we could expand the publishing. I think there was a slow change from script editors and writers not wanting to do their own stories as books, to them wanting to. Douglas Adams wrote to me at that time, and he was interested in doing something. I wrote back to say "Yes please," but it all went quiet and nothing happened.'

Two new authors who were contracted to write novelisations were actor Ian Marter, who had played the Doctor's companion Harry Sullivan in *Doctor Who* on television from 1974 until 1975, and *Doctor Who*'s producer Philip Hinchcliffe.

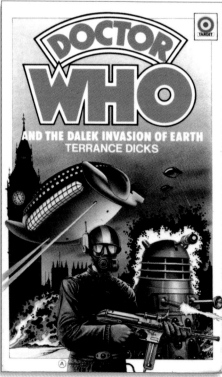

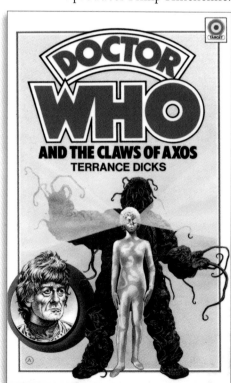

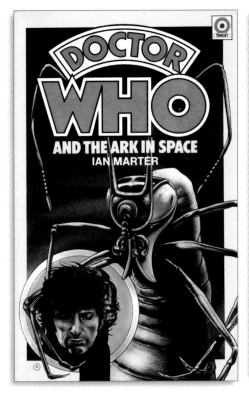

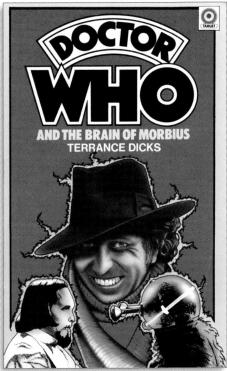

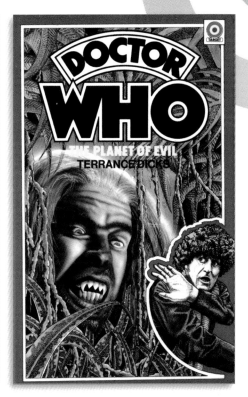

Marter was introduced to the publishers by Tom Baker, and, when he asked if he could write one of the books, they told him to send in a sample chapter. 'I chose "The Ark In Space" and "The Sontaran Experiment"', recalled Marter in 1984. 'I thought "The Ark in Space" was an excellent story and "The Sontaran Experiment" was its sequel – it was a two-parter also, which nobody else would touch. All the others I've been responsible for were the suggestions of the publishers as they have become available or as they have fitted into the schedules. I have a sneaking suspicion that I probably get the ones Terrance doesn't want to do!' Dicks remembers Marter apologising to him for doing the books, 'I told him it was fine by me,' laughs Dicks. 'I never considered I had the right of monopoly, and having done so many, I could hardly stand in the way of anyone else.'

Philip Hinchcliffe was the producer of *Doctor Who* from 1974 until 1977, and it was Barry Letts who suggested that he get in touch with the publishers as they were looking to bring more writers onto

'...like a car starting up...'

Gerry Davis, 1978

Doctor Who and the Tomb of the Cybermen

A sketch for an unused cover for *Doctor Who and the Mutants*. The artist is unknown, but it is thought the concept was scrapped when the *Doctor Who* production office requested that the novelisations only feature the image of the current Doctor (at the time Tom Baker).

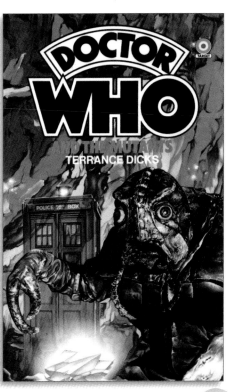

IAN MARTER

'It was a two-parter that nobody else would touch!'

Ian Marter, The Official Doctor Who Magazine *(number 93), October 1984*

Ian Don Marter was born in Keresley, near Coventry, on 28 October 1944. His father, Donald Herbert, was an RAF sergeant and electrician by trade, and his mother was Helen, *née* Donaldson.

In his early years he worked as, among other things, a teacher and a milkman. He became an actor after graduating from Oxford University, and appeared in repertory and West End productions and on television. He trained at the Bristol Old Vic. He was best known for playing companion Harry Sullivan in *Doctor Who* from 1974 to 1975, but had earlier appeared in the show as Lieutenant John Andrews in 'Carnival of Monsters' (1973). He had numerous other TV roles, including appearances in *Crown Court* and *Bergerac* ('Return of the Ice Maiden', 1985).

Marter got into writing the *Doctor Who* novelisations following a dinner conversation. He went on to adapt nine stories over ten years. He started with 'The Ark in Space', the television version of which he'd actually appeared in as Harry. He also wrote one of the *Companions* range, telling of the post-Doctor adventures of Harry in *Harry Sullivan's War*. Shortly before his death, he was discussing, with series editor Nigel Robinson, the possibility of adapting his unused movie script *Doctor Who Meets Scratchman* (co-written with Tom Baker) as a novel.

Alongside his *Doctor Who* writing, he penned movie adaptations of *Splash!* (1984), *Baby* (1985), *My Science Project* (published by Target, 1985), *Down and Out in Beverly Hills* (1986) and *Tough Guys* (1986) – in all but one case using the name Ian Don. His four books featuring the *Gummi Bears* were never published due to contractual problems.

Marter was married, with two sons. He died at the end of October 1986 at the age of 42.

the range. 'I had never written a book before,' Hinchcliffe said in 1981, 'but decided I would rather like to try. I did *The Seeds of Doom* first and Target liked it and said they would be happy for me to do others.'

This small image is the only existing evidence of an earlier cover for *Doctor Who and the Deadly Assassin*. The unused cover was by John Geary.

The books published during 1977 and 1978 were as follows; the author is noted where it was not Terrance Dicks: *The Carnival of Monsters*, *The Seeds of Doom* (Philip Hinchcliffe), *The Dalek Invasion of Earth*, *The Claws of Axos*, *The Ark in Space* (Ian Marter), *The Brain of Morbius*, *The Planet of Evil*, *The Mutants*, *The Deadly Assassin*, *The Talons of Weng-Chiang*, *The Masque of Mandragora* (Philip Hinchcliffe), *The Face of Evil*, *The Horror of Fang Rock*, *The Tomb of the Cybermen* (Gerry Davis), *The Time Warrior*, *Doctor Who – Death to the Daleks*, *The Android Invasion* and *The Sontaran Experiment* (Ian Marter).

Fan reaction to the new titles was on the whole positive, although Terrance

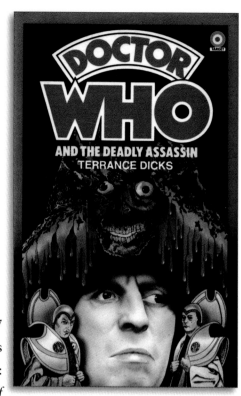

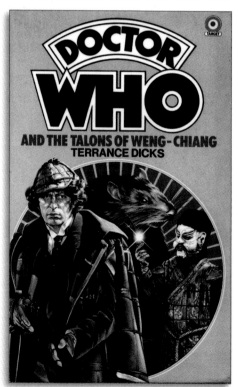

Dicks continued to come in for some criticism for his tendency to convert script to prose with little elaboration. As the '70s progressed, so more and more fan-produced magazines started to appear, and the range of publicly-aired views on the books likewise increased.

'I really must start off by saying how striking the cover of this book is,' wrote Keith Miller in the May 1977 edition of *Doctor Who Digest* about *The Carnival of Monsters*. 'I did like the additional fact … that "the Scope produced a mild hypnotic effect, making the viewer feel part of the scene he was witnessing." It gave the Scope a feeling of great complexity, rather than it just being an

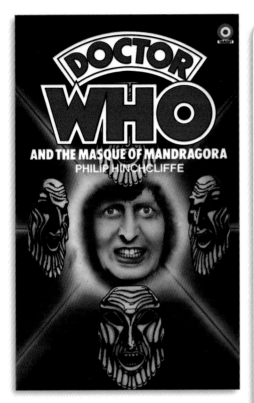

ALSO ON TARGET

Three of the authors for the *Doctor Who* range of novelisations had other books published by Target. Terrance Dicks had two original (and worlds apart) trilogies. First-up was *The Mounties*, telling the adventures of Rob MacGregor of the Canadian Mounted Police Force in the late 19th Century. Book one was *The Great March West*, followed by *Massacre in the Hills* and *War Drums of the Blackfoot*. Each book was published in hardback (by Allan Wingate) and in paperback during 1976.

Dicks' second trilogy was *Star Quest*, recounting the adventures of multi-national cousins Jan, Kevin and Anna who are kidnapped from Earth and become embroiled in the deadly struggle between the League of Sentient Lifeforms and their enemies. The first two books (*Spacejack* and *Roboworld*) were published by Target in 1979 and 1980 respectively, but there was a delay before the final book (*Terrorsaur!*) saw light of day in 1983. The covers were by Jeff Cummins and Bill Donohoe.

As well as adapting several *Doctor Who* stories, Ian Marter turned a number of movies into novels. Published by Target in 1985, and written under the pseudonym Ian Don, *My Science Project* was based on the Touchstone picture in which a group of students unleash havoc when they discover a time-jumping orb in a military junkyard. His other movie adaptations were published by Target's stablemate, Star Books.

Finally, in 1986, Donald Cotton saw Target publish his *The Bodkin Papers*, another told-first-hand tale in which a talking parrot recounts his adventures aboard Charles Darwin's ship *The Beagle*. Along with the text, Cotton also provided the book with a number of fine black and white illustrations.

elaborate TV set. One puzzling change … Why did Terrance change the Doctor's sonic screwdriver into a flare-pistol when he ignited the marsh gas in the dwelling place of the Drashigs? Perhaps he thought we would consider the sonic screwdriver a weapon, which the Doctor, as we all know, would never carry … Very entertaining.' Miller was less complimentary in the same issue about *The Seeds of Doom*: 'Enter *Doctor Who* producer Philip Hinchcliffe in his first attempt at writing Target books. Although his interpretation of a TV story is a bit more fluent than perhaps Mr Dicks's, he still fell into the dreaded 'script-to-book' style. I don't think I'll ever be happy until I find another Whitaker, Strutton or Letts … What I thought was absolutely *disastrous* was the omission of Amelia Ducat, possibly the best supporting character in a *Doctor Who* story for many years! One lousy mention, that's all. Sacrilege!'

PHILIP HINCHCLIFFE

'I had never written a book before but decided I would rather like to try. I did *The Seeds of Doom* first and Target liked it and said they would be happy for me to do others.'

Philip Hinchcliffe, Doctor Who Winter Special, *1981*

Philip Hinchcliffe was born in 1944 and educated at Slough Grammar School and Pembroke College, Cambridge. After a short spell of teaching, he began work as a story editor for ITV on a variety of programmes.

He joined the BBC in 1974 in order to take over from Barry Letts as producer of *Doctor Who*. It was Letts who encouraged Hinchcliffe to contact Target regarding novelising some of the Time Lord's adventures. Hinchcliffe's three *Doctor Who* titles were his only forays into the world of book writing.

He continued to oversee TV productions (including *Target* (1977), *Private Schultz* (1981), *Strangers and Brothers* (1984), *The Charmer* (1987), *The Gravy Train* (1990) and *Downwardly Mobile* (1994)) and produced the films *An Awfully Big Adventure* (1995), starring Hugh Grant, and *Total Eclipse* (1995), starring Leonardo Di Caprio. He then went on to act as executive producer on a number of television films and series, including *Taggart* (1999-2000) and *Rebus* (2000-2004).

JEFF CUMMINS

'I know, I know! It's the wrong Cyberman!!'
Jeff Cummins, jeffcummins.com

Jeff Cummins discovered his talent for art at school in the '60s. He grew up in North Wales before joining a London-based marketing company as a graphics artist in 1974. He moved on in 1976 and got commissions from pop artists such as Paul McCartney and Wings, Elvis Costello, Ted Nugent, Whitesnake and, with the design group Hipgnosis, Pink Floyd, Led Zeppelin, The Moody Blues and Peter Gabriel.

In 1976, he painted his first cover for the Target *Doctor Who* range. Alongside his ▶

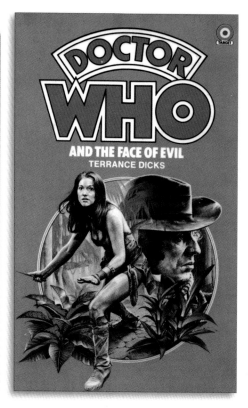

Ian Marter's debut was praised by John C Harding in the fanzine *Ark in Space*, published in 1983: 'At first glance, Ian Marter's adaptation of "The Ark In Space" looks encouraging; Chris Achilleos' cover art is impressive, one of the best Target covers of the time. The expectation this builds up is in no way dashed as Ian Marter turns in a fine adaptation. The important word here is adaptation. [The] writers are not there to turn out original novels, but neither are they there to commit the script to print verbatim, [and] Marter steers a middle road with a deft skill that returns an entertaining, readable account of a classic story.'

It was with *The Planet of Evil* that Dicks really seemed to falter, according to George G Milne in *Tardis*: 'After *The Brain of Morbius* and *The Dalek Invasion of Earth*, it looked as if Target books were on the way up again, however *Planet of Evil* was to shatter our hopes … Characterisation was non-existent except in the cases of Salamar and Sorenson … If you compare *Planet of Evil* with the other Marks/Dicks' book *The Day of the Daleks*, you see how the Target books have declined.' However, others had a higher opinion of the author's work. 'At last Terrance Dicks has excelled himself,' noted Simon Lydiard in a review of *The Deadly Assassin* in *The Doctor Who Files*. '[It is] a *Master*piece (get the gag).' And writing on the subject of *The Talons of Weng-Chiang* in the April 1978 edition of *Tardis*, Gary Hopkins opined: 'Terrance Dicks has done it again – in true style, he has written a book that, I feel certain, will be a gigantic success. [Dicks] has the ability to alter certain pieces of dialogue without losing the overall effect, sometimes even adding to it, and for this he became a writer with a difference … Robert Holmes must be very proud that yet another of his

*The original scriptwriter of both 'Planet of Evil' and 'Day of the Daleks' was Louis Marks.

excellent stories has been turned into a work of literary brilliance by one of his most talented contemporaries.'

Dicks's work on *The Time Warrior* and *Death to the Daleks* was similarly praised, while Ian Marter's second novel, *The Sontaran Experiment*, was appreciated by Peter Newell in the publication *23/11/63*: 'From the outset I intended to enjoy this novel, and I wasn't disappointed … I can only stop to wonder what Ian Marter would make of something like an early Bill Hartnell or Pat Troughton story. How would he fare with something like ["Inside the Spaceship"] or "The Rescue"? All in all, *The Sontaran Experiment* is a joy to read.'

Of the 1978 titles, it was really only Gerry Davis's *The Tomb of the Cybermen* that received a mixed reception: '*The Tomb of the Cybermen* is, to say the least, disappointing,' wrote an unknown reviewer in the fanzine *23/11/63*. 'Despite the apparent wealth of psychotics, neurotics and robotics (sorry!), the story is distinctly lacking in action. Finally, the question must be asked: is the book worth 60p? Well, if you are looking for nostalgia rather than a good story, the answer is yes. If not, then the answer, I'm afraid, is no.' However Chris Marton, writing in *Gallifrey*, had a contrasting opinion: 'In the best ever Target book concerning the exploits of the enigmatic, mythic astral drifter, Gerry Davis has penned the pick of this year's crop of novelisations, and put forward one of the best reasons for a few more older titles in the Target line-up per year. The writing is of an exceptionally high standard and the characters are especially well brought out.' This view was echoed by Chris Dunk in *Tardis*: 'The book was very atmospheric, and Gerry Davis's more descriptive way of writing suited the story down to the ground … The characterisation was

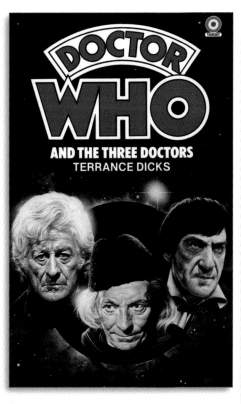

work on the novelisations, he provided covers for three titles in the *Doctor Who Discovers…* range (*Space Travel*, *Prehistoric Animals* and *Strange and Mysterious Creatures*) and for the first two books in Terrance Dicks' *Star Quest* trilogy, also published by Target.

His cover for 'The Time Meddler' (1988) marked a return to the range after almost a ten year break. It was his last project for Target, but he also painted eight covers for Virgin Publishing's range of original *Doctor Who* novels through the first half of the '90s – although he himself was less than happy with his work on these.

Around the time that he was producing his initial covers for Target, he was also working on artwork for a short-lived British SF poster magazine called *TV Sci-Fi Monthly* (1976). These were amongst his earliest commissions.

Cummins has gone on to paint covers and illustrations for dozens of books and magazines, including *Radio Times*. He has worked as a freelance illustrator and designer and produced ideas for children's animation. He now lives and works in Hertfordshire.

An early cover sketch for *Doctor Who and the Tomb of the Cybermen*. The artist is unknown, and it is assumed that the reason the cover was not progressed was that it featured an earlier incarnation of the Doctor, something the production team at the BBC were keen to avoid.

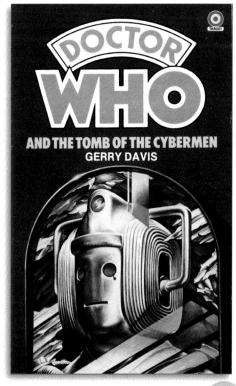

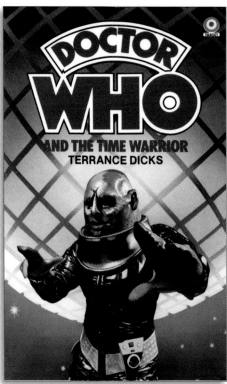

ROY KNIPE

Roy Knipe was born in Stafford in 1946 and graduated in 1971 from the Central School of Art and Design with a BA in Graphic Design. His first commission was for *Time Out* in 1971, and this was followed by work for various magazines and newspapers, including *Oz*, *Ink*, *Radio Times*, *New Society*, *Campaign*, *The Times*, the *Observer*, the *Telegraph* and the *Express*. He supplied cover artwork for *Time Out*, *Radio Times*, *Esquire Magazine* (New York), *Sunday Express* and the *Times Educational Supplement*. His work could also be seen in the magazine *TV Sci-Fi Monthly* (1976), illustrating shows such as *Star Trek*.

In 1976, Knipe joined the Spectron Artists agency and Art Box, and received commissions from leading advertising and design agencies all over the world. Clients included M & C Saatchi, Lowe Howard Spink, Abbot Mead Vickers BBDO, JWT, McCann Erickson and Publicis. ▶

very good throughout, although I noticed that there was not a single description of the second Doctor apart from his green eyes (?) … A great addition to my *Doctor Who* library, however, and a very hard act to follow for Terrance Dicks.'

As well as writing the books, Terrance Dicks was continuing to act as unofficial adviser to the range. He would decide which titles to do and, once agreement had been reached with the BBC (which was normally just the formality of an exchange of letters between the publishers and BBC Enterprises), he would either write them himself, or suggest someone else to handle them. This lightened the workload for the publishers, and was possibly one of the reasons that they did not immediately appoint a new editor on Elizabeth Godfray's departure.

When talking about the novelisations, Terrance Dicks is nostalgic. He agrees that his working method on the books changed as time went on. 'At first it was a great challenge. I'd never written a novel before, and so I tended to invent and fill out more stuff in the early books. Then, as the schedule grew more hectic and picked up pace, and it got to the stage where I was doing roughly one book a month, it became more of a technical exercise in taking a script and turning it into a book.

'I'm always kind of defensive about people thinking it's a piece of cake,' he comments when asked about the criticisms levelled at some of the books. 'You get two things from a script; you get what people do and what they say. You don't get what they look like, what they wear, what the weather is like, how they feel, what they're thinking, any of the visual aspects that are provided on television by the Costume and Make-up Departments and, indeed, by the actors themselves … All these things you have to recreate on the page, so the author has a lot of work to do in filling all this in.

'Certainly as time went on I added less and tried to put everything that was in the script into the book.'

Dicks also points out that when he started writing the books, there was virtually no commercial video and few repeats of *Doctor Who* on television. 'If you missed something on television, you'd missed it for good. Therefore the only chance you had to recreate the experience of seeing the show was to read the book, which is what I tried to allow for. My intention was to do an in-print video – the nearest thing you'd get to seeing the show again.'

Although Dicks's intentions were honourable, it was this principle that attracted the most criticism from fan readers. During the late '70s and early '80s, there seems to have been a shift in the fan base from wanting the novelisations to adhere strictly to the televised stories (witness *Doctor Who* Appreciation Society president Jan Vincent-Rudzki's comments, quoted above, regarding Gerry Davis's divergence from the televised version of 'The Tenth Planet' for his 1976 novelisation) to them openly embracing those novels (mainly, at the time, the Ian Marter-penned ones) that extrapolated from or presented a different slant on the source material. This shift can be partly attributed to the increasingly common availability of home video at the start of the '80s. If fans wanted to watch a story again, they could, as almost year-round repeats in Australia meant that many UK fans were able to import copies for themselves and their friends. There was also the fact that the initial fan base for the novelisations was growing up. The show on television was also arguably being aimed at a slightly more adult and intelligent audience – a fact noted by Brenda Gardner – but Dicks was still aiming his novelisations at the 11-14 age group originally intended for the Target range rather than at the more vocal and mature fan audience.

In 1984 he painted the prestigious Christmas cover for *Radio Times*, and in 1994 he designed a commemorative stamp for the Post Office to mark the centenary of the birth of R J Mitchell, designer of the Spitfire. His book covers have adorned titles by authors such as Paul Theroux, William Boyd and Hilda Von Stockum.

He has won several awards, and held many exhibitions of his work, he has also taught at the Addison Institute, Granville College in Sheffield, the Birmingham School of Art and the Norwich School of Art and Design.

He produced the covers for six books in the Target range during 1978 and 1979. So impressive was his cover for *Death to the Daleks* that it was released as a poster by W H Allen in the early 1980s and was also used on the cover of *Doctor Who Magazine* when they covered the Target book range in the '90s.

Knipe currently lives in France, and is still busy producing commercial artwork for a wide variety of clients, represented by the Thorogood agency.

MIKE LITTLE

Mike Little took over from Chris Achilleos as the principle cover artist on the Target range for a run of four books in 1977.

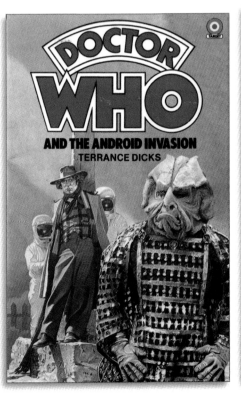

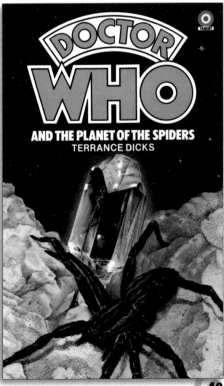

There were a few cases of books being rescheduled during this period: July 1977 was the original publication date for Gerry Davis's *The Tomb of the Cybermen*, but the manuscript was delayed and the book was eventually published in May 1978; and March 1978 was the date planned for publication of Terrance Dicks's own novelisation of his forthcoming TV story 'The Witch Lords', which ultimately fell through and was replaced – both on television and in the Target book schedule – by *Horror of Fang Rock*.

In the case of *The Time Warrior*, Dicks had persuaded Robert Holmes, the original scriptwriter, to tackle the novelisation. With no sign of the manuscript, W H Allen asked Dicks to chase it up, and he discovered that Holmes was having difficulties but still wanted to write the book. Then, after another long gap, three pages were sent by Holmes to Dicks with 'You finish it' written on the top. Dicks was very impressed with the three pages and often said that he wished he could write like that … but that at only three pages a year, it would be hard to make a living. Dicks used Holmes's work as the prologue to the eventual novel, and, as Holmes requested, wrote the remainder of the book himself.

There were also further points raised by the BBC regarding the cover artwork. They had previously queried both the use of a past Doctor on the cover of *The Web of Fear* and the fact that the Doctor did *not* appear on the cover of *The Space War*, and when presented with Chris Achilleos's cover for *The Claws of Axos* in November 1976, they again queried the use of a past Doctor. Initial cover designs for both *The Mutants* and *The Tomb of the Cybermen* were ultimately not used, presumably again as they both featured the appropriate past Doctor. In the case of *The Mutants*, the Controller of BBC1, Graeme McDonald, when he was consulted in Feburary 1977, demanded in very forceful terms to know why Tom Baker was not pictured on the cover. Any response to his note is not recorded.

During 1978, with the *Doctor Who* range continuing to do well, W H Allen started to look for more titles with which to expand the series. 'We did two junior books, and I'm sure Terrance may have suggested them,' recalled Gardner. 'There was the factual *Doctor Who Discovers* series, and we also later did a book on K-9 (*The Adventures of K9 And Other Mechanical Creatures*) and one on the Daleks (*Terry Nation's Dalek Special*). That was the first time I came across Terry Nation's agent, Roger Hancock. Very, very tough to work with. There was one point where we thought we wouldn't be allowed to use the Daleks on the cover or something. A very demanding man.'

The first title to be chosen for the new *Junior Doctor Who* range was *Doctor Who and the Brain of Morbius*, written by Terrance Dicks. The tentative publication date of July 1978 was swiftly changed to April 1979 and a second title, *Doctor Who and the Giant Robot*, was announced. This latter book ran into problems when producer Graham Williams commented that the likeness of Tom Baker in Peter Edwards' internal illustrations was very poor. At the start of 1979, the publication date for both titles was moved again, this time to December of that year. By July, the publication of *The Brain of Morbius* had been put back yet again, to 1980. *The Giant Robot* was finally released in hardback in December 1979, although readers had to wait until the following year before the paperback edition came out. After these two titles, no further *Junior Doctor Who* books were published.

With *The Ark in Space* in 1977, cover artist Chris Achilleos made his final contribution to the *Doctor Who* range. 'I had done so many,' Achilleos explained, 'and when Dom Rodi joined, I told him that I really wanted to give them up and explained my position to him. I think he reluctantly agreed.'

Dom Rodi was employed as art director for Star Books at W H Allen around 1975. 'I remember when I first arrived, going into the offices at the old Universal-Tandem offices at Gloucester Road and being told to create an art department,' he recalled. 'The first book I had to do was not a *Doctor Who*, it was a horror novel by Jefferey Konvitz called *The Sentinel*, and I had literally 24 hours to do it. I also did some Graham Masterton horror titles … They were great days.

'Taking over from Brian Boyle, Universal-Tandem's art director, I knew that Chris Achilleos was doing the *Doctor Who* covers, and he had set the standard. There was a working system for the *Doctor Who* covers there, which I saw no reason to change: the logo was set, it was just a case of refining the visual so that it was more the way that I saw them rather than the way Brian saw them.

'There came a point, and I can't remember why, where I made a change from Chris Achilleos to some new artists. Chris was starting to become very successful and was being commissioned for work all over the world. He was very kind, as I recall, and agreed to do more covers in order to give me the chance to find some other people

An unused and unfinished piece of art by Roy Knipe for *Doctor Who and the Planet of the Daleks*. This piece was commissioned from Knipe but the commission was cancelled before the art was completed and delivered. Knipe subsequently completed the artwork in the 2000s and sold it privately to a collector.

The Sentinel: the first cover edited by Dom Rodi.

ALUN HOOD

Alun Hood painted three covers for the Target range, all of them replacing artwork originally created by Peter Brookes. Other work included the cover for the paperback edition of Terrance Dicks' original children's novel *Cry Vampire!*

Hood painted album covers for 1970s British bands Budgie ('If I Were Britannia I'd Waive The Rules', 1976) and The Strawbs ('Deep Cut', 1976). He also worked on covers for books by Agatha Christie, Richard Adams, Brian Lumley and Sir Arthur Conan Doyle, amongst many others.

Hood died in the early 1990s.

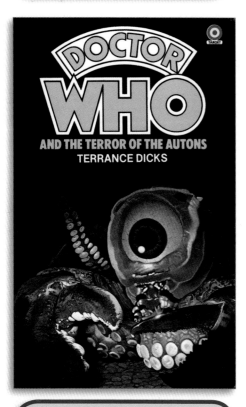

JOHN GEARY

John Geary contributed six covers to the Target range of *Doctor Who* novelisations in 1979. He also produced an alternative cover for *Doctor Who and the Deadly Assassin* that in the end was used purely in promotional literature.

In addition to his *Doctor Who* work, Geary provided a *Look-In* magazine cover illustrating the ITV fantasy series *Sapphire and Steel* and two covers for the tie-in novels for the BBC's science fiction radio series *Earthsearch*.

Alongside his cover work, Geary also contributed illustrations for *Radio Times*.

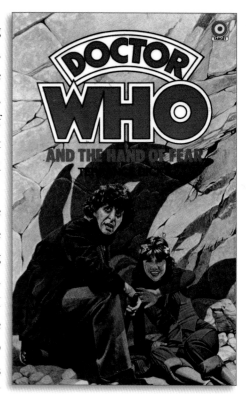

to work on them. What I was looking for was not another Chris Achilleos, because, even after all these years, there is no other Chris Achilleos, he's unique, but I was introduced to the work of Jeff Cummins through Martin Borland at Spectron Artists, who also represented Roy Knipe.'

Cummins, like Achilleos when he started, had not been long out of college and was touring the publishers trying to find work. 'I think I was put in touch with Dom Rodi, the art director at W H Allen,' remembered Cummins, 'and he asked me to do one of the *Doctor Who* covers as a sort of trial. That one was for *The Talons of Weng-Chiang*, and I remember trying very hard to get it as perfect as I could. After I had delivered that one, the call came in to do *The Mutants* at very short notice as another artist had fallen through or something. A similar thing happened on *The Tomb of the Cybermen*, and I ended up, as I later discovered, using the wrong sort of Cyberman on the cover.'

Rodi was looking for realism: 'Realism and the ability to render figures well. Jeff had a great feel for the texture of the subject, but with Chris, you also had an innate graphic design quality to his work, which made the compositions really stand out. The artists were working in the main with reference material derived from the BBC's archives, and sometimes there was very little of it. You might have a number of shots of Cybermen all taken from a given angle, but that might not be very dramatic or dynamic, and yet they had to try to make a cover out of what they had.

'I wanted to move away from the graphic feel that Chris brought to his paintings. With Jeff, it was very much creating a feeling of mood and illusion and atmosphere. I didn't see the *Doctor Who* range as a children's range of books. I don't think anyone did, from the sales people to the MD. It was always treated as an adult range, and from a design point of view, it was in a category of its own: sandwiched between the adult, thriller and horror books and other books that were specifically for children.'

Whereas Achilleos's cover paintings had been generally A3-sized, Cummins tended to paint his only slightly larger than the finished book. 'That was because it took longer to paint a bigger cover,' he says, 'and I had found that I could get all the detail on the smaller size – I was using brushes with two hairs on!'

Cummins painted nine covers for the range through 1978 and 1979, and contributed artwork and covers to a range of non-fiction *Doctor Who*-related books called the *Doctor Who Discovers* series, published in 1977 and 1978.

'I stopped doing the *Doctor Who* covers simply because I wanted to broaden what I did. I moved into doing record covers and worked with Paul McCartney (I did the inside spread for his *Wings Over America* LP), Rainbow, Ted Nugent, the Moody Blues and Elvis Costello amongst many others. Eventually I stopped doing that because all I seemed to be offered were Heavy Metal covers, and moved again into other areas. I've done a lot of work for the *Radio Times*, as well as video jackets, and character design for websites ... quite a diverse career, really.'

Dom Rodi left W H Allen in 1979 as he'd been offered a job with Sphere books; this lasted just a year before he was asked to join Artist Partners, an agency that handled a great many different artists. Replacing him as art director at W H Allen was Mike Brett, who was to oversee this aspect of the range for the next ten years.

1977 to 1979 saw several other artists working for the range. A programme of re-issuing the novelisations with new covers was started with a re-print of *The Three Doctors* in 1978, and over the next few years most of Achilleos's original covers were replaced as the books were reprinted. Alun Hood provided new covers for re-issues of three of the books originally jacketed with Peter Brookes's artwork (*The Auton Invasion*, *The Green Death* and *Planet of the Spiders*), while Cummins supplied a new jacket illustration for *The Giant Robot*, thus replacing Brookes's contribution completely. Mike Little worked on the new novelisations alongside Jeff Cummins, before Roy Knipe took over from Little. Another artist who contributed to the range was John Geary, whose work first appeared on a re-issue of *The Sea Devils* in 1979.

'If you look at their work,' explained Rodi, 'you can see what I was trying to do. Both Roy Knipe and John Geary have that graphical quality to their paintings. It's almost like trying to do film posters where you create something out of nothing. You might have two or three black and white photographs from the BBC for a *Doctor Who* cover and nothing else.'

It wasn't until later that year that another artist was found to look after the covers on a more regular basis. Andrew Skilleter was working as a freelance illustrator when he approached Mike

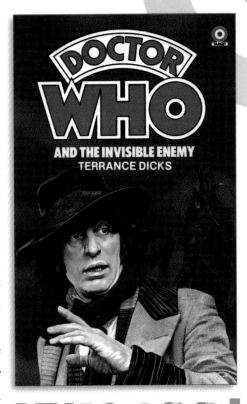

'...a peculiar trumpeting noise like a wounded animal...'

Philip Hinchcliffe, 1977
*Doctor Who and the
Masque of Mandragora*

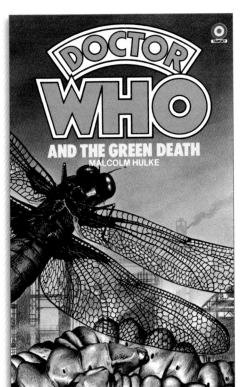

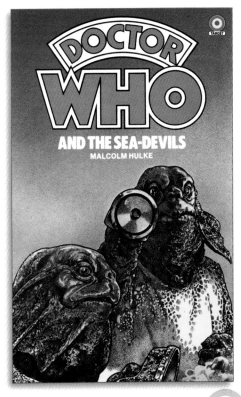

ANDREW SKILLETER

'One of the last covers I did in 1982, for "The Abominable Snowmen", I still regard highly today.'

Andrew Skilleter, writing in **Blacklight: The Art of Andrew Skilleter**, *December 1994*

Born on the Isle of Wight, Andrew Skilleter was captivated by illustration from an early age. He studied Graphic Design at Bournemouth and Poole College of Art and then pursued a career as a freelance illustrator, gaining commissions for magazines, children's books, advertising and merchandise.

His first mainstream cover illustrations were for W H Allen, including on the *Worzel Gummidge* and *Doctor Who* ranges. His first pieces of *Doctor Who* artwork were the cover and internal illustrations for *The Adventures of K9 and Other Mechanical Creatures* and *Terry Nation's Dalek Special* (both 1979). He contributed over 40 covers to the novelisation range between *Destiny of the Daleks* in 1979 and *The Mark of the Rani* in 1986. A handful of his video covers adorned the later Virgin reprints.

In the mid-1980s, he formed Who Dares, a publishing company that focused primarily on *Doctor Who*-related artwork. Products included prints, calendars, bookmarks and artcards. In 1988, the company published *Cybermen*, a collaborative work with actor-turned-writer David Banks, who had played the Cyberleader in several stories on television.

Skilleter dominated 1980s *Doctor Who* art. He painted 'The Five Doctors' cover for the *Radio Times*, the cover for Peter Haining's *The Key to Time* (1984), posters for *Doctor Who Magazine* and illustrations for Piccadilly Press's *The TARDIS Inside Out* by John Nathan-Turner (1984), and designed the colourful BBC tour bus that travelled the USA promoting the show throughout 1986.

In the 1990s, Skilleter provided *Doctor Who* artwork for BBC Video, five books in Virgin's range of original novels, a knitting pattern booklet and several large-format hardbacks, notably *Blacklight* (1995), the definitive collection of his *Doctor Who* artwork. He worked with writer Terrance Dicks again when he painted the covers ▶

Brett about the possibility of some work. Out of that meeting, he found himself supplying new covers for the original Barbara Euphan-Todd *Worzel Gummidge* books, followed by some covers for the Star list – including a reprint jacket for Graham Masterton's seminal horror thriller *The Manitou*. Eventually he was asked if he would like to tackle *Doctor Who*. 'I was asked to do not just the jacket but the whole K-9 special, all of which had to be done to an impossible timetable,' he told *Doctor Who Magazine* in 1983. 'It was my very first affair with *Doctor Who*, and all too rushed. Around the corner was the *Dalek Special*, to be followed by my first Target *Doctor Who* novelisation jacket, *The Destiny of the Daleks*, which went down very well.'

As *Doctor Who* was still doing well on television, pressure increased to link the publication dates of selected titles to the television transmission of the stories themselves. The first story for which this was attempted was *The Destiny of the Daleks*, the book's publication being planned for November 1979, just two months after the story would finish on television. When sent a proof of Andrew Skilleter's cover artwork in June 1979, producer Graham Williams commented that it wasn't very 'individual' and that as the story hadn't actually been made at that time, it was tricky to provide any photographic reference for it. He also noted that he hoped the publication date would follow the BBC's transmission of the story.

During 1979, the books went bi-monthly, for reasons unknown, and the titles published were *The Hand of Fear*, *The Invisible Enemy*, *The Robots of Death*, *The Image of the Fendahl*, *The War Games* (Malcolm Hulke), *The Destiny of the Daleks* and *The Ribos Operation* (Ian Marter). *The War Games* was to be the final contribution to the range from Malcolm Hulke as he died on 6 July 1979 after completing the book and before it was published.

Dicks was still receiving much praise for his work: 'Once more Terrance Dicks keeps to the successful formula and descriptive comments he has used throughout his adaptations of the Tom Baker stories, with few exceptions ...' wrote Graeme Wood in *23/11/63* about *The Hand of Fear*. 'Dicks provides an almost straightforward novel of the broadcast programme. Even the inconsistencies that

A series of Barbara Euphan-Todd's Worzel Gummidge novels, covers by Andrew Skilleter.

appeared in the TV showing are still apparent here … An enjoyable novel, although it is nothing really special,' *The Robots of Death* seems to have been enjoyed by just about everyone: 'Mr Dicks has managed to get across the atmosphere of the sandminer perfectly,' enthused Tim Munro in *Fendahl*. 'The weariness of the crew, and everybody's tetchiness with Uvanov came across just as well as in the TV series'. 'All in all, an excellent book,' agreed John C Harding, writing in *The Ark In Space*, 'and one of Terrance Dicks' best. As a representation of the story it excels itself.'

Paul Mount, however, writing in *The Doctor Who Review*, found a cause for concern regarding *The Robots of Death*: 'The major gripe about this excellent novel, is of course its size. After two years at the stable price of 60p, Target have at last been forced to increase to 70p, but the fact that they chose to do so with the novel with the lowest page count, at a mere 101 pages of actual printing, is rather unfortunate to say the least.'

Of the 1979 novels, it was perhaps *The War Games* of which the most was expected, but which was found most wanting, as these comments from Paul Mount in *The Doctor Who Review* exemplify: 'I feel that [Hulke's] adaptation of "The War Games" is not a fitting testament to his great and undeniable talent, and, in parts, comes across as little more than an extended Terrance Dicks effort … We are left with a long, involved story concentrated into a relatively short book, with an absurdly large cast of characters, most of whom remain hideously undeveloped … Basically, it is not a good book. It is not a good story. It is not the book it should have been, and it is certainly not the work that I shall remember the genius of Malcolm Hulke for.'

Perhaps the most significant event connected with the range came when Time-Life Films in America approached W H Allen in 1978 asking if they could distribute the *Doctor Who* books in the USA. W H Allen agreed to co-ordinate this, but it wasn't until Lyle Stuart took over distribution in 1983 that the titles became widely available there. The promotion of *Doctor Who* in the USA had started in 1978 when Time-Life Television distributed a package of 98 *Doctor Who* episodes comprising the first 23 Tom Baker stories. In fact, Chris Achilleos's artwork for *The Doctor Who Monster Book* was used to promote the launch of the series in America, an arrangement that the artist remembers well: 'W H Allen got in touch with me one day and asked if they could borrow some of the original artwork for publicity purposes. So I brought some in, including the piece for the first *Doctor Who Monster Book*, and then heard nothing for ages. When I eventually asked if they could let me have my artwork back, they kept making excuses and eventually admitted that they'd mislaid the *Monster Book* art. I was furious, of course, but then they suddenly said they'd found it, and told me that it

for the latter's *The Unexplained* series of original novels for older children.

Alongside his *Doctor Who* work, Skilleter has provided covers for titles by numerous adult and children's authors, including Ruth Rendell, Enid Blyton and Captain W E Johns (creator of *Biggles*). He has painted covers for audio, CD and video releases (including *Star Cops*), and created works based on the fantasy worlds of Tolkien, C S Lewis, Gerry Anderson and *Star Wars*. His book illustration work has been seen in *Stories from The Decameron of Baccaccio* (1980), a richly illustrated role-playing book, *Ten Doors of Doom* (1987) and a personal retelling of *Ivanhoe* (1997). A DVD devoted to his work was released by Reeltime Pictures (2005).

Skilleter continues to produce artwork, using both traditional and digital approaches, and in addition to professional work continues to paint private commissions and to sell his original art and limited edition prints. He is currently also writing and pursuing new creative directions.

'A very tall man with a mop of curly hair … He was dressed with a kind of casual Bohemian elegance in a long, loose jacket, gaily checked waistcoat and tweed trousers. The outfit was topped with a broad-brimmed soft hat, and an incredibly long multi-coloured scarf dangled round his neck.'

Terrance Dicks, 1979
Doctor Who and the Invisible Enemy

The Doctor Who Monster Book. The first and most popular factual title published under the Target imprint.

Chris Achilleos' distinctive artwork from *The Second Doctor Who Monster Book* was also used by BBC Worldwide to promote the series in America.

was in America.'

What had happened was that the BBC had asked W H Allen if they could supply some illustrations to help promote the sale of *Doctor Who* to American television. The BBC claimed, when challenged by Achilleos over the use of his art, that they had assumed that they had the rights to use it, and W H Allen stated that they had not known to what use the BBC intended to put the art.

Caught in the middle, Achilleos was understandably very upset. 'All W H Allen had bought was the right to use the art with regards to the book,' he explained. 'Certainly not to give to the BBC to launch the *Doctor Who* series in America, which I found out about only by accident when a friend sent me a television magazine with my work on the cover! I was not paid for any of that, and despite my complaints, no-one seemed to want to take it seriously.' At this time, Achilleos had stopped doing the *Doctor Who* covers on a regular basis but had hoped that he might do more in the future. 'This was a sad way to conclude my dealings with the publisher,' he admitted. 'I'd always hoped to stay on good terms with them.'

The sale of the *Doctor Who* television series to America was to lead to the American public's total acceptance of Tom Baker as the Doctor, and an exponential increase in *Doctor Who*'s fortunes in the USA. Before long it would emerge as a massive cult show, and, in the early '80s, the print runs for each novelisation's first edition paperback leaped from a not-insignificant 25,000 to 30,000 copies to a massive 50,000 or 60,000 copies.

Although the *Doctor Who* titles were doing very well for W H Allen, the company as a whole was in trouble. 'I don't really know what the cause was,' says Brenda Gardner today, 'but we all knew that there were problems – we hadn't made our targets or something, or someone, maybe an investor, was pulling out. Something was certainly up. They started letting the flat upstairs at 44 Hill Street that we used to use for parties, and several people had said to me that the company was looking for cutbacks. However, because the *Doctor Who* books were so successful, I didn't think I'd be affected.

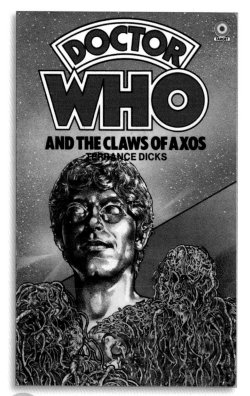

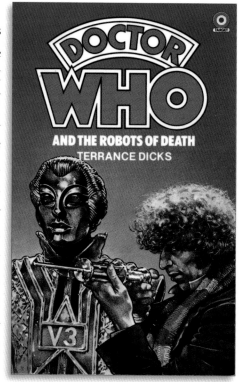

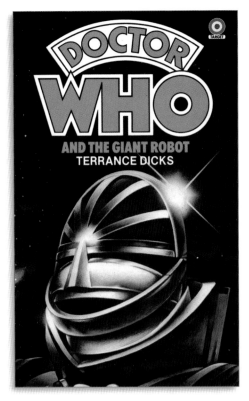

'Earlier in the year, when one of my colleagues – Jackie Lilley – left to join her husband in Greece, I decided to upgrade her job, allowing me to spend more time on the hardbacks and getting someone new in to look after the paperbacks. I told my boss I wanted to do this, and no-one told me I shouldn't, so again I felt that my place in the company was secure.'

During the summer of 1979, Ralph Fields, the owner of W H Allen, brought in Bob Tanner, a literary agent who had been Managing Director of the New English Library paperback imprint, to act as a consultant to the W H Allen publishing operation. W H

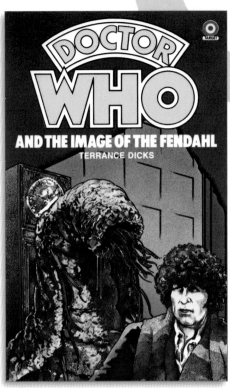

Allen's Managing Director, Francis Bennett, subsequently left the company to join Thompsons as the Managing Director of Sphere Books. His place was then taken at W H Allen by Tanner. Generally when a publishing company gets into financial difficulties, there are two possible remedies: slim down the workforce, or jettison a whole area. In the case of W H Allen at this time, the approach taken seemed to be a combination of the two, with the children's books division being especially hard-hit.

Brenda Gardner was made redundant in September 1979. 'I was called down to Francis Bennett's office and told that I was being made redundant. The person I had brought in to replace Jackie was also made redundant at the same time, and she'd only been there a week or so. It wasn't a very pleasant time.

'What they did was to cut the children's department right back and move the *Doctor Who* list to be under the responsibility of the adult editor – this was the excuse I recall, anyway, for why my job was not there any more.'

After she left W H Allen, Brenda Gardner joined E J Arnold, a Leeds-based educational publisher, to set up a trade list for them. 'I started a list called Pepper Press, and then a year later, they too had problems. We'd just launched the list and the company wanted to fold it, so I persuaded them to sell it on to another publisher called Evans, and I went to them with it. A year later, they folded as well, and hived off their trade division to a company called Bell and Hyman. By that time, I had decided to go it alone, and, after briefly housekeeping the list for Bell and Hyman, I left in July 1983 to start my own company, Piccadilly Press, which is still going strong today.'

Under Gardner, Piccadilly Press were responsible for a number of *Doctor Who-*

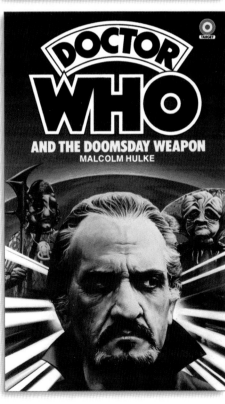

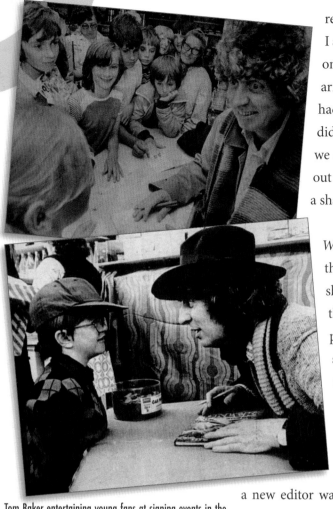

related books in the '80s. 'I had always got on well with Terrance, and I also liked Andrew Skilleter. I think it was Andrew who mentioned one day that John Nathan-Turner was dying to do a book, and so we arranged to meet … It wasn't the happiest of relationships, but we had Andrew to do the artwork, and the books did very well. We also did some *Doctor Who* encyclopedias with author David Saunders, but we couldn't complete the series – the paperback publisher dropped out and we couldn't afford to do them on hardbacks alone, which was a shame.'

Gardner's overriding memories of working on the Target *Doctor Who* list are, however, good ones. 'The nicest thing was the idea that you were publishing something that kids really wanted to buy,' she smiles. 'There was a ready market and people were dying for the books. That was a great surprise to me, because normally you publish and hope for the best. It was nice being a part of a success story. I found out a lot about working with people and about how the industry operated. We certainly had our good times. When we used to take people out to lunch, the "staff canteen" was either Langans Brasserie or The Greenhouse. Both Terrance and I remember those days with much fondness.'

With the departure of Brenda Gardner at the end of 1979, a new editor was eventually appointed to the range in the person of Christine Donougher. Also in 1979, Graham Williams moved on from producing *Doctor Who* on television, and his place was taken by John Nathan-Turner.

Tom Baker entertaining young fans at signing events in the late seventies.

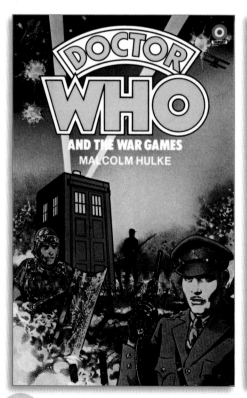

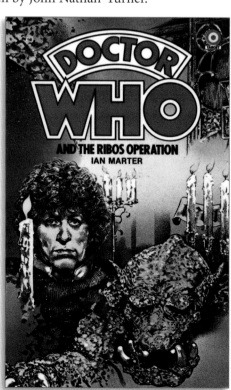

PART FOUR: PRISONERS OF SUCCESS

BY THE END OF 1979, THERE WERE 52 TARGET *Doctor Who* novelisations available, but the publishers could not afford to become complacent. 'I remember our licence was coming up for renewal,' recalls Brenda Gardner, 'and we took a couple of people from BBC Enterprises out to lunch as we were worried that they might want not to renew, and to keep the licence for themselves. To my amazement, there was no suggestion of this at all. We were very relieved, and pleased. We were expecting them to make us pay more royalties or something as the books were doing so well, but they were happy and we were allowed to carry on.'

The books did carry on, but under a different team following Gardner's redundancy in the shake-up instigated by new Managing Director Bob Tanner.

Tanner has a no-nonsense style, and an approach to business that may be seen as uncompromising by some but certainly gets results. He started his working life on the *Daily Mail* newspaper but in the early '60s was persuaded to go and work for the Scots

Andrew Skilleter's preparatory sketch for the figure of the Dæmon Azal for the reprint cover of *Doctor Who and the Dæmons*.

DAVID McALLISTER

'It was hard to get hold of reference material and Mike Brett was always very specific about what he wanted. I would've liked more freedom.'
David McAllister, interviewed by Tim Neal for The Target Book, *April 2007*

Belfast-born David McAllister studied at the Central College of Art and Design in London and started illustrating professionally in 1977. Moving on from design work, his first published piece of work was a *film noir* style cover for *Time Out* magazine. He painted covers for books throughout the '70s, '80s and '90s. He worked for a number of publishing houses including Penguin, Severn House, New English Library and Hamlyn, where he provided the covers for, amongst others, the *Blade* series of Westerns by Matt Chisholm. He provided the cover for Brian Hayles' non-*Doctor Who* novel *Goldhawk* in 1979.

McAllister was already working with Mike Brett at W H Allen on covers for a number of thriller and romance novels when he was given the opportunity to contribute to the *Doctor Who* range. He painted twelve covers in all during the '80s including two covers for *The Companions of Doctor Who* range. He also was commissioned for an artwork cover for fifth Doctor story 'The Visitation', but this was rejected by the BBC and as a result, photographic covers were introduced to the range.

Alongside his *Doctor Who* work, McAllister has painted other cult favourites like Bruce Lee, Robin Hood, *Star Trek*, *Star Wars*, *Indiana Jones* and antiques dealer David Dickinson, and has produced advertising material for the Disney Company and McDonalds.

As well as continuing to work in commercial illustration, he has spent time recently building up his portfolio of personal work, which has a tendency towards portraiture and black and white/*film noir* style pieces, with a view to exhibiting.

VWOORP! VWOORP!
'The sound was faint at first, but it quickly grew. It was an unmusical sound, a warning hoot...'
John Lydecker, 1982
Doctor Who and Warriors' Gate

entrepreneur John Menzies, whose book division he ran for about eight years. He eventually became a director of Menzies ('The first Sassenach to do so,' he recalled) but then was approached to join the newly-created New English Library publishing imprint. 'What happened was that New American Library (NAL) bought Four Square Books,' explained Tanner. Coincidentally, Four Square Books was the company from which came both Ralph Stokes and Brian Miles – the Managing Director and Sales Director of the Universal Tandem Publishing Company who in 1973 first initiated the Target list and started the whole range of *Doctor Who* novelisations off.

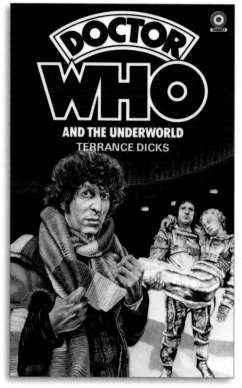

'Four Square Books were hopeless,' Tanner continued candidly. 'They hadn't made a profit in about 15 years, and NAL renamed the UK operation New English Library (NEL). Then NAL was bought out by the *Los Angeles Times*, so therefore the *Los Angeles Times* got NEL too. I was then approached to join NEL but I turned them down. They persisted and asked again, and I again said no. Then, on a Whitsun Sunday morning, up at Claridges Hotel in London, they asked me again … The man who was president of the book division at the *Los Angeles Times* asked

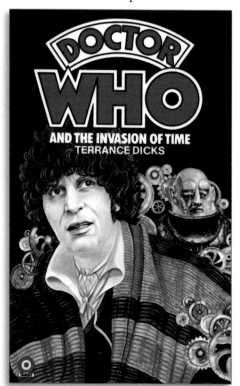

me to join, and I told him that they had problems – very bad overstocks; it was the talk of the trade how bad NEL was – and they'd need Jesus Christ to get them out of trouble, to which he asked me if He was available! I liked the man after this, and decided to think about the offer. I spoke to John Menzies, for whom I had very high regard, about it, and eventually decided to join them.

'I worked a year as Marketing Director for NEL and then took over as Managing Director, eventually becoming their longest-serving Managing Director ever. When I left to start up my literary agency, International Scripts, around 1968, within two years the NEL list was

sold to Hodder and Stoughton, where it continued to be published for many years. I got to know many publishers while I was at NEL, and among them were the Americans who owned W H Allen, Ralph Fields and Mattie Burdon.

'Then, in the mid-'70s, I went to the Los Angeles book fair and met up again with Ralph. He told me that they had four companies, among them W H Allen. They wanted me to join them to look after these companies. I looked over the paperwork and finances of the four, and reported that I thought three of them were hopeless, but that W H Allen could be saved. They asked me to look at the budget for the next year. I said that they'd never make it, and when they'd calmed down, I explained that they simply didn't have enough books being published to make the money they needed.'

As a result of Tanner's discussions with Fields and Burdon, changes were made to W H Allen's staffing structures, which culminated in the current Managing Director moving on from the company by his own choice. This left W H Allen without a Managing Director, but Fields and Burdon had their own plans.

'I went off on holiday to France,' recalled Tanner, 'and on my first day back

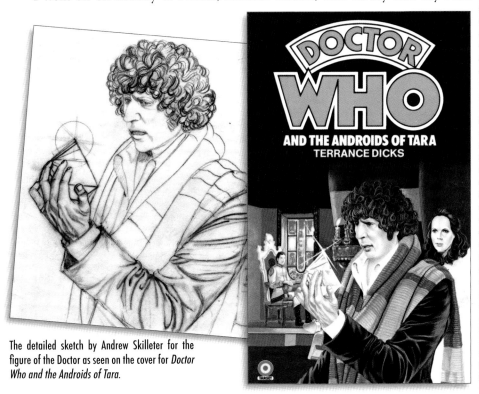

The detailed sketch by Andrew Skilleter for the figure of the Doctor as seen on the cover for *Doctor Who and the Androids of Tara*.

BILL DONOHOE

'With each commission, I went to the BBC photo library for reference images. Often there was little to go on, so a lot was made up.'
Bill Donohoe, interviewed by Tim Neal for **The Target Book***, January 2007*

William J Donohoe was born in 1956 and graduated from Brighton Art College in 1978. He travelled for a while before securing an agent in London and has worked consistently as an illustrator ever since. Some of his first commercial work was a run of four covers for the Target range in 1980/81. He also made one other contribution to the novelisations, providing the cover used only on the W H Allen hardback release of *Doctor Who and the Curse of Peladon* (1980).

Donohoe also painted the artwork used on the original 1981 editions of *The Doctor Who Programme Guide*. The same illustration was used again for various promotional pieces and on the first *Doctor Who Gift Set* box. His cover for *The Cybermen* was issued as a poster by W H Allen in 1985.

When, in the early 1990s, Virgin were working on David J Howe's thirtieth anniversary book *Timeframe*, they contacted Donohoe to seek permission to use artwork from some of his covers within the book. This led to him painting the covers for five of their original novels: *Blood Harvest* (1994), *Human Nature* (1995), *Head Games* (1995), *Death and Diplomacy* (1996) and *Damaged Goods* (1996).

Throughout the 1980s and 1990s, Donohoe produced traditional artwork for use on book and video covers, and illustrated a great number of educational books for children. Since 1997 he has moved mainly into computer-based artwork. He now lives in Brighton with his wife and two children.

STEVE KYTE

'I was gutted at never getting a crack at a Dalek cover!'

Steve Kyte, interviewed by Tim Neal for **The Target Book**, *January 2007*

Steve Kyte was born in London in 1958. Inspired by comic book artists and following the footsteps of his two older brothers, he studied Graphic Design and Illustration at Kingston Polytechnic, graduating in 1979. He set himself up as a freelance artist immediately after, and work began to come through in the form of illustrations for educational publications and children's books.

The Target *Doctor Who* covers were some of the first work he did. Alongside the three paintings used, Kyte also produced a cover for *Doctor Who and the Enemy of the World* that went unused in favour of one from Bill Donohoe.

Although a *Doctor Who* fan, Kyte's main love with regard to television fantasy has always been the work of Gerry Anderson. He joined and later helped run Fanderson, the official fan club, and has produced artwork (for video covers, jigsaws, comics, commemorative plates and so on) for *Thunderbirds*, *Captain Scarlet* and other Anderson shows, and also developed character designs for Anderson's Japanese animated TV show *Firestorm* (2003).

Kyte has also worked on *2000 AD* and provided the cover for a video release of the 1962 film version of *The Day of the Triffids*.

Since the 1980s he has developed an interest in Japanese anime, and a lot of his more recent work has been related to Manga-style illustrations, including those for the new edition of *The Anime Encyclopedia* (2006) by Jonathan Clements and Kyte's partner Helen McCarthy. Together with Helen, he started the first English anime fanzine, *Anime UK*, which went on to become a full colour international magazine, reflected in its name change to *Anime FX*.

In the late 1990s, he illustrated a series of children's books by Chris Wooding called *Broken Sky* (2000-2001). More recently, he has been working on ▶

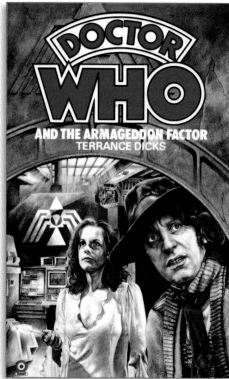

from holiday, Ralph was on the phone asking if I'd come round to see them. I'd told him after doing all the initial consultancy that I was happy running my agency and simply didn't have the time to run one of their companies as well, but he wanted me to come and see him, so I agreed to meet the next day.

'When I arrived, he took me down to the basement of 44 Hill Street, a huge ballroom-type room they used to entertain people and to hold parties and so on, and when I walked in, I saw that all the staff were assembled there. Ralph introduced me to them and said, "This is Bob Tanner, your new Managing Director!"

'I'd never agreed to this! I had no intention of taking over as Managing Director! But this was Ralph Fields. He pulled a blinder on me, and how could I then refuse?

'They had no money, things were in a terrible state, and every day people would arrive to try and take away typewriters and other equipment. I had no salary, they couldn't afford a car for me and it wasn't until I'd been there some six weeks that we discussed how much they were going to pay me. The first thing I wanted was a qualified accountant, and I managed to persuade the number two man at NEL to come and join me, which was one of the best moves I ever made. He was a tremendous help, as I'm not a financial man, and together we sorted the whole thing out.

'I'll tell you one thing. This big room in the basement I told you about … I arrived for the first editorial meeting, and it was over lunchtime. So I went down to this room, and there was a Bacchanalian feast going on – and this was a company with no money! I'd never seen anything like it in my life: spirits, beer, wine, heaps of food … We put a stop to that sort of thing.'

Among the people brought in by Tanner was Christine Donougher. 'I didn't think Christine had enough experience for the Editorial Director job we had advertised,' said Tanner. 'When I told Christine that we couldn't use her, she asked if there was another job, and so I said that we could take her on as an editor, and she agreed. Later on, Christine took on more responsibility and was a great asset to the company.'

Before Tanner could really get to grips with any pressing *Doctor Who*-related matters, the first thing he had to do was to sort out the next six months' worth of titles for W H Allen to publish and to keep the company afloat. As it transpired, he managed to source only enough books for five months – and to do that he had to go to New York to speak to agents, as the company owed so much money to agents in the UK that none of them was keen to supply books.

Tanner was aware that the *Doctor Who* range of novelisations were doing well, and he quickly became very fond of the subject. '*Doctor Who* was wonderful. I loved it. When you deal with a subject, you fall in love with it. When I think back to my days in publishing, what really made New English Library for me was Harold Robbins and gaining distribution of *Penthouse* magazine. Two big things. I was also very proud of a series of books called *Skinheads* – critically slammed, but they sold very well despite everything. And what made W H Allen? It was *Doctor Who*.

'I'd actually been at the launch of the Target list and the first *Doctor Who* titles in 1973, and I knew Ralph Stokes. *Doctor Who* was a minor part of W H Allen's output when I started. The books were cheaply priced at around 70 pence each, and they were publishing about one a month. I thought there was a great opportunity with *Doctor Who* as it was very popular.

'I suggested putting the price up, but the Marketing Director said that if we put the price up, we'd not sell any copies. But I insisted, and when the price went up, it made no difference to sales. I realised that we were onto something potentially big here, and decided that we needed someone to look after the *Doctor Who* titles properly.

'I asked Christine Donougher to look after the books, and I wanted to increase the number we were doing, but the problem was getting hold of the rights. We would buy the rights from the original scriptwriters, who had the option of writing the books themselves, but if they didn't want to, then we always had Terrance Dicks to fall back on, and he was happy to do them. Terrance's agent thought I

pre-production designs for a potential CGI science fiction/fantasy TV series.

Kyte has now taken a short break from illustration in order to rejuvenate his enthusiasm for the art, and has been working as a warden in a number of galleries in London.

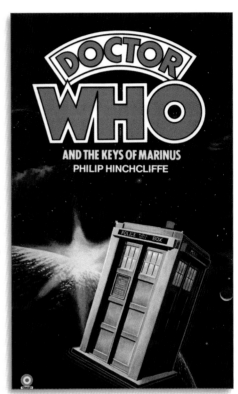

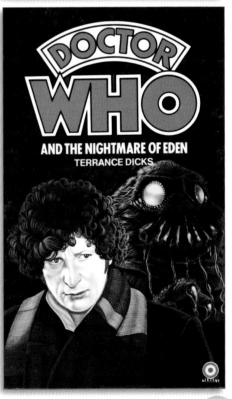

was wonderful with all this work that Terrance was bringing in. Christine was an excellent editor, and we were gradually getting on better with the BBC. They were always quite amazed when we sent them the royalties each half-year.'

By a curious coincidence, Tanner's replacement at NEL, Nick Webb, approached the BBC at the end of 1979. He said in his letter that he wanted to 'write a series of *Doctor Who* paperbacks with rather more substance, both in length and in detail than at presently published by W H Allen' and indicated that he had several skilled writers in mind who 'would combine to produce publications on a number of topics'. The BBC asked that Webb provide some sample chapters, but after looking further into the practicalities of publishing *Doctor Who* novels, Webb reluctantly decided that the project would take more time than could be afforded. Another factor was that the number of clearances that had to be obtained to do the novels was prohibitive. He therefore dropped the idea.

In 1980, the novelisations returned to pretty much a monthly schedule, with Terrance Dicks writing all but one of the titles: *The Underworld*, *The Invasion of Time*, *The Stones of Blood*, *The Androids of Tara*, *The Power of Kroll*, *The Armageddon Factor*, *The Keys of Marinus* (Philip Hinchcliffe), *The Nightmare of Eden*, *The Horns of Nimon* and *The Monster of Peladon*. The publishers were aware of the problems that having just one author handling all the books might cause, and so during 1979 had approached both Philip Hinchcliffe and *Doctor Who*'s first story editor David

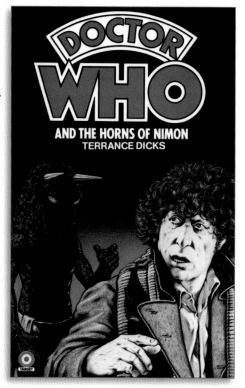

Whitaker about doing more of the books. While this led to Hinchcliffe writing *The Keys of Marinus* – which would be his last contribution to the range – Whitaker died on 4 February 1980 having managed to complete only some rough notes for a novelisation of his 1967 story 'The Enemy of the World' – a title that was eventually assigned to Ian Marter and published in 1981.

The covers for the books were now being handled by a number of artists. Andrew Skilleter completed most of them, but *The Keys of Marinus* was by David McAllister, *The Underworld* and *The Armageddon Factor* were by Bill Donohoe and *The Horns of Nimon* and *The Monster of Peladon* were by Steve Kyte.

Kyte remembered his first contact with the company. 'I just phoned up and asked for an interview with the art director. Having just left college, I was trying most publishers. I didn't have any hopes to work on the *Who* novels in particular.'

Three cover sketches by Steve Kyte for *Doctor Who and the Horns of Nimon.*

Having got the commission, Kyte found the working relationship fairly easygoing. 'There was no pressure to conform to any sort of house style or rules,' he explained, 'other than the rather silly one that no Doctors other than the current one could be shown, which caused inevitable problems on *The Enemy of the World*.'

'After the initial few covers, the *Doctor Who* work became a steady and enjoyable thread of my career,' said Skilleter. 'Having completed the jacket paintings for a number of years, I naturally felt more enthusiastic over some than others, and there were periods when I wondered why on earth I was doing *Doctor Who* jackets at all while engrossed in a huge project of Renaissance-style set-piece paintings, or working on artwork related to the *Star Wars* saga.'

David McAllister had been working for art director Mike Brett at W H Allen for some time before the first *Doctor Who* commission came up. 'I was doing

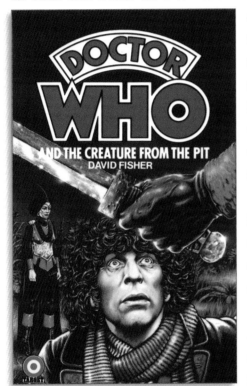

covers for thrillers, westerns, all sorts of things,' McAllister recalled. 'Mike knew that I could do figures and faces, and so the *Doctor Who* covers came along. I hadn't done that much science fiction work, and so it really was because of what I had been doing for Mike up to that point.'

McAllister had started illustrating in 1977 after studying at the Central College of Art and Design in London, and Mike Brett was one of the first art directors to use his work.

'With the cover for *The Keys of Marinus*, I remember I wanted to do something different, something that did not have people in it,' recalled the artist. 'I didn't have a reference picture for the TARDIS and so doing the painting was interesting. I was also not using an airbrush at the time, and so all the background – all that black, the planet and stars – was done with a standard paintbrush.'

Issue 33 of *Doctor Who Weekly* had reported that off-monitor photographs from the story had been sourced for the artist to create a cover for this book, and McAllister has a very vague feeling that the picture eventually used may have been originally intended for another project. 'Was there a *Doctor Who* calendar or something around at the time?' he mused. 'I really can't remember, but it's possible that the TARDIS in space was used on the book because something else fell through.'

Generally the books were well received, with commentators in the fan press consistently saying that they felt that Dicks's books were better than they had

Three cover sketches by Steve Kyte for *Doctor Who and the Creature from the Pit*.

JOHN LYDECKER (STEPHEN GALLAGHER)

'It seemed like the perfect opportunity for some of the original material to see the light of day.'

Stephen Gallagher, TARDIS, September/ October 1988

John Lydecker was the pen name for writer Stephen Gallagher. Gallagher was born in Salford, Lancashire, on 13 October 1954. He studied Drama and English at Hull University before getting a job as a documentaries researcher for Yorkshire Television. He then worked for Granada television and began writing scripts for Independent Local Radio. This led to work for BBC Radio 4.

His first commissioned TV work was the serial 'Warriors' Gate' (1981) for *Doctor Who*, followed two years later by 'Terminus' (1983). He wrote the two adaptations under the name of Lydecker to distinguish them from his body of work as an original novelist. The name came from a character in his radio play *An Alternative to Suicide* and had already been used on an adaptation of the movie *Silver Dream Racer* (1980). He used the name one more time when he wrote a short story for the 1992 *Doctor Who Year Book*. Other adaptations include the movie *Saturn 3* (1980) and *The Kids from Fame* (writing as Lisa Todd, 1983).

Gallagher adapted his own SF radio drama *The Last Rose of Summer* (1978), which was revised and rewritten as a stand-alone novel, *Dying of Paradise* (as Stephen Couper, 1982). A sequel followed (*The Ice Belt*, 1983).

Gallagher went on to a successful career as a science-fiction/thriller author. He wrote the novels *Chimera* (1982), *Follower* (1984), *Oktober* (1988), *Valley of Lights* (1987 – republished by Telos in 2005), *Down River* (1989), *Rain* (1990), *The Boat House* (1991), *Nightmare, with Angel* (1992), *Red, Red Robin* (1995), *White Bizango* (2002), *The Spirit Box* (2005), *The Painted Bride* (2006) and *The Kingdom of Bones* (2007). ▶

expected them to be. Fans were, however, split on whether Philip Hinchcliffe had made a good job of his book or not. Reviewers like Gary Russell in his fanzine *Shada* were disappointed: 'More than anything, it reads like Terry Nation's BBC storyline would have, it is so absolutely, well, skimpy. There is no animation; it is totally two dimensional … So what have we gained from this book? A basic storyline and the knowledge that if you tell an author he is really good and just what is wanted, he rests on his laurels and decides that anything goes. Well, Mr Hinchcliffe, I wait in absolute horror for your next book.' Other reviewers, though, were very impressed. Take, for

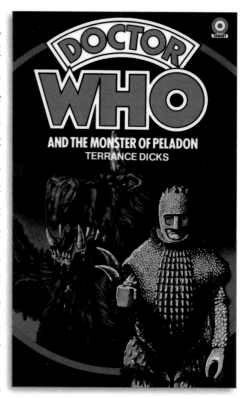

example, Paul Williams, writing in *Doctor Who: Views, News and Reviews*: 'The Keys of Marinus is quite a faithful rendering of the TV serial; it is an enjoyable read and a welcome change from the endless stream of Baker books published in recent years.' Or Ian K McLachlan in *The Doctor Who Review*: 'The Keys of Marinus is a book that belongs in the 1960s in the sense that it could have been written then, rather than in 1980. Nothing is included here that was unknown to the *Doctor Who* viewer of 1964 – and this I feel is one of the book's definite pluses … An excellent rendition of the original serial on which it was based.'

W H Allen continued to send proofs of cover artwork and completed manuscripts to the BBC for approval. John Nathan-Turner took a more personal interest than his predecessor Graham Williams in all *Doctor Who* spin-off material, and he shared Williams's general dissatisfaction with the quality of artwork presented for the covers. On 25 February 1980, he singled out the artwork for *The Armageddon Factor* and *The Power of Kroll* as being very poor; and then, on 9 June, he commented upon seeing the original artwork for the

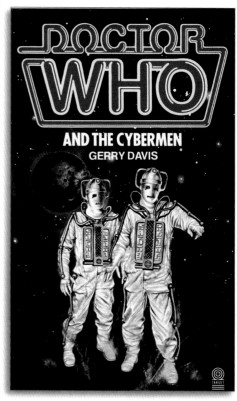

cover of *The Keys of Marinus* that the TARDIS should be blue and not grey and that the light on the top should be white and not red. These comments were not taken on board by W H Allen.

It was during 1980 that a potentially major problem arose that directly affected the *Doctor Who* range. The Writers' Guild of Great Britain wanted W H Allen to agree to a standard contract, and their main weapon was Guild member Terrance Dicks.

'The Writers' Guild was negotiating to get a standard contract agreed by the publishers,' recalled Dicks. 'They were fairly handicapped, because most of their members were scriptwriters and not book writers, so they didn't have a lot of leverage. But where they worked out they did have leverage was with me. I was doing a lot of books, and the Guild got in touch with me and said that they wanted me to take part in a strike; but this was going to affect me quite badly.

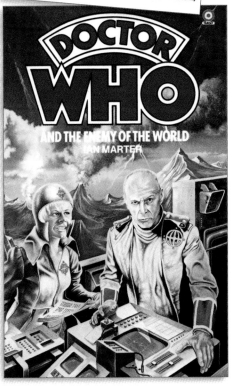

'I had a meeting with them about it, and tried my best to dissuade them. I told them that they were asking me to sacrifice myself and my career for their cause, but they said they were right behind me, and although I argued, I couldn't get anywhere. Also, having signed up to belong to the union, I didn't feel that I could blackleg. Malcolm Hulke, a good friend, had also been a very keen Writers' Guild member, and he would not have even considered not supporting them when they asked, and would no doubt have haunted me forever had I refused to help.

'I did feel that it was rotten luck on my part, though, and that the Guild were being a little unscrupulous. However, it wasn't too bad for me in financial terms, because you were allowed to work on things that were already under contract, and I had a couple of books in that position, and by the time that it would have begun

His novels *Chimera* and *Oktober* have both been adapted for television (Gallagher directing *Oktober* himself). He has written TV scripts for *Rockcliffe's Folly* (1988), *Chiller* (1995), *Murder Rooms* (2001), *Rosemary and Thyme* (2004-05) and *Eleventh Hour* (a series he helped devise, 2006). He was series consultant and occasional writer on the first three seasons of the BBC's *Bugs* (1995-97).

Gallagher and his family have lived in the USA and the UK. He continues to write original novels and short stories, and develop ideas for television and film. His new drama, *Lifeline*, was shown on the BBC in 2007.

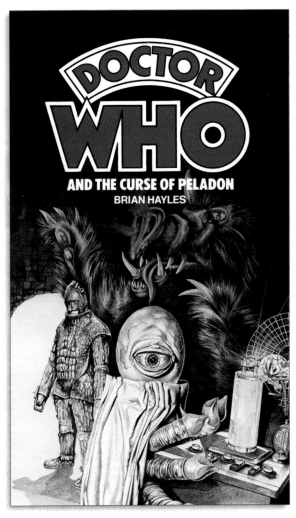

TOP LEFT: A cover sketch by Steve Kyte for *Doctor Who and the Enemy of the World*. The final cover was by Bill Donohoe.
ABOVE: The cover for a hardback edition of *Doctor Who and the Curse of Peladon*. This cover art by Bill Donohoe was never used on one of the Target paperbacks.

DAVID FISHER

'I made a lot of changes, but I should have changed a whole lot more!'

David Fisher, Doctor Who Magazine *(number 269), September 1998*

David Fisher started out as a script reader at Ealing film studios. After the studios closed in 1957, Fisher went into advertising and worked in Paris and Johannesburg. On his return to the UK, he got a job with Scottish Television where he served as a script writer for six years before going freelance.

Fisher first wrote for *Doctor Who* for the sixteenth season, penning two instalments of the search for the Key to Time ('The Stones of Blood' and 'The Androids of Tara', both 1978). Two more adventures followed ('The Creature from the Pit', 1979; 'The Leisure Hive', 1980). He also wrote the original scripts for the story that became 'The City of Death' (1979). His first two transmitted *Doctor Who* stories were novelised by Terrance Dicks, but Fisher himself did the work for his last two.

Prior to *Doctor Who*, Fisher had worked with script editor Anthony Read on *The Troubleshooters* (11 episodes, 1969-71). The association continued when Fisher wrote for the Read-script-edited series *Hammer House of Horror* ('Guardian of the Abyss', 1980) and *Hammer House of Mystery and Suspense* ('The Corvini Inheritance' and 'The Late Nancy Irving', both 1986).

Other TV series contributed to by Fisher include *Orlando* (1967), *Dixon of Dock Green* ('Whose Turn Next', 1969), *The Lotus Eaters* ('A Tiger in Bristol Street', 1972), *Sutherland's Law* ('The Dutchies', 1973) and *The McKinnons* ('Playboy of the Western Highlands', 1977).

Fisher and Read collaborated again throughout the 1980s and 1990s on a series of non-fiction books predominantly about the Second World War, after a planned TV series they were due to work on collapsed. The books were *Operation Lucy* (1980), *Colonel Z* (1985), *Deadly Embrace* (1988), *Kristallnacht* (1991), *The Fall of Berlin* (1992) *Berlin Rising (1994)* and *The Proudest Day* (on India's long road to independence, 1997).

to bite financially, the strike was settled and everything was back to normal. But I think that action made W H Allen realise that they rather had all their eggs in one basket and that I was the basket. It may therefore have become policy at that time to try to use other writers; but also, and coincidentally, I think the writers started to realise that the books were a good enough proposition to be worth doing.'

Ultimately Tanner met with the president of the Writers' Guild. 'They wanted standard terms and we wouldn't give it to them,' he recalled. 'I had lunch with them and we eventually managed to sort it all out.'

The result of this action was that in 1981 only four new *Doctor Who* titles were published: *The Creature from the Pit* (David Fisher), *The Enemy of the World* (Ian Marter), *An Unearthly Child* (Terrance Dicks) and *The State of Decay* (Terrance Dicks). In order to maintain a regular schedule of publications, hardback editions were released of some of the earlier books that had not been previously available in that format.

The suggestion to publish the novelisation of the first ever *Doctor Who* story,

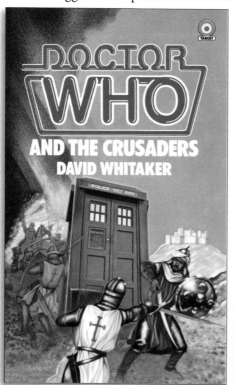

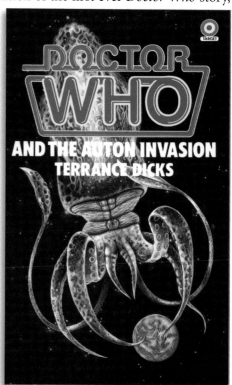

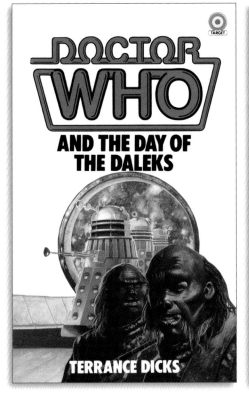

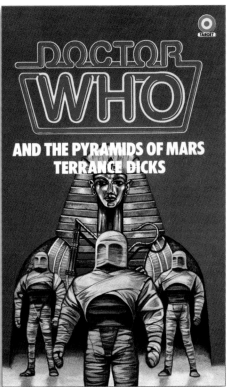

'100,000 BC' (at the time generally known by the title of its first episode – 'An Unearthly Child' – rather than the overall title used by the production office at the time of transmission) came from Nathan-Turner on 20 July 1981. The producer had managed to secure a short season of repeats on BBC Two, starting with this adventure. However, this left very little time to get the novelisation together.

'It was obviously an opportunity not to be missed,' explained Christine Donougher in an interview for *Doctor Who* Magazine in 1982. 'It gave us a chance to sell the book not only to those who remembered the programme when it was first shown, but also to a completely new generation of youngsters and to people who have become addicted to *Doctor Who* since 1963. I think *An Unearthly Child* was an excellent story to publish, and I was surprised it hadn't been done before.'

'We had a lot of problem chasing down the rights, as the author had died,' recalled Tanner, 'and we eventually found his widow living in Herne Bay on the south coast. Christine and I met her and she agreed that we could novelise the story. Of course, when we published it, we put the cover price up again.'

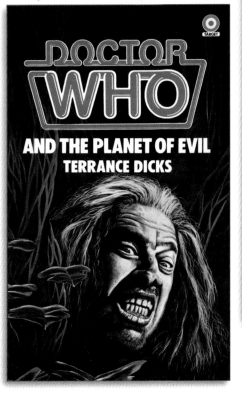

ERIC SAWARD

'I think *Doctor Who* works best when it thrills one moment and is funny the next. That's what I was attempting in that book.'
Eric Saward, Doctor Who Magazine
(number 148), May 1989

Eric Saward was born in December 1944 and attended grammar school until the age of 18. After working as an estate agent, he moved to Holland, where he lived for three years and was briefly married. On his return to England, he took a succession of jobs, including as a publisher's proof editor and as a bookshop sales assistant. He then trained and worked for a while as an English teacher. He also started to write, and found some success with drama scripts for radio, the first he had accepted being a play entitled *The Fall and Fall of David Moore*.

He gave up teaching in order to pursue a full-time writing career. To supplement his income he also filled in with some odd jobs, including a stint in the theatre as a self-taught electrician working on productions such as *Hair* and *The Canterbury Tales* at the Phoenix in Shaftesbury Avenue. He was then approached by *Doctor Who* script editor Christopher H Bidmead to submit some ideas to the series, having been recommended by the senior drama script editor at BBC Radio. This led to the 1982 story 'The Visitation', on the strength of which he was immediately appointed as script editor. He held the position for five years until he resigned partway through 1986, during which time he contributed three more stories ('Earthshock', 1982; 'Resurrection of the Daleks',1984; 'Revelation of the Daleks', 1985) and substantially rewrote and reworked others, including 1985's 'Attack of the Cybermen'.

He wrote the radio serial *Doctor Who: Slipback*, which was broadcast during 1985, and four novelisations for Target. His association with the show continued after his resignation when he wrote the linking narration for some of the BBC Radio audio releases of missing stories in the early 1990s.

Both before and since working on *Doctor Who*, Saward has written scripts for dramas broadcast on German radio.

Two cover sketches by Steve Kyte for *Doctor Who and the State of Decay*. The final cover art was by Andrew Skilleter.

Author Terrance Dicks was asked to handle the book, and, as he recalled, time was short. 'I found that I could quite easily complete a book within a month, and as time went on, I learned all the techniques to speed up the process. The quickest books to write were probably *The Five Doctors*, which they desperately wanted to get out to tie in with the show on television – in fact, they did so well that it ended up being available before transmission, and the production team got very cross about that – and *An Unearthly Child*, which they wanted to get out to tie in with the repeat. I think I was given about a fortnight to do that one.

'The pressure didn't feel phenomenal at the time – I was on my twentieth or thirtieth novel by then, and I was used to doing it. Around the start of

ESCAPE TO DANGER!

Part of the fun with the Target novelisations was spotting recurrent themes in the melodramatic chapter titles. Terrance Dicks was a particular master of this, and sometimes it was arguably unnecessary to read the actual story, as the arc of the chapter titles pretty much told you all you needed to know. Unfortunately, the imaginations of some authors wouldn't stretch to creating individual chapter titles; in particular, the novelisers of the seventh Doctor's stories just didn't play ball. Of course, this was nothing compared to Stephen Gallagher (writing as John Lydecker), who dispensed with chapters entirely for his two novelisations.

Best to start with something like 'The Terror Begins'[1] or to cut straight to the action as in 'Abandon Ship!'[2] (note also the early use of the exclamation mark for heightened dramatic impact). Pretty quickly we need our protagonists to put themselves into the action arena appropriate for our story: 'Into the …'[3] (insert as appropriate). These places are almost inevitably subterranean (caves, caverns, depths, chasms and so on). Or they need to embark on a 'Journey into Danger/Peril'[4].

To establish the pervading air of gloom, we recommend some early titles '… of Death'[5] or '… of Terror'[6], throwing in the occasional '… Peril …'[7] (which works at either end of a scene setting chapter title). Perhaps the whole predicament could be encapsulated as '(The) Nightmare'[8]. The reader should be warned of 'The Horror in the …'[9] (wherever is most atmospheric) and for intrigue 'The Secret of the …'[10].

We would need to establish the nature of the side the Doctor and his companions are joining: they may for example be 'The Fugitive(s)'[11]. Our hero is the catalyst for the story, so it should be that 'The Doctor Makes a …'[12] (as appropriate); or to really stir things up it could be that 'The Doctor Disappears'[13]. 'Face to Face'[14] often denotes a showdown between the Doctor and the bad guys.

Almost invariably there is a rotten apple within the barrel of good guys, someone who could be described as 'The Enemy Within'[15] or as 'The Traitor(s)'[16]. This person or these persons would be expected to conduct some 'Sabotage(!)'[17], to attempt a 'Takeover'[18] or to commit '(The) Betrayal'[19]. But more often than not, they would be instrumental in setting 'The Trap'[20] resulting in our heroes becoming 'Trapped(!)'[21]. Or if not going down the trap route, then maybe '(The) Ambush'[22].

As tock must follow tick, so a trap or an ambush must lead to one or more of our heroes being 'Capture(d)'[23], as a result of which they end up as 'The Prisoner(s)'[24] or '(The) Hostage(s)'[25]. This also opens up the opportunity for personalisation of the chapter title, as in 'Prisoner(s) of … (insert as appropriate)'[26]. However, we can rest assured that our heroes will manage to achieve '(The) Escape(!)'[27] – although occasionally with short-lived fortuitousness when it turns out to be an 'Escape (in)to Danger'[28].

Usually we can expect our heroine to be held against her will as '(The) Sacrifice'[29] or one of our heroes to face a 'Death Sentence'[30]. However, they need only wait for the next chapter, when they can expect '(A/The) Rescue'[31] – although soon after one disaster is averted, we can be fairly sure of a 'Return to Danger'[32].

Early, small-scale incursions by the bad guys may be flagged up under '(The) Intruder(s)'[33], but it's almost inevitable that sooner or later there will come 'The Attack'[34] or, for added intrigue, an 'Attack from the Unknown'[35]. Of course, this can always lead to a 'Counter-attack'[36].

The end draws near, signalled by '(The) Countdown'[37], possibly one as ominous as a 'Countdown to Doom'[38]. 'The Final Battle'[39] begins, possibly taking the form of a 'Duel to the Death'[40] or the Doctor leading the underdogs in an act of 'Rebellion!'[41] or with deployment of 'The Ultimate Weapon'[42].

And so we come to wrap up our story, perhaps with '(The) Farewell(s)'[43], certainly with 'Departure'[44], but perhaps also the more philosophical 'An End and a Beginning'[45].

the '80s I would have started getting a video of the story as well, and so that made it a little easier.'

With *An Unearthly Child*, cover artist Andrew Skilleter started a run (unbroken save for a few photographic covers during 1983) of 21 covers for the range. '*An Unearthly Child* was wanted so urgently,' recalled Skilleter, 'that not even a rough was requested, and the painting was completed over a weekend. There was often not the opportunity to give the work as much polish as I'd personally have liked to – but then that is so often the case with professional illustration.'

Fan reaction to the four 1981 books was mixed. *The Creature from the Pit* was liked by Gary Russell, who wrote in the fanzine *Shada*: 'The best, greatest, [most] amazingly enjoyable Target book of all time … Get it, or you'll actually believe that *The Destiny of the Daleks* is the best Target can do.' *The Enemy of the World*, on the other hand, was criticised by Chris Marton in *Wheel in Space*. 'Some of the writing has much to commend it, like the description of the TARDIS landing on the beach. However, vast chunks of the story have been cut. So have huge portions of dialogue. This is a pity, as it makes the book chop about so much that there is no natural flow, and this jars more than once.'

1 As used in *The Terror of the Autons*, *The Horror of Fang Rock* and *The Pescatons*.
2 *The Sea-Devils*, *The Myth Makers*.
3 *The Cave-Monsters*, *The Daemons*, *The Curse of Peladon*, *The Deadly Assassin*, *The Mind Robber*, *The Sensorites*, *The Pescatons*.
4 *The Chase*, *The Revenge of The Cybermen*.
5 *The Deadly Assassin*, *Earthshock*, *Marco Polo*, *The Dominators*, *Terror of The Vervoids*.
6 *The Zarbi*, *The Curse of Peladon*, *The Android Invasion*, *The Keys of Marinus*, *Inferno*, *The Wheel in Space*.
7 *The Abominable Snowmen*, *The Revenge of The Cybermen*, *Planet of The Daleks*, *The Carnival of Monsters*, *The Faceless Ones*.
8 *Death to the Daleks*, *Snakedance*, *Inferno*, *The Time Monster*, *The Chase*.
9 *The Auton Invasion*, *The Brain of Morbius*, *The Deadly Assasin*, *The Talons of Weng-Chiang*, *Arc of Infinity*.
10 *The Abominable Snowmen*, *The Tomb of the Cybermen*, *The Masque of Mandragora*, *The Destiny of the Daleks*, *The Nightmare of Eden*, *The Sensorites*, *The Faceless Ones*, *The Time Meddler*.
11 *The Dalek Invasion of Earth*, *The Mutants*, *The Invasion of Time*, *The Nightmare of Eden*, *The Monster of Peladon*, *The Sunmakers*, *The Space Pirates*.
12 *The Cave-Monsters*, *The Claws of Axos*, *The Brain of Morbius*, *Black Orchid*.
13 *The Auton Invasion*, *The Time Warrior*, *The Five Doctors*.
14 *The Doomsday Weapon*, *The Mark of the Rani*, *The Massacre*, *Time and the Rani*.
15 *Planet of The Daleks*, *The Horror of Fang Rock*, *Terror of The Vervoids*.
16 *The Cave-Monsters*, *The State of Decay*, *Arc of Infinity*, *Warriors of the Deep*, *The Faceless Ones*, *Mission to The Unknown*.
17 *The Ark in Space*, *The Seeds of Doom*, *The Robots of Death*, *Warriors of The Deep*.
18 *The Android Invasion*, *The Caves of Androzani*, *The Wheel in Space*.
19 *The Genesis of the Daleks*, *The Seeds of Doom*, *The Invasion of Time*, *The Curse of Fenric*.
20 *The Space War*, *Death to The Daleks*, *The Face of Evil*, *The Mutants*, *The War Games*, *The Sunmakers*, *The Faceless Ones*, *The Wheel in Space*.
21 *The Deadly Assassin*, *The Seeds of Doom*, *The Carnival of Monsters*, *The Celestial Toymaker*, *Harry Sullivan's War*, *The Edge of Destruction*, *The Seeds of Death*, *The Space Pirates*.
22 *The Doomsday Weapon*, *Death to The Daleks*, *The Time Warrior*, *The Horror of Fang Rock*, *An Unearthly Child*, *Harry Sullivan's War*.
23 *The Sontaran Experiment*, *The Android Invasion*, *The Face of Evil*, *An Unearthly Child*, *Vengeance on Varos*, *The Ark*, *The Space Museum*, *Warriors of The Deep*, *The Smugglers*, *The Faceless Ones*.
24 *The Cave-Monsters*, *The Destiny of the Daleks*, *The Sunmakers*, *Arc of Infinity*, *Harry Sullivan's War*, *The Space Pirates*.
25 *The Destiny of the Daleks*, *The Monster of Peladon*, *The Mind of Evil*, *Warriors of the Deep*, *Mutation of Time*.
26 *The Day of The Daleks*, *The Terror of The Autons*, *The Planet of The Spiders*, *The Genesis of The Daleks*, *The Talons of Weng-Chiang*, *The Androids of Tara*, *The Keeper of Traken*, *Meglos*, *Frontios*, *The Reign of Terror*, *The Time Meddler*.
27 *The Sea-Devils*, *The Green Death*, *The Loch Ness Monster*, *The Dinosaur Invasion*, *The Planet of The Daleks*, *The Mutants*, *The Destiny of the Daleks*, *The War Games*, *State of Decay*, *Snakedance*, *The Mind of Evil*, *The Caves of Androzani*, *The Massacre*, *The Mysterious Planet*, *The Macra Terror*, *The Space Pirates*.
28 *The Daleks*, *The Zarbi*, *The Curse of Peladon*, *The Genesis of The Daleks*, *The Keeper of Traken*, *An Unearthly Child*, *Vengeance on Varos*.
29 *The Daemons*, *The Claws of Axos*, *Death to the Daleks*, *The Masque of Mandragora*, *The Talons of Weng-Chiang*, *The Stones of Blood*, *The Power of Kroll*, *Meglos*, *Warriors of the Deep*, *The Seeds of Death*, *Mission to the Unknown*.
30 *The Invisible Enemy*, *Arc of Infinity*, *Snakedance*, *Inferno*.
31 *The Daemons*, *The Time Warrior*, *The Space Museum*, *The Massacre*, *The Krotons*, *The Seeds of Death*.
32 *The Day of the Daleks*, *The Time Warrior*, *Inferno*.
33 *TheUnderworld*, *The Monster of Peladon*, *The Leisure Hive*, *The Keeper of Traken*, *Warriors of the Deep*, *The Space Pirates*.
34 *The Doomsday Weapon*, *The Mutants*, *The Power of Kroll*, *The Nightmare of Eden*, *Meglos*, *Kinda*, *The Mind of Evil*, *The Krotons*, *Warriors of The Deep*.
35 *The Three Doctors*, *The Horror of Fang Rock*.
36 *The Ice Warriors*, *The Time Warrior*, *The Invisible Enemy*, *Warriors of The Deep*.
37 *The Android Invasion*, *The Hand of Fear*, *The Power of Kroll*, *Time and The Rani*, *The Seeds of Death*.
38 *Inferno*, *The Space Pirates*.
39 *The Auton Invasion*, *The Abominable Snowmen*, *The Deadly Assassin*.
40 *The Sontaran Experiment*, *The Deadly Assassin*, *The Masque of Mandragora*.
41 *The Revenge of the Cybermen*, *The Genesis of the Daleks*, *The Dalek Invasion of Earth*.
42 *Meglos*, *The Myth Makers*.
43 *The Dalek Invasion of Earth*, *The Mind of Evil*, *Paradise Towers*.
44 *The Face of Evil*, *The Destiny of the Daleks*, *State of Decay*.
45 *The Planet of the Spiders*, *The Deadly Assassin*, *The Mysterious Planet*, *The Wheel in Space*.

ANDREW SMITH

Andrew Smith hailed from Rutherglen in Scotland. His early work included scripts for BBC2's *Not the Nine O'Clock News*, Radio Scotland's topical comedy programme *Naked Radio*, Radio 4's satirical *Week Ending* and an original play called *Thieves* in Scottish Television's *Preview* series.

He was a fan of *Doctor Who* prior to writing for it. In his first season as producer, John Nathan-Turner was keen to encourage new writing talent, and Smith was a beneficiary of this policy. He was just 19 when he wrote 'Full Circle' for Season 18 in 1980. He adapted the serial for Target shortly after. The writer contributed at least one more idea to the show, but this was not taken up.

CHRISTOPHER H BIDMEAD

'I found the novels a wonderful way of realising the story exactly as you wanted it. I put all I had into them and I'm very proud of the results.'

Christopher H Bidmead, Doctor Who Magazine *(number 109), February 1986*

Christopher Hamilton Bidmead was born in 1941. He trained as an actor at the Royal Academy of Dramatic Arts and appeared on stage, television (*Emergency Ward 10*) and radio (*Waggoner's Walk*) before moving in the 1970s to writing for radio and television (including scripting for two Thames Television shows: *Harriet's Back in Town* and *Rooms*).

He was appointed as script editor on *Doctor Who* by producer John Nathan-Turner, having been recommended ▶

Terrance Dicks's two offerings received both bouquets and brickbats, perhaps proving that you can't please everyone. 'This is not a meaty, compelling novel of *The Dæmons* vein,' John Manning commented in *Peepshow* about *An Unearthly Child*. 'At 128 pages, it is far from that; nevertheless, it is a change from the weakly-written rubbish that we have been subjected to over the last couple of years … The story is told simply and lucidly, undoubtedly aimed at a ten to 14 age group; but don't let this put off older readers.' However Stephen P Boa, writing for *Definitive Gaze*, was not happy: 'Oh dear! What a disappointment!! … Don't bother with this book at all, as it has very little to offer.' *State of Decay* also found opposing views, the first from an unknown reviewer in the fanzine *Meglos*: 'The word "rubbish" comes to mind. Usually when novelising one of his own stories Terrance is excellent – like *The Brain of Morbius*. This book, fine for *Jackanory* … is as bad as *Horns of Nimon* – itself a 30-minute read. Something must be done – and now … We can't just sit back and watch the reduction or total removal of these books.' At the opposite end of the scale, Stephen P Boa was positively ecstatic in *Definitive Gaze*: 'This novel is the best *Doctor Who* book since *The Tomb of the Cybermen*. Never in my wildest dreams did I think I would have enjoyed a book adapted from a Tom Baker adventure as much as this … This really is a must for any *Doctor Who* fan's library and will no doubt be in many fans' top ten Targets'.

1982 saw a further eight titles being published, with only three being by Dicks: *The State of Decay*, *Warriors' Gate* (written by Stephen Gallagher under the pen-name John Lydecker), *The Keeper of Traken*, *The Leisure Hive* (David Fisher), *The Visitation* (Eric Saward), *Full Circle* (Andrew Smith), *Logopolis* (Christopher H

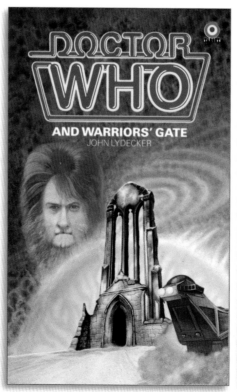

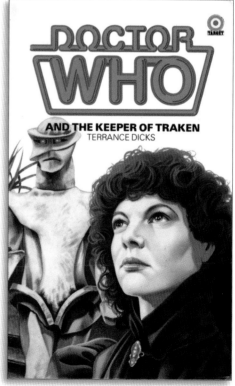

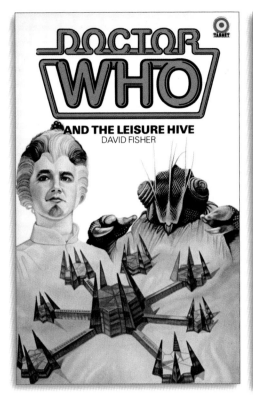

by fellow writer and script editor Robert Banks Stewart. In addition to script editing the 1980/1981 season of *Doctor Who*, he contributed three scripts to the show, all of which he later novelised.

There was one final script for *Doctor Who*, 'Pinacotheca' – a Greek word meaning gallery of pictures – but this was never produced. He was approached about novelising the story as part of W H Allen's *Missing Episodes* series of books, but felt that the financial incentive wasn't great enough.

Bidmead had worked as a journalist specialising in scientific and technical subjects prior to his time on *Doctor Who*, and this is the career he has focused on since. He has written for *New Scientist*, *Wired* and *Personal Computer World*, amongst others, and has a regular column in *PC Plus*.

Recently he has returned to writing fiction, with an audio script for the Big Finish range of *Doctor Who* CDs, 'Renaissance of the Daleks' (2007).

Bidmead) and *The Sunmakers*. *The Sunmakers* was the last original novelisation to have the prefix '*Doctor Who and the …*' in the title. From this point on, all the books were simply titled '*Doctor Who –*' followed by the story title, and this notation was also used for *Full Circle* and *Logopolis*. For convenience in this text, however, this has been omitted.

Nathan-Turner continued to take an active interest in the books, and amongst other comments he requested that an epilogue contained within Andrew Smith's novelisation of *Full Circle* be deleted. However, things were going well enough that BBC Enterprises extended W H Allen's licence to publish *Doctor Who* fiction for a further five years from 21 August 1981.

'The BBC took on a very good producer in John Nathan-Turner,' recalled Tanner. 'I'd meet him for lunch and he'd always arrive dressed very flamboyantly, wearing a pink shirt with white spots, a blue bow tie and so on. He also smoked, and on one occasion, he went to light his cigarette with a great flourish and this great flame shot out from his wristwatch and lit his cigarette. I decided not to comment – it was too obvious – but then of course

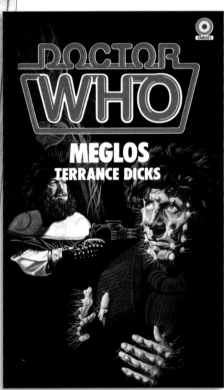

LEFT: Andrew Skilleter's cover rough for *Doctor Who-Meglos*.

DOCTOR WHO
FULL CIRCLE
ANDREW SMITH

'...then a sort of chuffing and groaning...'
Christopher H Bidmead, 1982
Doctor Who – Logopolis

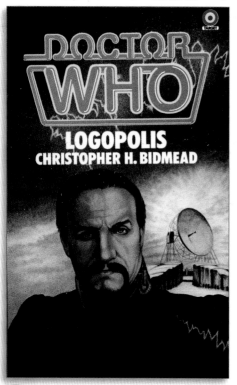

DOCTOR WHO
LOGOPOLIS
CHRISTOPHER H. BIDMEAD

he did it again, and I had to say something. "Oh!" he exclaimed, beaming all over his face, "have you noticed?"

'He was keen on publicity, and he helped us organise signings and so on. Nathan-Turner also shared the same agent as Peter Davison – John Mahoney – and so when he was organising pantomimes, he could get Davison to appear in them. A nice man.'

The cover for *The Visitation*, the first novelisation to be published of one of the stories starring Davison as the Doctor, proved problematic. Artwork was commissioned from artist David McAllister but this was rejected by Davison's agents on the grounds that they felt the likeness of the actor was not good enough. As a result, the finalised cover featured instead a photograph of Davison – the first time that a photograph had ever been used on a Target *Doctor Who* book cover.

Bob Tanner, however, does not recall the dispute over the artwork and feels that the move was more to do with trying a new image for the Davison books, just as the TV series was trying a new image for the Doctor.

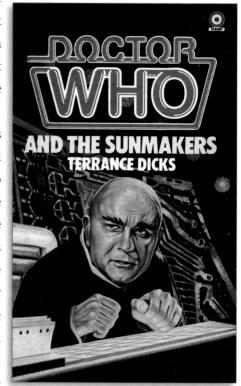

DOCTOR WHO
AND THE SUNMAKERS
TERRANCE DICKS

'We went to photographic covers as they were changing the Doctor and we thought it would be a good idea to use photographs to tie in with that,' he explained. 'Then we started to get the agents and the artistes coming to us and saying that if we were going to use their photograph on the cover, then they wanted paying for it. Sometimes we would pay in books – if they got books, they were happy … well, the actors were, but the agents weren't. And finally we had to stop using photographs and went back to artwork, as we just couldn't afford it. They wanted a royalty for us to use the photograph, as well as a lump sum and also a royalty on sales of the book, and we just were not going to agree to that. All the extra accounting and work to administer it … We were just not going to do it.'

Therefore the photographic covers gave way to artwork images once more, for the very reason that artwork rather than photographs had been used when the range first started.

The fans were, as usual, forthright in their views, and generally the books met with approval. 'I really wanted to do a hatchet job on *Warrior's Gate* but will just say the truth … *Wow!*' wrote Stephen P Boa in *Definitive Gaze*. Stuart Donaldson, reviewing *The Leisure Hive* in *Shada*, commented: 'It is one of the best Target novels in recent years …' This was a view shared by Stephen P Boa: 'The only thing I can suggest about this novel is to go out and buy it; it's so good, it's a disgrace to call it a children's fiction, and when I think about it, there's not many *Doctor Who* books I can say that about.' *The Visitation* did not fare so well, however. David Owen noted in *Shada*: 'Reading the book depresses me rather a lot, since it concerns dull-witted villagers, the plague, bad smells, rats and a singularly unimaginatively-thought-out alien. Given these ingredients, Saward makes a competent job of weaving a story around them, but they are not particularly exciting or pleasing ingredients, which tends to make for dull reading … Sorry, Eric, better luck next time …'

Andrew Smith's *Full Circle* was received slightly better, with Andrew Martin noting in *Shada*: '[It is] not the world's best novelisation, nor is it the worst … It isn't a bare re-rendition of the original script, yet it doesn't offer a host of new insights and angles we might previously only speculate on. It has the myriad faults of a first novel without the spontaneity and freshness, yet there are new, bright splashes of humour and descriptive prose.' *Logopolis* too found favour with Steven Redford, writing in the same fanzine: 'Target seem, at long last, to have realised the way to publish a good *Doctor Who* novel is to use the original writer, as they used to … [*Logopolis* is] a horror story of universal proportions, [and] there is a feeling of doom throughout …'

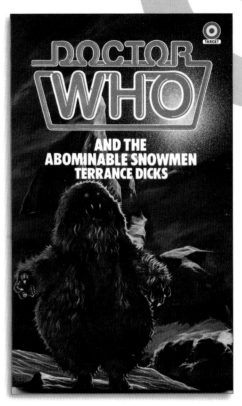

Finally *The Sunmakers*, like many Dicks novelisations, seems to have polarised the readers. *Shada*'s Jon Bok loved it: 'Dicks paints an extremely vivid picture of the different environmental settings via his words … I found this book a lovely read from cover to cover and certainly worth the £1.25 it cost to purchase it. Truly excellent, your Superlative!!' On the other hand, Russ Mould, writing in *Eye of Horus*, hated it: 'This book is, unfortunately, one of the very few of the Target novelisations that I actually detest… [It has a] positively grotty front cover. Not a bad likeness, I suppose, of the Collector, but aren't front covers meant to try and entice the consumer to buy the book? As to the writing of the book itself, it is of the usual Terrance Dicks standard: short but acceptable. Unfortunately the author has kept a lot of the over-jokiness of the story, making it even more unbearable than the almost "hammy" plot of the original.'

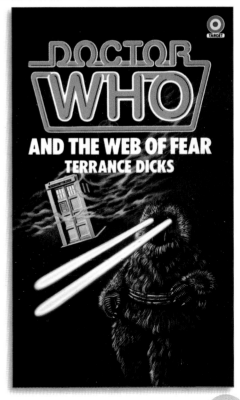

DOCTOR WHO: A CELEBRATION
Two Decades through Time and Space

Illustration copyright W.H. Allen.

W.H. ALLEN CELEBRATES THE 20TH ANNIVERSARY OF BBC TV'S SPECTACULARLY SUCCESSFUL DOCTOR WHO PROGRAMME WITH A FITTING TRIBUTE TO A TRULY REMARKABLE PHENOMENON.

This unique volume also marks many years of happy co-operation between the BBC and W.H. Allen, the official publishers of the Doctor Who novelisations.

If you have any difficulty in obtaining this title, please use the order coupon below.
To: W.H. ALLEN SALES 44 Hill Street, London W1X 8LB
Please send me ☐ DOCTOR WHO: A CELEBRATION at £10.95 (inc. p&p)
I enclose a cheque/postal order for £_____

Whilst every effort is made to keep prices low, it is sometimes necessary to increase prices at short notice. W.H. Allen reserve the right to show new retail prices on covers which may differ from those advertised in the text or elsewhere.

Name _____
Address _____
_____
_____

Please write in BLOCK CAPITALS   Also available at your local bookseller

One of the header cards used on dumpbins for the books in this period.

1983 saw the twentieth anniversary of the television series (and also the tenth anniversary of the Target book range), and, while plans were being made to celebrate the event on television with a special story, and in public with a massive convention held at Longleat House in Wiltshire, at W H Allen, the one thing that Bob Tanner had always wanted to achieve with regards to the *Doctor Who* books was finally realised: distribution to America.

'Getting America and Australia was essential,' he commented. 'No-one realised how big *Doctor Who* could be in America. From my days at NEL when I looked after *Penthouse*, I knew all the people in Australia to talk to about getting the books out there. I did a good deal with Australia, and our sales were going up. There was one point when the export sales were greater than the home sales.

'But getting into America was always a problem, and the BBC were getting a little tetchy about it all. But *Doctor Who* was on fairly infrequently in America and I tried a number of big publishers but they weren't interested. Then I contacted a friend of mine out there called Lyle Stuart, and initially he said he couldn't do it and so on, but I persisted until he finally agreed to try some.' Stuart eventually took over on 7 September 1983 the stockholding, sales, distribution and invoicing of all the Target *Doctor Who* titles in America on W H Allen's behalf.

'There was going to be a *Doctor Who* convention for the October Thanksgiving holiday in 1983,' recalled Tanner. 'Christine and I went out to this convention, and they had all the Doctors, loads of fans out there … an amazing experience. What Lyle did was to pile all the books he got from us like bricks in an enormous heap, and I watched this pile vanish as the weekend went on and the copies were sold. Incredible.

'Lyle eventually sold his business for about 11 million dollars and went on to set up Barricade books. At the time he, like so many other people, did not realise the potential scope of *Doctor Who* in America.'

As with the novelisation of '100,000 BC', Nathan-Turner was keen that the novelisation of 'The Five Doctors', the twentieth anniversary story, should be released to tie in with the transmission on BBC television in November. He nevertheless made it very clear in advance to the publishers that the book should not go on sale before the official publication date of 26 November, and – as noted above – was greatly annoyed when he learned that copies had been on sale as early as two weeks prior to transmission. This came on top of grievances that Nathan-Turner had regarding some of the factual books (in particular, corrections not being made to the *Doctor Who Crossword Book* and mistakes in *The Doctor Who Programme Guide*) and also problems with other areas of merchandising, like the World Distributors' *Doctor Who Annual*. As a result of all this, in an internal BBC memo on the anniversary date itself, 23 November, Nathan-Turner requested a meeting with BBC Enterprises to discuss the merchandising of *Doctor Who* in general. In the same memo, he suggested that Brian Gearing, editor of *Radio Times*, who had been very supportive of *Doctor Who* in publishing a special magazine to mark the twentieth anniversary, might be interested in discussing the possibility of editing and publishing the novelisations through the BBC's own imprint. Ultimately the growing unease between W H Allen and *Doctor Who*'s producer was smoothed over, and the licence to publish the novelisations stayed where it was.

The Five Doctors was hastily written by Terrance Dicks from an early version of his scripts for the TV special; and, in line with Tanner's policy of pushing the price whenever possible, this book cost £1.50. (The other novelisations were at the time £1.35, with the exception of *Terminus*, which was also priced at £1.50 as it was significantly longer than the others.) As usual with Dicks' novelisations, fan reaction hit both extremes: 'This is a really good book, and deserves all the credit it can muster,' wrote Russ Mould in *Eye of Horus*. 'It shows effort, time and imagination, with some nice descriptive work, and even a passage that wasn't … filmed. Well done Terrance Dicks.' However, an unknown reviewer in a fanzine 'celebrating' the anniversary story commented: 'Terrance Dicks has, in my view, become stale. He has now written so many of the Target selection that fans can expect nothing new from his books. In my view, he should adopt a different style, leaving behind his "recite the facts" manner of today … The main problem with this book is that it fails to stir any excitement in the reader.'

The other novelisations published in the anniversary year were *Time-Flight* (Peter Grimwade), *Meglos* (Terrance Dicks), *Castrovalva* (Christopher H Bidmead), *Four to Doomsday* (Terrance Dicks), *Earthshock* (Ian Marter), *Terminus* (Stephen Gallagher as John Lydecker) and *Arc of Infinity* (Terrance Dicks). Dicks' domination

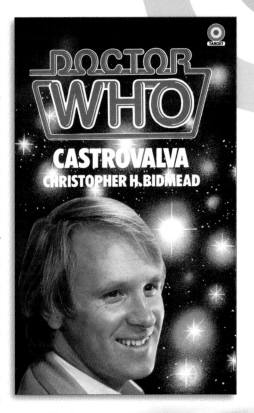

'The Doctor, now in his fifth incarnation, was a slight, fair-haired figure with a pleasant open face, and an air of mildly-bemused curiosity. He wore the garb of an Edwardian cricketer: striped trousers, fawn blazer with red piping, a cricket sweater bordered in red and white, and an open-necked shirt. There was a sprig of celery in his lapel.'
Terrance Dicks, 1985
Doctor Who–The Caves of Androzani

of the writing chores seemed to be drawing to a close, with the majority of newer adventures being novelised by their original scriptwriters. The notable exception here was Ian Marter handling *Earthshock*, the story having been originally scripted by Eric Saward.

As previously, Marter's and Lydecker's books were generally praised. Peter Grimwade's debut was also well liked, including by Robert Franks in *Shada*: 'An immensely enjoyable book and an undoubted success for Peter Grimwade. I have read better books, but I have also read far, far worse. I highly recommend it.' The same title, however, was positively hated by Howard Bull in *Tardis*: 'I can honestly say that I think this is one of the worst, if not the worst *Doctor Who* book ever written.'

Meglos was similarly criticised by some: 'In *Meglos*, Dicks appears to stop at nothing to avoid such painstaking little details as characterisation, description or explanation, in what must be one of his least adventurous books to date,' wrote Alec Charles in *Shada*, while in the same magazine Steve Mercer went even further: 'Each criticism that has ever been levelled at Mr Dicks could be levelled at this book, and be just as valid as it ever was. There are no changes of any significance from the televised version to generate any spark of interest, his descriptive work is at best rudimentary, more often non-existent, all the old pat phrases crop up with such unfailing regularity that I'm beginning to

As *Doctor Who* grew in popularity, so the marketing by W H Allen increased. Illustrated here are two of the header cards used on dumpbins for the books in this period, as well as a cardboard standee Dalek also used for promotional purposes.

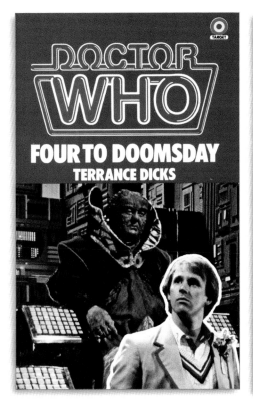

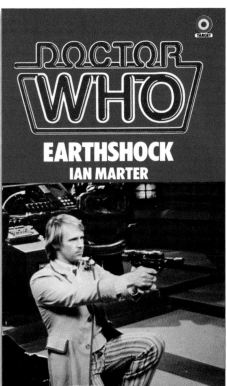

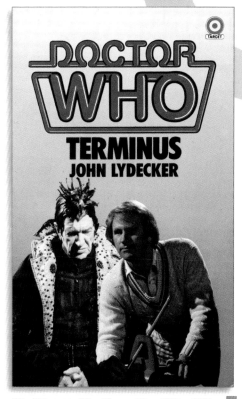

wonder if he isn't just using these adaptations as a means of extracting the urine from anyone daft enough to buy them – in short, this book is the pits.'

On the other hand, Christopher H Bidmead seemed to have got it just right with *Castrovalva*. 'Here, just for you, is another really classy book, from another really classy writer,' enthused Russ Mould in *Eye of Horus*. 'This novelisation has really done tremendous justice to his truly superb script ... and has filled any anxious moments concerning the translation ... The book has only one fault; which is the state of the cover ... A smashing book, full of life and entertainment. I really enjoyed it.' Paul Vanezis, writing in *Arc of Infinity*, echoed this view: 'It is truly a novel, of novel proportions. You never want the story to end, which is exactly what a good book should be like. In my opinion, *Castrovalva* is the best example of a *Doctor Who* book I have ever read, and I challenge anyone to name a *Doctor Who* book by a different author that is better.'

'...with a final series of raucous shrieks a battered blue police box materialised...'

Ian Marter, 1983
Doctor Who–Earthshock

Whatever the fans thought of their relative literary merits, all the novelisations were doing phenomenal business. For 1983 alone, the 2.5 per cent royalty earned by BBC Worldwide on sales of all the W H Allen *Doctor Who* titles was nearly £36,000 – making net takings of the books just under 1.44 million pounds. Each paperback enjoyed a first edition print run of around 10,000 copies, with an average reprint print run set at around 17,000 copies.

Starting with the paperback release of *Terminus*, the books carried a number proclaiming them to be part of the Target *Doctor Who* Library. *Terminus* was number 79, *Arc of Infinity* was not numbered (although was counted as number 80) and then from *The Five Doctors* (number 81) onwards the books were numbered in publication order. The first book to be numbered was actually *Time-Flight*, which

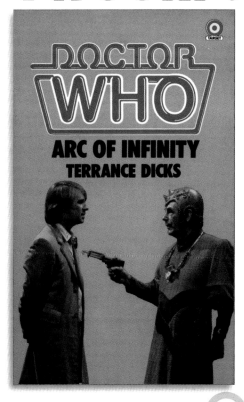

PETER GRIMWADE

'The novel is a way of directing it yourself – you can try to embellish it with any ideas that didn't come across in the TV version.'
Peter Grimwade, Opera of Doom
(number 1), February 1985

Peter Grimwade was educated in Cornwall and attended the University of Wells, following which he did a post-graduate course in Bristol studying drama. He joined the BBC in Bristol as a trainee and then moved to London to train as a film editor.

He worked at the BBC as a production assistant on dramas such as *Tinker, Tailor, Soldier Spy*, *All Creatures Great and Small* and *Doctor Who*. He directed an episode of *The Ωmega Factor* ('Out of Body, Out of Mind', 1979) before moving on to direct four *Doctor Who* stories in Seasons 18 and 19 (1980-1982). He then wrote three scripts for the series, in the process creating and writing out the character Turlough, and adapted all three for Target shortly after transmission.

In 1986, Grimwade wrote and directed *The Come-Uppance of Captain Katt* for the *Dramarama* slot on tea-time ITV. The drama was about the behind-the-scenes tussles between the star and producer of a long-running TV science fiction show, something of which Grimwade had first hand experience.

Grimwade wrote one further novel, *Robot* (1987), for W H Allen before his death. Publication of the book was offered to Grimwade by way of a good will gesture on the part of the publishers. They had licensed from the BBC the rights to produce an original fiction piece based on the character Turlough (*Turlough and the Earthlink Dilemma*) – rights that the BBC did not in fact own but Grimwade did. *Robot* has *Doctor Who* references scattered throughout.

Grimwade died, following a battle against leukaemia, on 15 May 1990.

was number 74. However the number did not appear on the first edition of the title and was included on the second printing later in 1983. Earlier published titles were simply listed alphabetically and then numbered from 1 to 73, these numbers appearing on reprint editions from 1983 onwards. The decision to start numbering the books came from Tanner: 'It came to me one day,' he explained, 'that with the Mills and Boon titles, people don't ask in the shops for the books by title, they ask for book number 36 or whatever. So I thought that if we numbered the *Doctor Who* books, the same thing would happen. It was my idea, I'm afraid.'

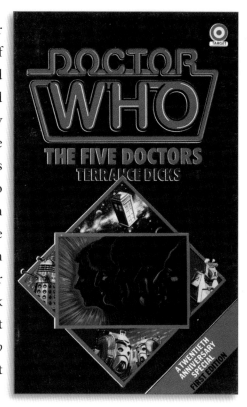

The idea may have been sound, but the numbering system caused several problems for successive editors when manuscripts arrived late and books that had

been announced and had their covers printed had to be moved around in the schedule. Perhaps the worst culprit was Philip Martin's novelisation of 'Vengeance on Varos', book number 106, which was eventually published around two years after it was originally announced, between books 128 and 129.*

In a further celebration of the twentieth anniversary of the TV show in 1983, Tanner commissioned Peter Haining, who had been his editorial director at NEL, and who was one of the writers represented by his literary agency, to write a history of the show. The result, a large format hardback called *Doctor Who: A Celebration*, would go on to sell over 100,000 copies, making it one of the most successful *Doctor Who* titles ever published.

---

*See Appendix B for details of the Doctor Who Library.

PART FIVE: THE FINAL BATTLE

BY THE END OF 1983, W H ALLEN'S TARGET RANGE of *Doctor Who* novelisations was doing great business, despite the cover price being raised whenever the increase could be justified either by a 'special' story being novelised, or by the book containing more pages than usual.

Christine Donougher, the range editor, eventually decided that she wanted to move on from *Doctor Who* – a subject that reportedly was never one of her favourites – and so a new editor was brought in. This was Nigel Robinson, who later became a prolific and respected author of young adult fiction with numerous titles to his name, including two novels for Virgin Publishing's range of original *Doctor Who* fiction. At the time he joined W H Allen, Robinson had previously written *The Doctor Who Quiz Book* for Target, and was a self-proclaimed fan of *Doctor Who*. 'When I left university, I wrote *The Tolkien Quiz Book* as a laugh with a friend; we literally wrote all the questions down the pub,' reveals Robinson. 'We first took it to Allen and Unwin – who were the publishers of all Tolkien's own books – and they turned it down, but it was then picked up by Star, the mainstream paperback division of W H Allen. I knew that W H Allen also published the Target books, so I came up with the idea of a *Doctor Who* quiz book. I liked the show, had watched it since it started, and had bought the Target novels. I wasn't involved in any fan clubs or conventions or anything like that, but I was a fan of the series.

'Christine was officially in charge of the *Doctor Who* books at the time. I don't think it's a secret that she couldn't stand working as *Doctor Who* editor. She didn't have much time for the books, she didn't have much time for the fans, and she was looking for a way out. I think she saw me as a godsend for the novels.'

Robinson was initially asked to proof-read the novels as a freelancer, and

'At this stage in his lives, in his sixth incarnation, the Doctor was a tall, strongly built man with a slight tendency towards overweight. Beneath the mop of curly hair, the face was round, full-lipped and sensual, with a hint of something catlike about the eyes. The forehead was broad and high and the jutting beak that was his nose seemed to pursue the Doctor through most of his incarnations. This Doctor was a solid, powerful figure, exuding confidence and energy, yet with something wilful and capricious about him. The extravagent side of his nature was reflected in his costume, which was colourful to put it mildly.'

Terrance Dicks, 1988
Doctor Who–The Mysterious Planet

BARBARA CLEGG

'They asked me to do it a little time after the story went out, and I was delighted.'
Barbara Clegg, Doctor Who Magazine *(number 267), July 1998*

Barbara Clegg started out as a theatre actress, then won the role of Nurse Jo Buckley in the long-running ATV soap *Emergency Ward 10* (1957-67). She also appeared in the 1963 Tommy Steele movie *The Dream Maker*.

She moved on to writing, contributing seven episodes to the long-running soap *Coronation Street*, which were transmitted in 1961. She wrote for the radio shows *Waggoner's Walk* and *Mrs Dale's Diary* and authored a tie-in novel for *Waggoner's Walk*, published in 1975. For television, she contributed scripts to *Crossroads* and *Together*. She co-wrote the ATV children's TV series *Once Aboard the Lugger* and *Strange Concealments*. Clegg's dramatisation of John Wyndham's *The Chrysalids* was broadcast on radio in 1981.

When Clegg was commissioned by Eric Saward to write 'Enlightenment' for the 1983 season of *Doctor Who*, this gave her the distinction of being the first woman to write for the show (the only other contender, Lesley Scott, having apparently made little or no contribution to the story on which she was co-credited, Paul Erickson's 'The Ark' in 1966). She later adapted her story for Target books, becoming the first female author on the range.

She went on to contribute to the Thames series *Gems* in 1986 and to work prolifically in radio.

the first that he recalls looking at was either *Kinda* or *Snakedance*. A couple of months after that he was asked to handle some of the editing as a freelancer. 'Shortly after that, in July 1984, I was called into the office for a chat and was offered the position of junior editor at Target. I had been working in numerous temporary jobs and I was actually working at the BBC when they offered me the editing job, organising transport for BBC shows. Funnily enough, I organised all the transport for "Attack of the Cybermen" …

'Looking back on it now, I think I was invited in to take over from Christine, although I wasn't told so at the time. I was just asked to be a junior editor, but about four weeks after I joined W H Allen, I was handed the Target editorship, which effectively meant the *Doctor Who* books as they comprised at the time around 75% of Target's output.

'When I joined, I took over lots of books from Christine that she had already commissioned, like *Fury From The Deep*, and some of the others, but as far as I remember, the first book I saw through from contacting the author, sending the contract out and seeing it through to publication was *The Two Doctors* by Bob Holmes, the one hundredth Target *Doctor Who* book.

'*Doctor Who* was seen by the publishers as one of two big moneymakers. The other was W H Allen's series of erotic books: anonymous Victorian erotica. Without the erotica and *Doctor Who*, W H Allen would not have survived for as long as it did. It was a real moneyspinner, and yet it was regarded as something that was

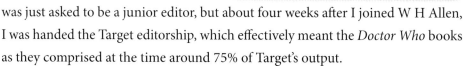

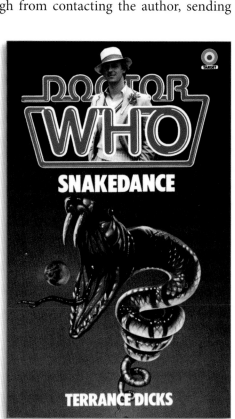

For the first time in 1985, Target took a stand at the UK's annual *Doctor Who* convention, PanoptiCon, organised by the *Doctor Who* Appreciation Society.

A concept cover for *Doctor Who-Mawdryn Undead*.

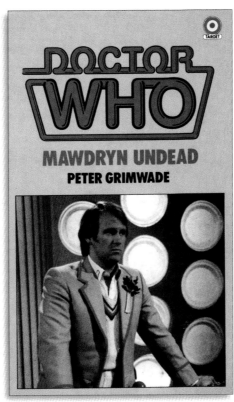

NIGEL ROBINSON

'I don't think the book is a straightforward translation of the TV version, and I've tried to add a lot more character into it.'
Nigel Robinson, DWBulletin (Winter~Spring Special), December 1986

Nigel Robinson's first book was published shortly after he graduated from university. This was *The Tolkien Quiz Book* (1981), a collaborative effort with his school-friend Linda Wilson. He began his association with *Doctor Who* in a similar vein when he wrote the first in a series of three *Doctor Who Quiz Books* (1981-85) and *The Doctor Who Crossword Book* (1982) for Target.

He went on to take over editorship of the Target range from 1984 until April 1987. He wrote four novelisations based on serials from the 1960s and also completed *The Rescue* after Ian Marter died with the book incomplete. After the Target range came to its end, he wrote two of Virgin Publishing's original *Doctor Who* novels (*Timewyrm: Apocalypse*, 1991, and *Birthright*, 1993).

Robinson has also written novelisations based on the TV shows *Baywatch* (four books, 1993), *The Young Indiana Jones Chronicles* (four books, 1993), *The Tomorrow People* (four books, 1995) and *Dragon Flyz* (four books, 1996-97), and tie-ins for the *Free Willy* films.

His original fiction for young readers includes the science fiction trilogy *First Contact* (1994), *Second Nature* (1996) and *Third Degree* (1997), a series of horror books (seven books, 1994-95) and the *Luke Cannon Showjumping Mysteries* series (four books, 1996). His writing came full circle in 2005 when he wrote a quiz book based on *The Chronicles of Narnia*.

always there and that was always going to be making money. So they just let it carry on making money without giving it any thought or direction.

'I fought for more PR for the range, and we organised a big promotion at the Edinburgh Festival with author Terrance Dicks, and we also had a Dalek trundling around Birmingham airport. The *Doctor Who* Appreciation Society's annual convention was in Brighton in 1985 and that was the very first convention where

Target/W H Allen had a stall to promote the books. When you consider that the show and the books had been very, very big since the late '70s, it took a long time for that to happen. I think the *Doctor Who* Target books were underrated and taken for granted an awful lot.'

A push to novelise older stories had been started by Donougher, who had commissioned titles like *The Aztecs*, *The Enemy of the World*, *The Dominators* and *Inferno*, and this had, according to Robinson, originally been suggested by John Nathan-Turner as a means of keeping the publishing programme going. Robinson continued Donougher's initiative and oversaw a major schedule of novelising all the older stories that had

'...reminiscent of a camel in the last stages of dementia praecox...'
Donald Cotton, 1985
Doctor Who-The Myth Makers

ERIC PRINGLE

'The novel was based entirely on the two-part story as shown on screen – novelisations generally have to be faithful to the televised serial.'

Eric Pringle, Doctor Who Magazine *(number 172), April 1991*

Eric Pringle was born in Morpeth, Northumberland. He went to Nottingham University and left with a degree in English and American Literature. After an unhappy spell working in the City of London, he tried farming in Gloucestershire before settling for life as an insurance salesman.

Having moved to the Lake District with his wife and two children, he tried his hand as a creative writer, having also to work as an editor on specialist publications in order to make ends meet. He wrote scripts for HTV's historical drama *Pretenders* (1972) and *The Carnforth Practice* ('The Tattered Anarchist', 1974) as well as a number of radio dramas. He won a Sony Award in 2001 for his Radio 4 play *Hymus Paradisi*, about the creative but tragic life of the composer Herbert Howells.

In 1984, he contributed 'The Awakening' to *Doctor Who*; he later adapted it for Target.

In 2001, Bloomsbury published Pringle's first children's book, *Big George*. Set in 1103, it retells the story of George and the Dragon with an outer-space twist. This was followed by *Big George and the Seventh Knight* (2002) and *Big George and the Winter King* (2004). This led to Pringle being proclaimed 'the new Roald Dahl of the millennium' by *Bookseller* magazine.

JOHN LUCAROTTI

'I've been accused of cutting out Marco's fight with Tegana to save Kublai Khan at the end, but I just thought that the way I ended the book was a better way; it was sharper, yet more subtle than going through and rigging a swordfight, which is TV and not book stuff.'

John Lucarotti, Doctor Who Magazine *(number 124), May 1997*

John Lucarotti was born in 1926 in Aldershot and spent nine years in the Royal Navy. He then went to North America to work for Imperial Oil. It was here that he began writing. Later, he scripted an 18-part series about the life of Marco Polo for the Canadian Broadcasting Corporation. ▶

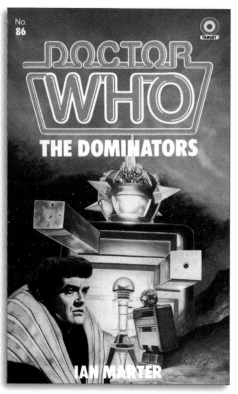

No. 86
DOCTOR WHO
THE DOMINATORS
IAN MARTER

not up to that point been done. Many of the authors of the original scripts came to pen the books, with Terrance Dicks and Ian Marter picking up those for which the original author declined or was unavailable to do so.

Robinson remembers that attracting new writers to the range was not a problem. '*Doctor Who* to a great extent looked after itself. New shows would be on television each year and, as a matter of course, we would contact the original scriptwriters about the books. By that time, *Doctor Who* as a whole was making big money, especially from the States, so people were keen to do it.

'Some of the authors – Glen McCoy springs to mind – actually contacted us before we contacted them, on the advice of either John Nathan-Turner or the show's script editor, Eric Saward. Everything we did had to be approved by John, and he was very good at passing ideas our way, as well as comments back on the manuscripts and artwork we sent him.'

By 1983, the BBC was making a lot of money out of the Target books, and W H Allen was making even more. Regular Target author Terrance Dicks remembers the mid-'80s with both fondness and some degree of pain, as over half of the 82 titles published by this time had his name on. 'Around that time, it was raining money on me,' he smiles. 'I thought this was very nice. The problem was that this money was rolling in and I was cheerfully spending it, and also I was going off to America once a month to conventions. They always paid for your air ticket and accommodation but in time they started to pay fees as well when they became more commercial, and so you'd get a few hundred or maybe even a few thousand pounds on top of a free holiday in America. I was living the life of Riley, really. I even took the family out to Fort Lauderdale to a big

DOCTOR WHO
WARRIORS OF THE DEEP
TERRANCE DICKS

convention there, and also to Chicago one year.

'What I had not taken into account, and this is a classic trap that many freelancers get into, was that this money had to have tax paid on it; and, of course, tax demands arrive a year or 18 months later. So there came a time when the money coming in from the *Doctor Who* books was declining as I was writing less of them, and the sales were starting to tail off a little, but the tax bills were still going up. I was very nearly ruined by this, and I had a very tight time for a couple of years as I tried to juggle the accounts. It happens to freelancers all the time – it just didn't occur to me to keep some money back for the taxman.'

The titles published in 1984 were as follows: *Mawdryn Undead* (Peter Grimwade), *Kinda* (Terrance Dicks), *Snakedance* (Terrance Dicks), *Enlightenment* (Barbara Clegg), *The Dominators* (Ian Marter), *Warriors of the Deep* (Terrance Dicks), *The Aztecs* (John Lucarotti), *Inferno* (Terrance Dicks), *The Highlanders* (Gerry Davis) and *Frontios* (Christopher H Bidmead).

Generally the fan press was much kinder about the titles than in previous years. Terrance Dicks' work, long the subject of both bouquets and brickbats, this year drew a largely positive response from members of the *Doctor Who* Appreciation Society (DWAS), as comments in their newsletter *Celestial Toyroom* showed. Daniel Blythe enjoyed *Warriors of the Deep*: 'I particularly liked the past history that Solow and Maddox were respectively given. However Mr Dicks would do well to consult a thesaurus to find alternatives for "pleasant open face", the words with which he has described the Doctor in all six of his Davison novels so far.' John Logan agreed: 'While it is by no means

By the late 1950s he had taken Canadian citizenship, and then returned to England, where he became involved in TV work, including writing *City Beneath the Sea* (1962), *Secret Beneath the Sea* (1963) and *Dimension of Fear* (1963), all for ABC Television. He had recently moved to Majorca in 1963 when story editor David Whitaker approached him to write for *Doctor Who*. Remembering his CBC series, he chose Marco Polo as his subject and followed this with the stories 'The Aztecs' (1964) and 'The Massacre of St Bartholomew's Eve' (1966).

He later wrote the TV serials *Operation Patch* (1976) and *The Ravelled Thread* (1980), and contributed scripts to *The Avengers* (five episodes, 1961-65), *Ghost Squad* (three episodes, 1963), *Joe 90* ('Child of the Sun God', 1969), *Paul Temple* (two episodes, 1971), *Moonbase 3* (two episodes, 1973), *Star Maidens* (two episodes, 1976) and *Into the Labyrinth* (two episodes, 1981), amongst others.

Lucarotti novelised his own serials *Operation Patch* (1976, also published by Target) and *The Ravelled Thread* (1980) before tackling his three *Doctor Who* scripts in the mid-1980s.

He contributed the first 'Brief Encounter' short story for *Doctor Who Magazine* in 1990, which featured the author himself meeting the first Doctor.

Lucarotti died on 20 November 1994.

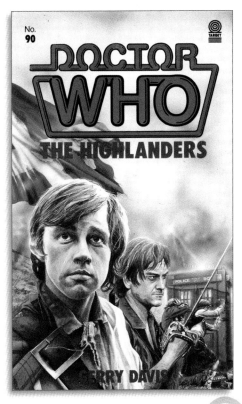

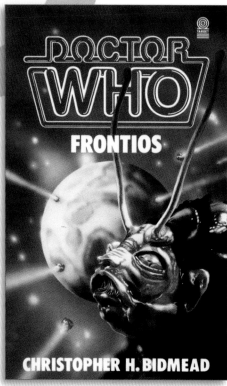

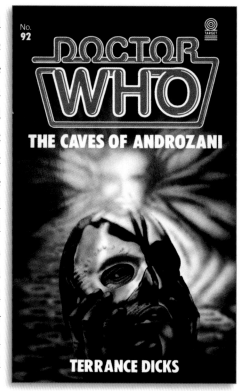

one of Dicks' best novelisations, I found it the most enjoyable since *The Invasion of Time*. Let's hope he can keep up the standard, even improve on it, then perhaps *The Caves of Androzani* will read like *The Auton Invasion*.' Robert Flint found much to enjoy in *Inferno*: 'A great boost to those of us who knew Terrance Dicks could still write if he put his mind to it,' he opined. 'He remains untroubled by too much description or background, except where it's very necessary. In compensation, he has brushed off his old skill of storytelling, to the extent that by halfway through the book I had stopped thinking about its literary credits and debits and started simply enjoying it.'

Kinda, however, was the target for some somewhat haughty criticism from Matthew Christmas writing in the fanzine *Cloister Bell*: 'I expected *Kinda* to be written as badly as usual; and it was … Now although I am doing A-level and may be considered to be way above the age bracket that requires such large print and can't read long words, I do feel that *Doctor Who* novels are worthless, except as tedious reference books for fans and young children.'

For the books by other authors, the reception was again mixed. Barbara Clegg's *Enlightenment* received much praise from DWAS members. 'The general air of excitement and adventure makes this one of the most enjoyable books to come out of Target for quite a while,' enthused Mark Benoy, and Darren Short commented: 'A lot of care and indeed affection seems to have gone into this book … A very pleasant read, more enjoyable than *Terminus* or *Snakedance*, and [it] fully enhances a truly original and imaginative classic.' Martin Day was also full of praise, despite having hated the television story: 'The novel of "Enlightenment" is brilliant … like a walk in the sun – simple and enjoyable.

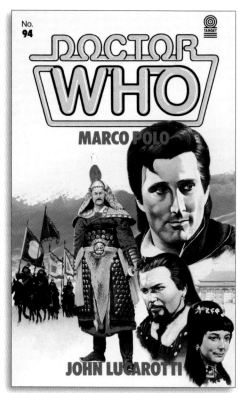

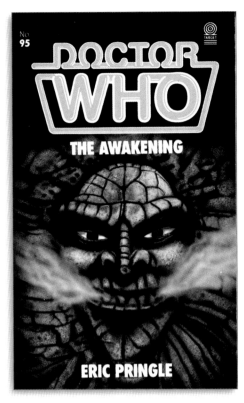

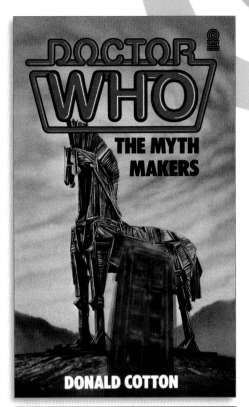

This is one of the best books this year, and well worth the money if only to prove how good it could have been on television.'

Ian Marter's *The Dominators* was, however, not overly liked, and not simply because with this title the cover price rose from £1.35 to £1.50. 'The book is passable, I suppose, but isn't Ian Marter overrated?' asked Gareth Lonnan. 'Give me David Fisher, Chris Bidmead or Philip Hinchcliffe any day.' Mark Benoy was similarly disappointed: 'This book highlighted the fact that fans of Ian Marter will blindly praise every word and full stop he uses, to the detriment of objective, clear thinking. Ian Marter throws away any chances he has to elaborate "messagey" elements of the plot. The subsequent slow action on the scantily-described Dulkis (very appropriately named) populated with almost Dicks-like characterisations, makes one wish for a copy of *The Horns of Nimon* – a far more enjoyable book.'

Finally for 1984's titles, John Lucarotti's *The Aztecs* incited wildly differing views: 'This was the story I was looking forward to …' mused Ian K McLachlan,

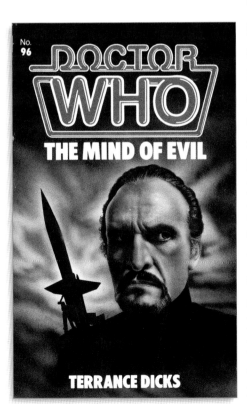

'but oh dear, I must confess that for me it is the most disappointing novel of them all, and by far and away the poorest Hartnell novelisation … It is written very childishly and yet it could have been an excellent story if, say, Ian Marter had novelised it.' Leslie Bray was particularly harsh: 'Do you suffer from insomnia? If your answer is yes, read this book. John Lucarotti has not really put any effort into this book. The characters are very dull and lifeless and you get more action from the *Beano*.' Springing to the defence were Denis Harrison and John Peel: 'It's different, it makes a change, I like the idea, I like the whole book – one of Target's best,' claimed Harrison, while Peel was especially pleased with the book:

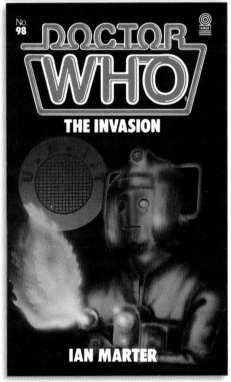

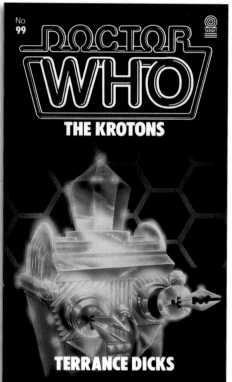

Andrew Skilleter's initial sketch for the Kroton on the cover of *Doctor Who–The Krotons*.

DONALD COTTON

Donald Henry Cotton was born on 26 April 1928 and went to Nottingham University to study zoology and English philosophy. While there he developed an interest in acting and writing.

He wrote for the stage and radio, contributing several scripts (often with a comedic bent) to BBC Radio's Third Programme. These were broadcast in the late 1950s through to the mid 1960s. His first television work was a musical adaptation of *A Christmas Carol* for ITV in 1955.

He was brought into *Doctor Who* by script editor (and old radio colleague) Donald Tosh. His first script was 'The Myth Makers' (1965) which was followed by 'The Gunfighters' (1966). A third script ('The Herdsmen of Aquarius') was rejected by script editor Gerry Davis. Cotton adapted both of his broadcast scripts for Target 20 years later, and also wrote the novelisation of Dennis Spooner's 'The Romans'.

In the late 1960s, he helped develop the fantasy-tinged series *Adam Adamant Lives!*, before leaving television work behind and focusing on the theatre, both as a writer and an actor. He retired from acting in 1981 but continued to write.

In 1986, Target released Cotton's original children's novel *The Bodkin Papers*. It told the story of a 150-year-old parrot that travelled with Charles Darwin. The book is written, typically, in first person based on a conversation between the parrot and the author, and features a series of black and white sketches by Cotton himself.

Cotton died in January 2000.

'The best novelisation for many a long year, and I enjoyed the changes from the original teleplay immensely. *The Aztecs* is fascinating, well-crafted (if economical) and amusing. It's terrific to read an artist at work.'

1984 also saw the first W H Allen 'Bonanza Competition' being run, in which the lucky winner could get their hands on a copy of a leather-bound edition of Peter Haining's follow up factual book to *A Celebration*, *The Key To Time*, and have lunch with Terrance Dicks. Entrants had to answer ten questions about the show, and to say in not more than 20 words which of the Doctor's companions they would most like to be and why. The following year, another 'Bonanza Competition' was run. This time, entrants had to complete a short *Doctor Who* story in less than 300 words, and the first prize was a trip to the *Doctor Who* studios, lunch with the Doctor, a video and ten signed *Doctor Who* novels. There were also 25 runner-up prizes of copies of *The Key to Time*.

As noted above, with publication of *The Visitation* in 1983, W H Allen started to use photographs on the covers of the books rather than artwork. *Mawdryn Undead* at least went through one rejected variant before the final cover was chosen. Even after this policy was reversed, in the light of actors requesting payment for the use of photographs, problems continued to arise. Janet Fielding, who played the Doctor's companion Tegan in the series, complained to Equity, the actors' union, over the fact that the actors were not getting any payment when artwork of them was used. Equity took this up with the BBC and, in October 1984, following months of discussion, the BBC decreed that clearance was needed by any actor or actress whose likeness was featured on the cover artwork used on the novels. Furthermore, if the artwork had been copied from a photograph, clearance from the owner of the photograph's copyright was also required. These stipulations subsequently formed part of the BBC's standard contract with its licensees and affected many *Doctor Who* licence holders. In addition, the BBC on behalf of the aggrieved artistes claimed back-payment of copyright fees for the use of photographs from both

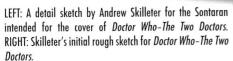

LEFT: A detail sketch by Andrew Skilleter for the Sontaran intended for the cover of *Doctor Who-The Two Doctors*. RIGHT: Skilleter's initial rough sketch for *Doctor Who-The Two Doctors*.

Marvel Comics (publishers of *Doctor Who Monthly*) and World International (publishers of the *Doctor Who* Annual). The BBC later clarified their guidelines over the use of artwork following some legal challenges. Legally it was all right to use likenesses, they now said, and the clearance aspect was more a courtesy to the artists involved.

These BBC 'guidelines' were to influence the subject matter of the covers to the end of the range, with artists who refused permission or who would not accept W H Allen's standard fee, being left off the covers. In the case of Colin Baker, his agent contacted the publishers to ask what the payment would be and W H Allen, immediately assuming that the payment they were prepared to offer would not be sufficient, made the decision not to use Baker's image at all, without even responding to Baker's agent. This was somewhat ironic as, according to Baker, his agent was simply asking out of interest and would most likely have accepted the standard fee. Unfortunately this decision meant that an already-completed cover for *The Twin Dilemma*, the first

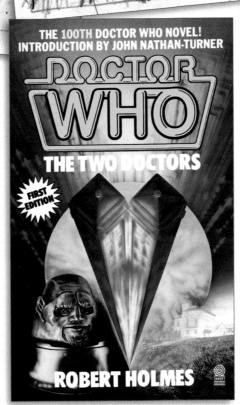

ROBERT HOLMES

Robert Colin Holmes was born in 1928 and was the youngest ever commissioned officer in the Queen's Own Cameron Highlanders, serving in Burma. After demob he joined the police and passed out top of his year at Hendon Police College. He eventually moved to court work, and left the force to become a court reporter and journalist. His work as a sports reporter took him to the Midlands, where he became the final editor of *John Bull Magazine*, at the same time submitting material to Granada TV for *Knight Errant 60* (1960).

Other early TV work included *Emergency Ward 10*, *Ghost Squad*, *Public Eye*, *Undermind* (his first science fiction) and *Intrigue*. His first work for *Doctor Who* was a commission to write 'The Space Trap', later retitled 'The Krotons' (1969). Subsequently he went on to become one of the series' most popular writers, responsible for 15 televised stories from 1969 to 1986.

He served as script editor on the show between 1974 and 1977, working alongside producers Philip Hinchcliffe and Graham Williams. Although he made a start on adapting his 1973/4 story 'The Time Warrior' for Target in 1977, it wasn't until 1985 that he completed a novelisation for the range ('The Two Doctors').

He scripted much TV drama during the '70s and '80s, including episodes of *Doomwatch* ('The Inquest', 1971), *Dead of Night* ('Return Flight', 1972), *The Regiment* ('Depot', 'North West Frontier', both 1973), *Warship* ('The Drop', 1973), *Blake's 7* (four episodes, 1979-81), *Into the Labyrinth* ('Shadrach', 1981; 'Dr Jekyll and Mrs Hyde', 1982), *Juliet Bravo* ('A Breach of the Peace', 1982) and *Bergerac* (three episodes, 1983-87). He adapted the BBC's 1981 science-fiction thriller serial *The Nightmare Man* from David Wiltshire's novel.

He was working on further *Doctor Who* episodes when he died, after a short illness, on 24 May 1986.

TONY ATTWOOD

'My *Companions* novel *Turlough and the Earthlink Dilemma* got a very similar reaction to that of *Blake's 7: Afterlife*. The committed fans did not like it at all. Some of the people who just watched the series and who took the trouble to write, were more complimentary. But I began to think maybe the fans were right, and I just shouldn't be trying to write in this little niche of TV continuation that I had carved out for myself.'

Tony Attwood, personal website, May 2002

Tony Attwood was born in 1947. He has worked as a teacher, musician, company director and writer.

He was commissioned by W H Allen to write the official companion to the BBC science-fiction series *Blake's 7* while the programme was still being made in the early 1980s. He interviewed several stars and programme makers, and communicated with series creator Terry Nation, who went on to write the introduction. *The Blake's 7 Programme Guide* was published in hardback by W H Allen in 1982 and in paperback by Target in 1983.

When *Blake's 7* ended, Attwood wrote the first of two intended sequels. *Blake's 7: Afterlife* was published by Target in 1984, but the sequel, *Blake's 7: State of Mind*, was put on hold indefinitely due to contractual difficulties.

Instead, Attwood became the first author with no professional or fandom-related links with *Doctor Who* to write an original *Doctor Who* novel: this was *Turlough and the Earthlink Dilemma*, the first in the short-lived *Companions of Doctor Who* range from Target.

Attwood has written over 80 titles, mostly related to educational techniques and methods, and is primarily known for his work on raising response rates in direct mail, which led in 1995 to the first publication of the Unified Theory of Direct Mail – an approach that offers 'the most comprehensive vision to date of why some direct mail works and some does not'. After a period spent writing books ▶

sixth Doctor story, and the first to be novelised, featuring a painting of Baker by Andrew Skilleter, was scrapped and a replacement commissioned.

Robinson, although the editor of the range when these events occurred, is uncertain of the facts behind this decision: 'The new cover for *The Twin Dilemma* was Bob Tanner's decision. I didn't see the correspondence from Colin Baker's agent asking for money, because what happened at W H Allen was that when the mail arrived in the morning, it was all opened and read by Bob. He would scribble on some of the letters and send them on to the people to whom they were addressed. But other stuff was kept and dealt with by him personally, so I never got to see the correspondence about the cover. But I do know that Bob insisted that rather than paying any more money to use the cover we already had, we got another cover done. It was a matter of principle to him, and Bob was ultimately in charge. He had the final say.

'A similar thing happened with *The Mark Of The Rani*. Kate O'Mara wanted some money, but Bob said no, so the image on the cover was painted by Andrew Skilleter so that it was not Kate O'Mara, it was an old crone.'

The publishing schedule for 1985 kicked off with a small treat for the fans as the standard length of the books was upped from around 120 pages to around 130 or 140 with, for once, no matching increase in cover price. The titles published during the year were: *Planet of Fire* (Peter Grimwade), *The Caves of Androzani* (Terrance Dicks), *Marco Polo* (John Lucarotti), *The Awakening* (Eric Pringle), *The Mind of Evil* (Terrance Dicks), *The Myth Makers* (Donald Cotton), *The Invasion* (Ian Marter), *The Krotons* (Terrance Dicks) and *The Two Doctors* (Robert Holmes).

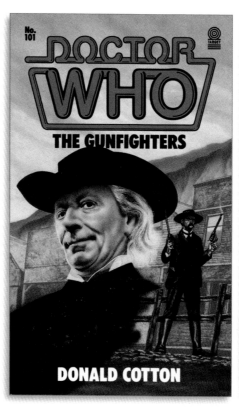

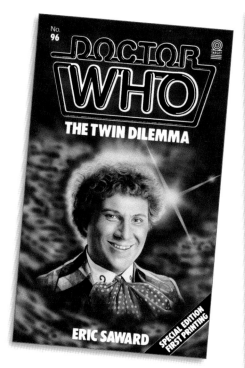

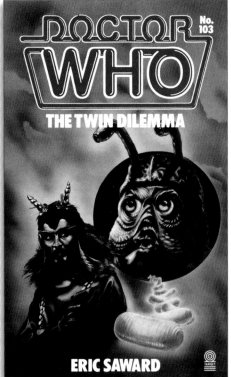

The original cover for *Doctor Who - The Twin Dilemma*. This was scrapped when it was realised that actor Colin Baker's agents may require paying for using his likeness, and a second cover was hastily prepared for the actual book's release.

Only Dicks' *The Krotons* was poorly received this time round. Andrew Thompson, writing in *Sci-Fi Times*, commented: 'At 121 pages and with a somewhat staid story, *The Krotons* is scarcely an inspiring read. Terrance Dicks, after the excellent *The Mind of Evil* and *Inferno*, has gone back to the rather bland method of barely elaborating on the script's framework. The book could have been a lot better.' Ian Bresman, writing in *Celestial Toyroom*, additionally claimed: 'Terrance Dicks never seems to tackle his characters with much conviction. His assumption that everyone knows the TARDIS crew could be substantiated, but there is no excuse for flat, uninteresting supporting characters … The novel is a series of superficial excerpts, transferred dialogue and only brief moments of inspiration.'

The other novels were however broadly praised. Mark Wyman, writing in *Opera of Doom*, liked *Planet of Fire*: 'Grimwade's structure is a far cry from the usual scene-by-scene transcription. Chapters are devoted to coherent strands in the plot … The overall effect is much less fragmented than we are used to, and I feel it to be a considerable improvement.' Andrew O'Day, writing in three editions of *Sci-Fi Times*, was pleased with the year's offerings: 'Do you want a good read? Then hurry out and buy [*The Caves of Androzani*] … A must for your bookshelf and your bedside table … [*The Mind of Evil* has] a very enthralling plot, which is very well executed by the author … *The Invasion* might win my award for the best book of the year, so far … [it] was at no time rushed by Marter. It was handled at just the right pace. I'm upset that the book ever had to end.'

Wholook's reviewer liked *Marco Polo* and went so far as to say it was one of the best *Doctor Who* novelisations to date: 'A true thoroughbred written by that

on other topics, Attwood returned to the theme in 2005 with *Education Marketing: The Theory And Practice Of Selling Into Schools*.

Attwood lives and works in Northamptonshire, where he is chairman of Hamilton House Mailings plc.

WILLIAM EMMS

'Something I've never told people is that the last ten pages were written when I was sick as a dog. I'd just come out of hospital and I wasn't feeling too good, but a deadline is a deadline. So if the ending is a bit out of this world, it's because I was!'
William Emms, Doctor Who Magazine
(number 156) January 1990

William Emms served in the Navy and taught English in London's East End before turning to writing. Throughout the 1960s, he contributed scripts to several ITV shows including *Redcap* ('It's What Comes After', 1964), *Public Eye* ('But the Joneses Never Get Letters', 1965), *R3* ('One Free Man' and 'Good Clean Fun', both 1965), *Mr Rose* ('The Golden Frame', 1968), *Callan* ('The Running Dog', 1969; 'God Help Your Friends', 1970) and *Ace of Wands* ('The Mind Robbers', 1970). He wrote 'Galaxy 4' for the 1965 series of *Doctor Who*. He was a fan of science fiction (having been brought up on H G Wells) and had watched *Doctor Who* regularly before he submitted his first script outline.

'Galaxy 4' was Emms' only commissioned script for *Doctor Who* and his only novelisation, which followed 20 years later. In 1986 his *Make Your Own Adventure with Doctor Who* book, *Mission to Venus* was published, based loosely on his plans for a 1966 script called 'The Imps'.

Emms died in 1993.

A detailed sketch by Andrew Skilleter for the figures of the Drahvins on the cover of *Doctor Who-Galaxy Four*.

brilliant historical writer John Lucarotti … The book allows you to imagine the glorious scenes and costumes now apparently lost to us forever.' Gordon Roxburgh in *Celestial Toyroom* was enthusiastic about *The Awakening*: 'Eric Pringle is very descriptive in his writing, and succeeds very well in capturing each character's feelings in the situation, especially Will Chandler to his new 20th Century surroundings. This must rank as one of the best-adapted *Doctor Who* novels, as well as being one that is very faithful to the original teleplay.' *The Myth Makers* was praised by M R Englander in *Sci-Fi Times*: 'I think this is a lovely novel … told with gusto and considerable skill. It is an imaginative reconstruction of the famous story – well told and very gripping. By the time I was half way through, I almost believed myself that it was the Doctor who had started the saga of the Trojan War and Helen that had launched a thousand space ships. Surely that is the ultimate test of a good novel. I challenge you to put this book down once you have started reading it.'

Finally, while discussing the one hundredth Target *Doctor Who* novel, *The Two Doctors*, Dominic May in *Celestial Toyroom* was impressed by Robert Holmes' first solo contribution to the range: 'Holmes has produced a novel that once you pick up, you never want to put down. Sometimes he writes with the conciseness of Terrance Dicks and the gore of Ian Marter, but what shines through above all is his own sense of humour and bawdiness.'

Not surprisingly given that it was the one hundredth book, the cover price for

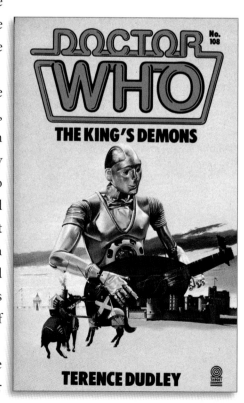

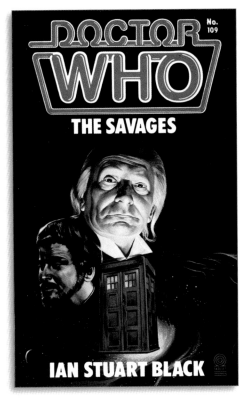

The Two Doctors increased by 25 pence to £1.75, although it then dropped back a little to £1.60 for subsequent books. Artist Andrew Skilleter recalls that the cover posed some problems. 'This was one of the rare times that I met with Nigel Robinson, and together with Mike Brett we discussed the inability to use the Doctors on the cover, hence the graphic image of two TARDISes. It turned out to be a powerful image, with some interesting effects that anticipated digital work, and the Sontaran head that anchors the rest of the imagery.'

The Myth Makers and Marco Polo had the honour of receiving the highest first edition print run for any of the Target Doctor Who titles, both having 65,000 copies printed. Both Tanner and Robinson recall that The Two Doctors had a first edition print run of 100,000 copies, however records from the publishers indicate that the true number was 60,000. These 60,000 copies sold out instantly (the bulk of them going to the USA) and an immediate second edition was produced, the print run for which is unknown.

With the novelisations now being published at the rate of around nine or ten a year, Robinson realised that before long, every televised story for which W H Allen could get the rights would be in print. He therefore approached the BBC on 18 October 1985 about the possibility of commissioning some original Doctor Who novels. Nathan-Turner replied that he was not happy to consider this at the time, and suggested deferring the decision to January 1987.

Undeterred, Robinson started up a range of original fiction anyway. 'I'd already suggested launching a series akin to the later Virgin Missing Adventures, which had been vetoed by the BBC for various reasons, when I started a series of Companions books

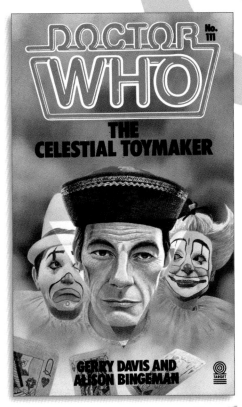

'...like the cry of a horse in pain...'
Terence Dudley, 1986
Doctor Who– The King's Demons

A cover rough by Andrew Skilleter for Doctor Who–The Mark of the Rani. The face of the Rani was obscured and made to be the 'crone' version to avoid having to pay the actress Kate O'Mara for use of her image.

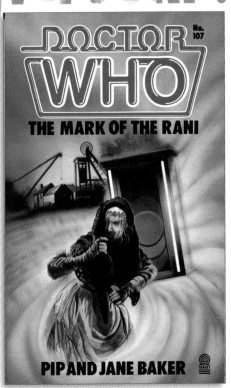

GLEN McCOY

'Having written the story and seen it as being very visual, it seemed like a chore to now have to do the whole lot again but in another form. But I far preferred to write it myself than let someone else do it and probably make a completely different story of it.'

Glen McCoy, Doctor Who Magazine
(number 210), March 1994

Glen McCoy was born in Bangalore, India, on 10 April 1954. His family returned to Britain when he was a young boy. After grammar school, he attended teacher training college in Eastbourne before training to be a paramedic as a stepping stone to getting into medical school.

He remained a paramedic for ten years, and wrote about his experiences in the book *Ambulance!* (1982). He also wrote the guide *Jobs in the Ambulance Service and Hospitals* (1984) before moving into more creative work. Because of his background, McCoy's agent first approached the BBC soap opera *Angels,* set in a Birmingham hospital, which led to the writer penning two scripts for the show.

The 1985 *Doctor Who* story 'Timelash' was his next commissioned work, which came about after he submitted an unsolicited story featuring the Daleks. He novelised the serial immediately after transmission, taking the opportunity to reinsert sequences omitted from the TV version.

He went on to write scripts for the soap operas *EastEnders* (three episodes, 1984/85, four episodes, 1998/99), *Eldorado* (seven episodes, 1992/93) and *Emmerdale* (15 episodes, 1994-97). He also submitted a storyline for police drama *The Bill* (1996).

McCoy has turned his creative skills to management consultancy, designing and leading training events on the principles and practicalities of customer service and sales for large-scale blue-chip companies. He also wrote *Getting Out of Debt* (1992).

He returned to the world of *Doctor Who* 20 years after 'Timelash', when he contributed the short story 'Dream Devils' to the anthology *Short Trips: The Centenarian* (2006).

with the Turlough, Harry and K-9 books.'

These titles were published in 1986 and comprised three novels. *Turlough and the Earthlink Dilemma* was written by Tony Attwood, with Mark Strickson, the actor who played Turlough on television, credited with 'character guidance'. *Harry Sullivan's War* (which had the working title *Harry Sullivan and the War of Nerves*) was written by Ian Marter, who had played Harry on television. Finally, *K-9 and Company* was a novelisation by Terence Dudley of his script for the K-9 Christmas special of 1981. Like all the non-*Doctor Who* series novelisations and factual books published by W H Allen, these had to be separately agreed and licensed by BBC Worldwide.

'Sales of these weren't phenomenal compared with the novelisations, but they were respectable and they made a profit,' muses Robinson. 'The plug was pulled on them all the same. "These books appeal only to fans," said the then-regime on the top floor. "Who else would buy them?" A great shame, really, as Janet Fielding had approached me [about contributing to the range] and we had a chat about it mid-1986. She was genuinely interested in the idea and was going to submit a proposal for a Tegan book, but ultimately never did. Ian Marter was going to pen a sequel to *Harry Sullivan's War* and Sarah Jane Smith, Victoria, Jamie and UNIT books were all on the cards.' Gerry Davis had been approached about writing the Jamie book, while then-unpublished writer Adrian Rigelsford had suggested a novel involving the Brigadier, which was eventually rejected by Sara Barnes in 1987.

W H Allen's Managing Director Bob Tanner remembers that the push to do original novels was very strong. 'We were running out of stories and we didn't know what to do. We started to go back to earlier ones and then ran out of those. When Nigel Robinson came in, we were getting so short that we proposed to John Nathan-Turner making up our own stories, which we'd never done before, and we then took one or two characters and made books around them. It was Nigel's project, and he was very skilful at it.

'It was built into W H Allen's overall budget that we had to have a new *Doctor Who* book each month, and we had to meet our royalty and licence payments to the BBC as well, so it was very important to us that we kept the books coming. I remember at one point Ralph Fields and Mattie Burdon, W H Allen's American owners, thought they could sell the *Doctor Who* list off separately to another publisher, and I was completely against this as it was such a major part of our budgets. They even went and took legal advice on this, but discovered that although the books belonged to W H Allen, the *Doctor Who* logo and all the characters belonged to the BBC and they couldn't sell one without the other.'

Robinson has specific memories on some of the titles he published: not always good. 'I was very pleased with *Inferno*, which was, I thought, Terrance at his very best. That was commissioned by Christine but I edited it. *Fury From The Deep* was also one of my favourites. Again, I didn't commission it, but I received the

A concept sketch by Paul Tams for the cover of *Doctor Who - Fury from the Deep*. This was scrapped when the BBC asked that no Doctor other than the current be pictured on the covers of the books. The final cover was by David McAllister.

manuscript and I edited it. It was very long and I tried to cut it, and worked with the writer, Victor Pemberton, on it for quite a long time. In the end we decided that we couldn't cut it, so we decided to release it as a bumper volume at £1.95, and I think it was worth it.

'I read all the reviews in the fan magazines and I did take notice of them. When certain books are reviewed badly it can hurt … I'll mention two titles: the fans seemed to dislike Donald Cotton's *The Romans*. It was my idea to get Donald to do that – a Dennis Spooner script – and I have to admit it didn't work out how I thought it would work

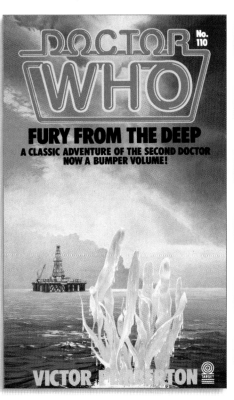

PIP and JANE BAKER

'We've got to provide the pictures for the readers; at least we've got to provide the signals that will form the pictures in their minds. That's what novelists do.'

Pip and Jane Baker, Doctor Who Magazine *(number 103), August 1985*

Husband and wife writing team Pip and Jane Baker have enjoyed an extensive career as novelists, playwrights and film and television writers since the early 1960s. The first film they worked on was *The Third Alibi* (1961). Others included *The Painted Smile* (1962), *The Break* (1963), *Night of the Big Heat* (1967) and *Captain Nemo and the Underwater City* (1969). For television they wrote episodes of *The Expert* (1976), *Z-Cars*, *Detective* (1968) and *Space: 1999* ('A Matter of Balance', 1976).

The Bakers worked on *Doctor Who* in the second-half of the 1980s, writing two stories for Colin Baker's Doctor and the introductory story for Sylvester McCoy. They also rounded off the epic *The Trial of a Time Lord* story after the death of Robert Holmes, the scriptwriter originally scheduled to write the conclusion, and the abrupt departure from the show of script editor Eric Saward. They novelised all of their scripts shortly after transmission and also wrote a *Make Your Own Adventure with Doctor Who* book, *Race Against Time* (1986).

After *Doctor Who*, the Bakers wrote a science fiction serial for children called *Watt on Earth*, which ran for two seasons (BBC, 1991-92). They also wrote a book based on the series.

In 1999, they scripted *The Last 28*, an independent video production starring Louise Jameson; and, in 2000, they wrote the *Doctor Who* spin-off audio play *The Rani Reaps the Whirlwind*.

TERENCE DUDLEY

Terence Dudley joined the BBC in 1958 and worked with them throughout his life in various capacities. He started out as a playwright and soon moved into scriptwriting, his early credits including *The River Flows East* for the BBC in 1962. He became a BBC staff producer/director in the early 1960s and thereafter pursued parallel writing and directing careers. In 1963 he was invited by *Doctor Who*'s original producer, Verity Lambert, to write the series' very first story, but declined.

Amongst other projects, he was a producer on the SF-flavoured *The Big Pull* (1962), *Doomwatch* (1970-72) and *Survivors* (1975-77).

He worked as a director throughout the '60s and '70s and into the '80s, including on episodes of *Out of the Unknown* (1969), *Doomwatch* (1970-72), *Colditz* (1974), *Survivors* (1977), *Secret Army* (1978), *All Creatures Great and Small* (1978-83), *To Serve Them All My Days* (1980) and *Doctor Who* ('Meglos', 1980).

He wrote for *Doomwatch*, the *Wednesday Play* ('A Piece of Resistance', 1966), *Survivors*, *Doctor Who* ('Four to Doomsday', 1982; 'Black Orchid', 1982; 'The King's Demons', 1983) and the 1981 *Doctor Who*-spin-off *K-9 and Company*. He novelised for Target three of his four *Doctor Who* stories. ('Four to Doomsday' was adapted by Terrance Dicks.)

Prior to his *Doctor Who* novelisations, Dudley had written two adventure books for children: *Darcy and his Snake* (1984) and *Darcy and the Colonel's Goat* (1986).

Dudley died on 25 December 1988 after a long battle with cancer.

IAN STUART BLACK

'I thought that as long as I could tell a good story and make an entertaining book, the fact that it wasn't always identical to what was on screen wouldn't matter.'
Ian Stuart Black, Doctor Who Magazine (number 170), February 1991

Ian Stuart Black's career as a writer spanned 40 years, and he wrote plays, books and radio, television and film scripts. He was born in London in 1915, went to school in Edinburgh and studied philosophy at the University of Manchester. After National Service, he worked for the Rank Organisation for three years, before moving into television. ▶

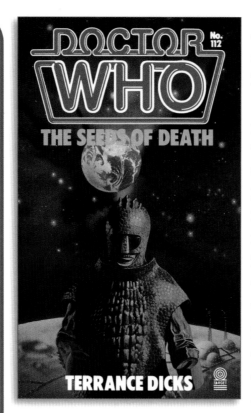

out, but nevertheless it was a great, fun novel. I can't see what there was not to like. However I thought the criticism *The Celestial Toymaker* received was totally justified. I was immensely disappointed with that book. I felt very let down by Gerry Davis as he was badgering me to let him do it, which I did, and in the end I imagine it was solely written by Alison Bingeman rather than by him.' Alison Bingeman, real name Alison Beynon, was a young, aspiring American author who at the time was a close friend and protégée of Davis's. She has since gone on to a highly prolific and successful career as a writer and producer in American television, generally credited as Alison Lea Bingeman, including on such hit series as *Relic Hunter*, *CSI: Miami* and *Whistler* – making her now, ironically, one of the biggest-name writers ever to have contributed to the Target range.

For other titles, Robinson recalls that he had difficulties in convincing some of the original writers of facts about the series. 'When Peter Ling delivered his manuscript for *The Mind Robber*, the character of Zoe was described as having long blonde hair like Alice from the Lewis Carroll novels, and I told him, sorry, but Zoe's got short dark hair. He wouldn't believe me, and in the end I arranged for a copy of the video to be sent to him. He apologised after that, which was nice. He later took me out to lunch and we talked about another book he wanted to do, set in a hotel, a big blockbuster type novel. A lot of authors did that; they saw *Doctor Who* as a springboard to go on to other things. Peter Grimwade was another. After we published Tony Attwood's *Turlough and the Earthlink Dilemma* in the *Companions* series, we discovered that the BBC did not own the rights to the character of Turlough, and that Grimwade, his creator, was

understandably upset that he had not been involved in any of the discussions or received any money from the project. From our point of view, we were totally blameless – how were we supposed to know what arrangements the BBC had made with the writers of the TV series unless they told us? Anyway, as a pacifying gesture to Peter, we offered to publish a non-*Doctor Who* novel he was writing called *Robot*. After that, we got on really well, and Peter wanted to do a big blockbuster called *Tin*, set in Cornwall over two centuries, about the decline of the Cornish tin mining industry, and we worked on that together for a time before he died.'

1986 saw the following titles released: *The Gunfighters* (Donald Cotton), *The Time Monster* (Terrance Dicks), *The Twin Dilemma* (Eric Saward), *Galaxy Four* (William Emms), *Timelash* (Glen McCoy), *The Mark of the Rani* (Pip and Jane Baker), *The King's Demons* (Terence Dudley), *The Savages* (Ian Stuart Black), *Fury from the Deep* (Victor Pemberton), *The Celestial Toymaker* (Gerry Davis and Alison Bingeman) and *The Seeds of Death* (Terrance Dicks).

Once again, fan comments were generally positive. Patrick Mulkern in *Celestial Toyroom* liked *The Gunfighters*: 'A splendid book in that it transforms what on screen was unmitigated offal to what on paper is a masterpiece of entertainment.

The cover for Peter Grimwade's novel *Robot*, issued under the Star Books imprint.

His list of TV credits covers a impressive range of acclaimed action and adventure serials of the 1950s, '60s and '70s: *Fabian of the Yard*, *The Adventures of William Tell*, *The Invisible Man*, *The Champions*, *The Man in Room 17*, *Man of the World*, *The Sentimental Agent*, *Sir Francis Drake*, *Adam Adamant Lives!*, *Star Maidens*, *Out of this World*, *The Saint* and *Danger Man* (which he helped devise). He contributed three scripts to *Doctor Who* in the 1960s and adapted them for W H Allen 20 years later.

He began writing original novels in the 1950s, with *In the Wake of a Stranger* (1953), *The Passionate City* (1958), *The Yellow Flag* (1959), *Love in Four Countries* (1961) and *The High Bright Sun* (1962). Both *In the Wake of a Stranger* and *The High Bright Sun* were turned into films. When he left television in 1975 he continued his novel writing with titles such as *The Man on the Bridge* (1975), *Caribbean Strip* (1978), *Journey to a Safe Place* (1979), *Creatures in a Dream* (1985) and *Cry Wolf* (1990).

One of Black's last written works was his contribution to the thirtieth anniversary (very) short story collection *Drabble Who*, edited by David Howe and David Wake and illustrated by Colin Howard.

Black died on 13 October 1997.

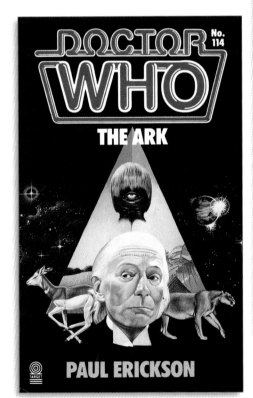

An example of the catalogue promotions being printed by W H Allen in this period.

TONY MASERO

'I will always remember entering the gloomy marble hallways of W H Allen, which were like a set from the *Rocky Horror Show*, and then going up the impressive stairway to the art department, where strips of brown parcel tape held the carpet together.'

Tony Masero, interviewed by Tim Neal for **The Target Book**, *January 2007*

Tony Masero was born in London during the Second World War. His father, Gino Masero, was a renowned woodcarver, and the young Masero's interest in art was heartily encouraged. He studied Graphic Design at Hornsey College of Art, although a request to transfer to Illustration was dismissed by the headmaster. After graduation in 1963, he found employment as a graphic designer for a number of advertising agencies around the vibrant Soho area in London.

Masero hawked his portfolio around several publishing houses with little success until David Larkin, art director at Pan Books, gave him some advice that eventually led to a commission from the art director at New English Library, Cecil Smith. The work was providing the covers for a series of NEL horror novels.

Other early work included covers for NEL's Western series *Edge* and *Adam Steele* in the 1970s. Throughout the '70s, '80s and '90s, Masero juggled producing book covers with supplying illustrations for advertising. In the mid-1980s, W H Allen's art director Mike Brett commissioned him to produce ten covers for the Target range of *Doctor Who* books. What would have been his final cover for the series ('Time and the Rani') went unused in favour of a photographic substitute. He also painted the covers for two large format W H Allen hardback specials by Peter Haining, *The Doctor Who File* (1986) and *The Time-Travellers' Guide* (1987).

Other work for W H Allen included covers for titles in the 'Target Classic' range, including *The Adventures of Professor Challenger* (1985), *Allan Quatermain* (1986) and *Ayesha* (1986). Masero returned to *Doctor Who* ▶

The level of wit and humour Donald Cotton manages to derive from such a sombre occasion is astounding. The book is quite faithful to the teleplay in that only the utter dross is omitted and all the fun scenes are retained.' Michael Duncan, again in *Celestial Toyroom*, was pleased with the characters in *The Time Monster*: 'The Master is superb – Dicks really has got that character perfect, he is by far the most interesting character in the story. The Doctor … well Terrance makes him appear as a bit of a crank, instead of the dashing, all-action hero we know the third Doctor to be.' Peter Ware, writing in *Chronic Hysteresis*, liked *The King's Demons*: 'A very enjoyable novelisation, although I must admit to having enjoyed the televised version anyway … Also worth watching out for is the word "whipping", guaranteed to have Mrs Whitehouse reaching for her quill pen and bottle of venom. But I can honestly say that, even if you didn't like the TV version, you will love the book.' Keith Topping was particularly taken with *Fury from the Deep* in his review in *New Whovical Express*: 'Pemberton has a wonderfully vivid storytelling technique that

uses highly visual, graphically haunting and utterly appealing lines of prose to interweave with his excellent dialogue … Best book ever? Possibly not, for Don Cotton's two Hartnell stories are something else entirely, but to say that *Fury from the Deep* pushes *The Myth Makers* and *The Gunfighters* close is the highest compliment I can possibly make to a quite remarkable book and an utterly fascinating story.'

The Mark of the Rani marked cover artist Andrew Skilleter's last original contribution to the Target novelisation range (although some of his BBC Video artwork was subsequently used on reprints). 'Things had become strained with Mike Brett, W H Allen's art director,'

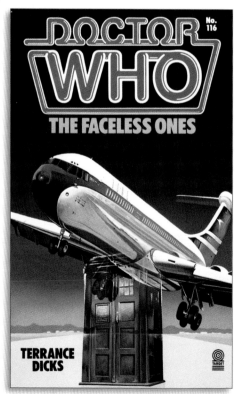

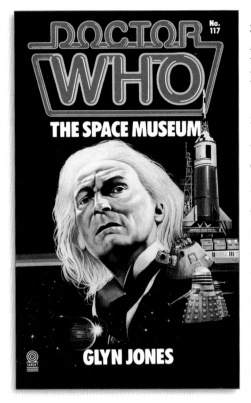

Skilleter recalls, 'and in 1985 my own publishing company, Who Dares, peaked with the publication of *Doctor Who* posters, artcards, bookmarks, two major books and the first of the art-based *Doctor Who* calendars. All this and my commissioned illustrative work, which included seven Target covers! It really is difficult to believe. But there was a price to pay – I think it's fair to say that there was a resentment from W H Allen about Who Dares, and I recall I was a long time delivering what must have been the cover for *The Mark of the Rani*, and Mike made it clear, probably justifiably, that he was very unhappy. I cannot recall the exact way the break came about, but he didn't ask me to do any more covers and I didn't chase any more work. I remember saying at the time that I should have given up the Target covers earlier, but it was difficult to let go. *The Mark of the Rani* was farcical – I can't remember a great deal, but I secured good photographic reference for the Rani, and when it came to it I couldn't even use her face, so there was no powerful focus for the cover. So I guess it was one cover too far. I notice that, strangely, I was paid more for that cover than the previous ones, a fact I cannot account for. Maybe it was a gesture of bravado on my part to up the fee, but I doubt it. I didn't talk to Mike again for many years, until out of the blue he rang me from Virgin, where he continued working briefly, as friendly as ever.'

Skilleter continued with his freelance work and Who Dares, going on to publish and illustrate the 1988 *Doctor Who* book *Cybermen* (written by David Banks) as well as providing illustrations for 1992's *Doctor Who Monsters* (written by Adrian Rigelsford) and 1995's *Black Light: The Doctor Who Art of Andrew Skilleter*, which he also wrote. He also published several *Doctor Who* calendars until 1989 when Who

when he was commissioned for the covers for six of Virgin's original novel range in the mid-1990s.

These days, Masero paints in oils and makes use of digital technology both in his preparatory roughs and to enhance some images. His pieces are, on the whole, realistically representational, although he still produces the odd piece painted in the style of a book cover. Exhibitions of his work have been held in both the UK and Portugal, where he now lives.

GRAHAM POTTS

Graham Potts was already providing covers for W H Allen when he began working on their *Doctor Who* range. His work included paintings for three early books from horror writer Shaun Hutson (*Slugs*, 1982; *Spawn*, 1983; *Erebus*, 1984).

His first piece of *Doctor Who* artwork was the cover for the twentieth anniversary special *Doctor Who – A Celebration* (1983), a large format hardback by Peter Haining. The same artwork was then used on many promotional items and for the box cover of the *Seventh Doctor Who Gift Set*. He also painted the cover for Gary Downie's *The Doctor Who Cookbook* (1985).

His sole cover for the Target range was for 1986's *The Celestial Toymaker* (voted the best cover of the year in the 1986 *Doctor Who Magazine* poll).

In the mid to late '80s, Potts also illustrated a series of Ladybird books based on the *Transformers* TV show.

Throughout the '90s, Potts produced the covers for the UK novels of horror/ fantasy author Dean R Koontz. He has provided cover artwork for many other authors, including Brian Lumley, Stephen Laws and Michael Slade.

NICK SPENDER

Nick Spender produced four covers for the Target range during the mid-1980s.

He returned to the universe of *Doctor Who* in 1996 when he painted the cover artwork for Lance Parkin's original novel *Just War*.

He has also illustrated game books and provided illustrations and covers for a number of books for children.

VICTOR PEMBERTON

'I don't think readers would think the novel was an unfair version of the story, even if the missing tapes were ever found.'

Victor Pemberton, Doctor Who Magazine *(number 146), March 1989*

Victor Pemberton's career started in radio when a friend, David Spenser, challenged him to write a play because he was criticising another. The result was *The Gold Watch*, the first of many radio scripts. His first television script was for Rediffusion's *Send Foster*, concerning the exploits of a junior reporter on a local newspaper. He also worked as a bit-part actor to supplement his writing income, and had a role in *Doctor Who* ('The Moonbase', 1967). He then served as script editor on 'The Tomb of the Cybermen' (1967) before writing the serial 'Fury from the Deep' (1968), which he adapted for Target 20 years later.

Pemberton also contributed scripts to *Adventure Weekly* (1968), *Timeslip* ('The Day of the Clone', 1971), *Ace of Wands* ('The Power of Atep', 'Sisters Deadly', both 1972), *The Adventures of Black Beauty* (1972-74), *New Scotland Yard* ('Error of Judgment', 1972) and *Within These Walls* (1975). He created the children's adventure series *Tightrope* (1973) and was a consultant on the UK version of Jim Henson's *Fraggle Rock* (1983-87). He wrote 20 original dramas and adaptations for radio between 1961 and 1987.

In 1976 he wrote the first original *Doctor Who* audio play, *Doctor Who and the Pescatons*, starring Tom Baker and Elisabeth Sladen. He adapted the story as one of the last Target novelisations in 1991.

Pemberton ran his own production company, Saffron Productions, from 1987 to 1997 with David Spenser. The company produced documentaries for the BBC and Anglia Television.

Since the early 1990s, Pemberton has been busy writing romance novels, set across the 20th Century. These started with *Our Family* (1991), based on his three-part Radio 4 series of plays, which were retellings of events involving Pemberton's own family. His fourteenth such book, *A Long Way Home*, was published in May 2007.

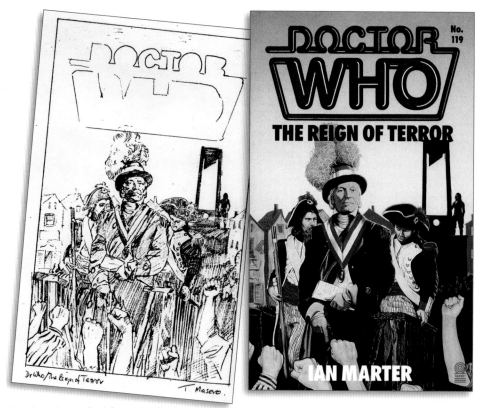

Tony Masero's cover sketch for *Doctor Who – The Reign of Terror*.

Dares was wound down, as well as contributing artwork to over two dozen of the BBC's *Doctor Who* video releases between 1991 and 1995. In 1995 he joined an agent who handled children's artwork but who was also a literary agent, and this led to his writing and illustrating a 1997 re-telling of the *Ivanhoe* story.

He continued to work as an illustrator, mainly on children's books and teenage covers. 'I hadn't realised the extent to which the new digital art technology had decimated traditional illustration as we knew it,' he reflects. 'The craftsmanship side of cover illustration is now dead – one can no longer tell what is hand- and what is digitally–rendered, so the integrity has gone – the only thing that matters now is the final cover image. For myself, I'm trying to bend my traditional techniques, particularly with the airbrush, to match digital imagery, but I see my longer term future developing illustrated and written properties for the children's areas.' In 1996, Skilleter started working for Brenda Gardner at Piccadilly Press, providing cover paintings for a young adult paranormal series called *The Unexplained*, written by Terrance Dicks. 'It's strange,' he laughs. 'After all that time, and I was painting covers for the same author and editor as when I started in 1979.'

Replacing Skilleter as the Target range's regular *Doctor Who* artists were David McAllister and Tony Masero, who handled the bulk of the covers. Other titles were assigned to Nick Spender (who painted covers for *The Aztecs*, *Inferno* and *The Highlanders* in 1984, and *The Sensorites* in 1987) and Graeme Potts (who contributed the cover for *The Celestial Toymaker*).

'My first contact with the *Doctor Who* covers was through a Mike Brett commission at W H Allen,' recalls Tony Masero. 'I was already an established illustrator at the time, having moved over from an earlier career as a graphic designer in the early '70s. My first book work was for New English Library, under the art direction of Cecil Smith, and from there, I went on to do jacket artwork for many of the major UK publishing houses. Looking back, it can be seen that from the '70s to the '80s was a heady time for illustration, but the advent of computer technology (amongst many other factors) meant a gradual decline of illustration in the accepted form of brush and paint. In those days, when there were fewer illustrators around, art directors would actually take time to see artists' portfolios, were mature enough to have had some life experience, could interpret a pencil rough as it stood and would give genuine artistic direction. The later policy of editors intruding into the responsibilities of the art director was, for me, the beginning of the end. Quite frankly, whilst most of these people were excellent with the written word, their expertise did not extend to the visual arts.'

Like other artists, Masero remembers that the reference material supplied for him to do the *Doctor Who* covers was limited. 'We were given just the jacket blurb, together with copies of the *Doctor Who Magazine* – and, if we were lucky, the issues contained relevant pictures. The magazines were cheaply printed on coarse paper and with a heavy screen dot. When working in a tight, representational style, accurate and clear reference is essential, and there was a constant demand to make a silk purse out of a sow's ear. It was a depressing source of many inaccuracies.

PAUL ERICKSON

Born in Cardiff on 22 November 1920, Paul Erickson spent most of his childhood and adolescence in San Diego, California, returning to England at the age of 18. After service in the RAF, he started out as an actor and worked fairly regularly in supporting roles on stage as well as in films and occasionally on TV.

During the 1950s he turned to administrative work in the theatre and spent about seven years with the Katharine Dunham and Jose Greco dance company, travelling widely. It was also in the '50s that his writing career started, and over the next two decades he contributed scripts to a wide variety of TV shows including *Crossroads, Emergency Ward 10, Out of the Unknown* ('Time in Advance', 1965), *The Saint* (five episodes, 1965-66), *The Inside Man* (1969), *Paul Temple* ('Re-Take', 1970), *The Rivals of Sherlock Holmes* ('The Affair of the Avalanche Bicycle and Tyre Co Ltd', 1971) and *Rogue's Rock* (1974).

His sole contribution to *Doctor Who* came in 1966 in the form of 'The Ark'. The story is credited to Erickson and his wife at the time, Lesley Scott, although she did not actually contribute to the writing. His last published work was the novelisation of his *Doctor Who* adventure in 1986, 20 years after its broadcast.

Erickson died suddenly on 27 October 1991, following a stroke.

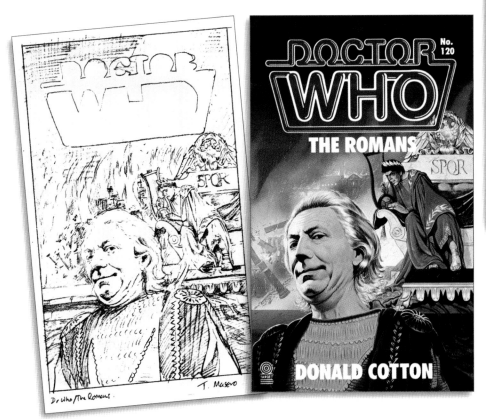

A cover sketch by Tony Masero for *Doctor Who–The Romans*.

'...as if some vast primitive being were in torment...'
Ian Marter, 1987
Doctor Who–The Reign of Terror

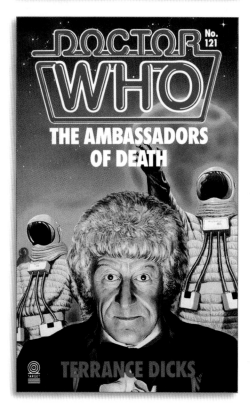

TOP: The original artwork by Tony Masero for *Doctor Who- The Ambassadors of Death*. The artwork was changed at the request of Jon Pertwee who felt that his hair was too dark on the original.

As I worked on the covers, I built up a *Doctor Who* file of my own, with pictures from *Radio Times* or wherever possible. Often there was no reference at all, as for instance with *The Macra Terror*, which is why I simply painted a real crab!'

One cover that had to be reworked was that for *The Ambassadors of Death*. 'I believe *The Ambassadors of Death* was the first cover to use Jon Pertwee's face for some time, and the publishers were very concerned that the actor was kept happy, as they presumably wanted to use him on subsequent covers. I was only a lowly illustrator, and the information that filtered down from on high was that Mr Pertwee was somewhat particular about his appearance and wanted his hair to be shown in all its snowy splendour. It was a bottom-lit portrait, so the hair was necessarily dark, but the man was insistent, so it was repainted, and the result was not to my liking, losing much of its early drama.'

Another cover that caused some problems was that of *The Romans*. 'As the variety of demands on an illustrator's reference resources is enormous (e.g. Monday a frog on a lily pad for a computer company, Tuesday a *Woman's Own* historical romance set in China …), a huge file of pictorial information is necessary. I once had a full filing cabinet, although nowadays it's all kept burned onto CDs. The total absence of any reference pictures for the cover of *The Romans* meant a trip to the filing cabinet, and the result was based on a movie still from, if memory serves, *Quo Vadis*, with Peter Ustinov as the crazed Nero. I particularly enjoy historical subjects and figure work, so I was always pleased to do those titles that involved this sort of subject matter.

'My favourite cover is not strictly speaking one of the Target series, although I do have a fondness for my first one, *The Seeds of Death*. My overall favourite is the one I did for a coffee table book published by W H Allen and written by Peter Haining: *The Time Traveller's Guide*. It was a large piece of artwork, front and back, with a great deal of detail, showing objects relating to each of the Doctors covered in the book. A small cheat on this was on the back cover, where I snipped a black and white picture of the first television title sequence and pasted it on the television screen shown there.'

Masero eventually moved to Portugal ('Why Portugal? Well, as I write this, my old house in Lewes, East Sussex, is under four foot of flood water and I am sitting in glorious sunshine … Reason enough, I think.') and continued working as an illustrator, mainly on print and web design. 'The glory days of illustration, with all their challenges and skills, appear to be over, so it's a matter of adapting to survive, but then, you never know …

'I will always remember entering the gloomy marble hallways of W H Allen, which was like a set from the *Rocky Horror Show*, and then going up the impressive stairway to the art department where strips of brown parcel tape held the carpet together. One image that sticks in my mind is the large wine glass full of cigarette butts standing in pride of place on Mike Brett's desk. The whole place had a kind of aged Dickensian feel of clutter about it. Virgin was a different kettle of fish altogether. Smart modern offices and younger staff, who were always changing. Very tight briefs and better reference. A much more serious attitude towards the covers which were by then reaching a wider market. And a lot better paid!'

Although the *Doctor Who* books had, over time, grown to become the mainstay of the Target range, they were not the only titles published under that banner; in fact, they comprised only half the stock list. By 1985, this list included tie-in novelisations to series like *Street Hawk*, *The A-Team*, *Automan*, *Airwolf*, *Blake's 7* and *Knight Rider*, titles related to films like *My Science Project* (one of several novelisations written by Ian Marter under the pseudonym Ian Don), *Dune*, *Return to Oz* and *The Last Starfighter*, and numerous others. Aside from the first three *Doctor Who* titles (*The Daleks*, *The Crusaders* and *The Zarbi*), the only other book still listed from the early days was *The Story of the Loch Ness Monster* by Tim Dinsdale. 'Loch Ness Monster books sell,' shrugs Robinson. 'Along

TOP: A selection of Target titles for this period. Editor Nigel Robinson had revived the brand to include more than just the *Doctor Who* novelisations. BOTTOM: The four Target posters issued at this time. The posters were offered for sale in the backs of the books. Two Target cover art pieces were included: Roy Knipe's impressive exploding Dalek from *Doctor Who–Death to the Daleks*, and Bill Donohoe's image of two Cybermen from the reprint cover of *Doctor Who and the Cybermen*.

Two further series added to the Target list by editor Nigel Robinson.

PETER LING

'Occasionally I came across a line of dialogue and thought "I don't remember writing that, that's a terrible line," but that's inevitable.'

Peter Ling, Doctor Who Magazine (number 177), September 1991

Peter Ling was born in Croydon in 1926, the son of a magician and a school teacher. He worked in advertising and served in the army before beginning his career as a writer. In 1950 he wrote comedy material for Jon Pertwee and between 1953 and 1959 he contributed to the *Eagle* comic.

Work for television included contributions to *Whirligig* (1950), *Dixon of Dock Green* (1955), *Crime Sheet* (1959), *The Avengers* (three episodes, 1961-63), *Sexton Blake* (1967-71) and *The Pathfinders* ('The Fog', 1972). In 1968 he wrote 'The Mind Robber' for *Doctor Who.*

His real strength lay in his contributions to radio and television soap operas. He worked with Hazel Adair on the soap opera *Compact* (1962) and together they created *Crossroads* (1964), which ran for 24 years. W H Allen/Star printed Ling and Adair's *Crossroads Cookbook* (1977), featuring recipes rustled up by Meg Mortimer and the staff of the Crossroads Motel. He also created *Waggoner's Walk* for BBC radio, which ran for 11 years (1969-80).

He wrote two novels in the 1950s (*The Three J's and the Pride of Northbrook*, 1957; *Angela has Wings*, 1960) and, under the pen-name Petra Leigh, three bodice-rippers in the late ▶

with books about Marilyn Monroe, the Titanic and cats. Don't ask me to explain that.' Other titles still in print from Target's early days included *Abandoned!* by G D Griffiths (which was indeed about a cat) and Spike Milligan's illustrated tales *Badjelly the Witch* and *Dip the Puppy* (neither of which was about the Titanic or Marilyn Monroe).

'Target aimed to publish four or five books a month,' explains Robinson. 'One was usually a *Doctor Who*, and one was usually another TV tie-in, because we had a deal with MCA Television in the States through which we got stuff like *Knight Rider* and *The A-Team*. We also did a "classic" a month, which was my idea, because they were cheap to do as there were no rights to pay – all the books were out of copyright. It was also nice to get the classics out to children, like Conan Doyle's Professor Challenger series or the H Rider Haggard books, which were difficult to find otherwise. The other strand of publishing at that time was the original fiction. This included a series called *The Starr Family Adventures* by G P Jordan, which I was pleased with, but the publishers would not put any money behind them and the books were not pushed or promoted.

'It was good fiction, but morale was very low at W H Allen through 1986, as they kept cutting back and wouldn't spend any money on anything. I finally left in April 1987 out of frustration, really, and went freelance. I commissioned myself to write *The Sensorites* and *The Edge of Destruction*, as I was building myself an income from royalties after I left. I actually went to Bob Tanner, quaking, to ask if I could do it, and he said: "Of course you bloody well can; I'm surprised it's taken you so long to ask." So he was all for it.

'I think that anyone who watched the show and who was a fan, wanted to write a *Doctor Who* novel. We received a lot of unsolicited manuscripts from fans, and the general feeling at the publishers when I arrived was that the fans were tiresome, spotty anoraks who bombarded the office with their own treatments for not-yet-novelised stories, which Terrance Dicks was contracted to write anyway. I tried to turn this around as best I could, but it was an uphill struggle. One of those "tiresome spotty anoraks" was a guy who sent in an excellent novelisation of the classic Marvel *Doctor Who* comic strip *The Tides of Time*. I couldn't do anything with it, but encouraged him to send in more of his material. His name was Mark Morris, and he is now one of the country's best horror writers, and author of several *Doctor Who* novels published by the BBC.'

As part of these efforts to encourage writers from within the series' fandom, Robinson initially invited Stephen James Walker to tackle the novelisation *The Edge of Destruction*, but Walker declined, partly due to other commitments and partly due to the daunting prospect of expanding a two-part story to novel length – a decision he subsequently regretted. This was another reason why Robinson eventually decided to take on that title himself.

Eventually, after three years, Robinson decided to leave the company. 'There were lots of reasons why I wanted to move on, but basically I felt I was bashing my head against a brick wall. In terms of *Doctor Who*, I didn't think it was being taken as seriously as it should be by the publishers, and I also thought that some of their decisions were somewhat cynical. Also there was very little faith in the Target range outside of *Doctor Who*.

'Within four weeks of leaving W H Allen, I joined Bantam books as a consultant editor, and worked in children's fiction publishing books with people like TV presenter Phillip Schofield. One of the first things I did at Bantam was to approach John Nathan-Turner to see if he was amenable to Bantam doing some original *Doctor Who* fiction. However John said no, as he felt first refusal on that should go to Target.

'There were quite a few things that I wanted to publish while at W H Allen that I couldn't, and things that I was told to commission that I didn't want to. It wasn't my choice. I was told that if we were given anything that was half-way decent then to do it. There were a lot of things that Christine commissioned that I had to see through although I would not have considered them. Bob was very protective of *Doctor Who* as a money spinner. He also got very annoyed when people, as he saw it, betrayed him. He got cross when he heard that I'd approached John Nathan-Turner when I started at Bantam books. Bob didn't like it when people tried to get their own hands on *Doctor Who*.'

'When I heard someone else was going to do a *Doctor Who* book I got very upset about it, because we were the *Doctor Who* publishers,' says Tanner firmly. 'We were the ones dealing with the BBC, we were the ones who dealt with John Nathan-Turner. I wanted as close a relationship as possible with the BBC. We were doing all the legwork and making the *Doctor Who* books a success all over the world. It was my love and I didn't want to share it with anyone.'

Robinson, despite his frustration at the time, has happy memories of working on the *Doctor Who* range. After thinking for a long time about what the high points were, he admits that it would have to be a selection. 'I was happiest working on Donald Cotton's books, although I commissioned only one of them. Probably the most enjoyable time was working on Jeremy Bentham's factual book *The Early Years*. It was just enormous fun. Because I'm a fan as well, seeing the original illustration for a Dalek, and actually handling the blueprints, was fabulous. Meeting the designer of the Daleks, Ray

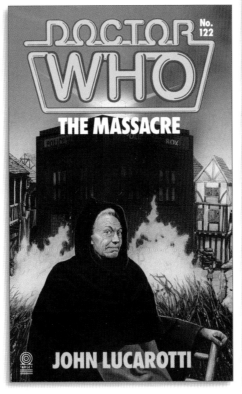

1970s (*Garnet*, 1978; *Coral*, 1979; *Rosewood*, 1979). He wrote his *Doctor Who* novelisation under his own name in 1987 and followed this up with two trilogies and two stand-alone novels (The *Crown House* trilogy, 1988-96; the *Watermen* trilogy, 1991-93; *Halfway to Heaven*, 1994; *Happy Tomorrow*, 1995).

He was married (to actress Sheilah Ward, in 1954) and they had four children. Ling died on 14 September 2006.

GLYN JONES

'I tried to write the novel with a sense of humour, which I hope comes through, especially with characters like the chess-playing robot.'

Glyn Jones, TV Zone (number 27),
February 1992

Glyn Jones was born in Durban, South Africa, went to drama school there, and came to England in the 1950s aged 22. In between acting jobs, he worked as a junior copy-chaser on *The Sunday Times*, at which point he also wrote his first play. Subsequently, he pursued parallel careers in acting and writing.

He wrote 'The Space Museum' for *Doctor Who* script editor David Whitaker in 1964 and contributed another idea that new script editor Dennis Spooner didn't take up. He appeared in *Doctor Who* when in 1975 he played the part of Krans, one of the astronauts in 'The Sontaran Experiment'. He finally novelised his one script contribution in 1987.

Other writing credits include *A King's Story* (1965) and *The Gold Robbers* (1969) for TV, and the Children's Film Foundation short *The Magnificent Six and ½* (1968). Other TV acting credits include appearances in *Strange Report* (1969), *Barlow at Large* (1974) and *Escape* (1980).

Jones was script editor for children's show *Here Come the Double Deckers*, which ran from September 1970 to January 1971. Alongside script editing, scriptwriting and writing some of the songs for this show, Jones penned a novelisation published by Pan (1972). He has also had a book of children's poems published (*Hildegarde H and Friends*, 1972).

He currently lives on the island of Crete.

1985 saw more promotion for W H Allen's hardback and paperback book ranges. These pages are from a publisher catalogue at the time.

Cusick, and just working on the book with him as well was brilliant. The guy that designed the book, a chap called Cecil Smith, wasn't a *Doctor Who* fan, far from it, but he got carried away with the whole project as well.

'John Nathan-Turner was also a total delight to work with. We had to go through him to check everything, under the terms of the contracts with BBC Worldwide. He approved everything we did apart from one thing, which was in John Lucarotti's novelisation of *The Massacre* when we had the Time Lords appearing in it. I sent it to John Nathan-Turner, and he asked what they were doing there. I replied, explaining why they were there, and he came back with an okay. As long as he knew what was happening, he was fine to work with. He was always very keen to promote *Doctor Who*. Very keen.'

At the end of 1986, with sales soaring, the BBC renewed W H Allen's licence to publish the books for a further five years. However, at this time, it was very apparent to Tanner and Robinson that there weren't another five years' worth of novelisations to be published, and that something would have to be done to address this.

1987 saw 11 more titles added to the *Doctor Who* range: *Black Orchid* (Terence Dudley), *The Ark* (Paul Erickson), *The Mind Robber* (Peter Ling), *The Faceless Ones* (Terrance Dicks), *The Space Museum* (Glyn Jones), *The Sensorites* (Nigel Robinson), *The Reign of Terror* (Ian Marter), *The Romans* (Donald Cotton), *The Ambassadors of Death* (Terrance Dicks), *The Massacre* (John Lucarotti) and *The Macra Terror* (Ian Stuart Black).

This time, it was Ian Stuart Black's contribution that generally received the thumbs down from readers, although a reviewer in the fanzine *Wholook* quite liked *The Macra Terror*: 'As a literary work, I can't say it isn't pro rata the TV broadcast; the book is primarily a good read because of the story … I'd give the interpretation six out of ten.' However Gordon Roxburgh, writing in the Doctor Who Appreciation Society's newsletter, was disappointed. 'The story is a more interesting one than Ian's previous novel *The Savages*, but sadly is not a better written adaptation, and I was generally left with a feeling of disappointment, because the potential was there for an excellent novel from an exciting story, but unfortunately it falls flat.' Robinson in fact had tried to encourage Black to develop *The Macra Terror* using a more adult style than he had used for *The Savages*, emphasising the mind-control angle, but these suggestions apparently were not taken on board by the author.

All the other books, especially those novelised by the original scriptwriters, were broadly praised. *Wholook* asserted that *Black Orchid* was 'certainly the best novelisation of this era, followed closely by *The King's Demons* also penned by Dudley.' Of *The Ark*, the same magazine commented: '[It has] much more action in the book than on screen and it is [consequently] more enjoyable. As with most translated literature, much better to read than to watch.' This view was echoed by Ian K McLachlan in *Celestial Toyroom*: 'Even if you have seen *The Ark*, don't neglect its novelisation. It is much better than the TV serial and deserves its place on your bookshelf!' Peter Ling's *The Mind Robber* also found favour with *Wholook*: 'The book has all the colourful information to set a story about telling stories, but with imaginative novel touches added.' Gillian Green, writing about the same book in *Celestial Toyroom*, said that she was 'captivated, entertained and very impressed … This is a brilliant book. Buy it!' Glyn Jones' and John Lucarotti's contributions were also praised, with Ian K McLachlan commenting in *Celestial Toyroom* about the former that 'it seems to be the case again that a poorer TV story has provided us with one of the better novels.'

Of the remaining books, Nigel Robinson's *The Sensorites* received a mixed reaction. 'A total mish-mash of '50s pulp prose,' claimed *Wholook*'s Andrew Engelfield, while Julian Knott writing in *Celestial Toyroom* had other criticisms: 'The book is written with a well polished hindsight that is both irksome and irritating, and is virtually devoid of any intentional humour, surely a requisite for any Hartnell novel.'

Terrance Dicks' work was very much appreciated by correspondents to *Celestial Toyroom*. 'From the very first page, Terrance Dicks grabs the reader and never lets up … Simple but effective,' enthused Dominic May about *The Faceless Ones*. Tony Jordan meanwhile found that, after a shaky start, *The Ambassadors of Death* was very much to his liking: 'A great challenge is to be found in reading *The Ambassadors of Death* – it is to reach chapter two without cringing at Terrance Dicks' archetypal clichéd opening narrative and descriptions. If you succeed, then you will be well rewarded, for there then proceeds to develop a well-paced, exciting adventure that stands as a fine tribute to the Pertwee era, whose novelisations it completes.'

The book that caused the most reaction, however, was Donald Cotton's re-working of *The Romans*. 'Whilst I agree that it bears no passing resemblance to the original story, I beg to differ on its main point, its enjoyment factor,' argued Gary Wales in *Wholook*. 'We all need a little frivolity now and again, don't we? Well here it is … The book is as fresh in its approach as the televised version was, both unusual in the *Doctor*

Two covers from the Target catalogue in 1985, including promotion of a reprint of 1975's *The Doctor Who Monster Book*.

Author Douglas Adams. His contributions to *Doctor Who* remain un-novelised in the Target range as the author was not prepared to accept the money that W H Allen could offer to write them, and declined to allow another author to do them on his behalf.

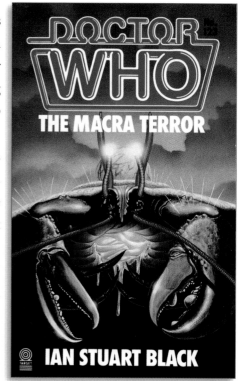

Who context.' However, the feelings of many were summed up by Gillian Green in *Celestial Toyroom*: 'Whatever this book was (entertaining, amusing and very silly), it wasn't a *Doctor Who* book.'

As noted by Tony Jordan in his review, *The Ambassadors of Death* marked the final Pertwee adventure to be novelised. *Meglos* was the last available Tom Baker story published, in 1983, and *Black Orchid* in 1987 brought the available Davison era to a conclusion. By the end of 1987 there were only a further 28 then-televised stories to be transferred to the printed page (counting 'The Trial of a Time Lord' as four stories). Douglas Adams was unwilling to let anyone else novelise his scripts ('The Pirate Planet' and 'City of Death') and too busy to do so himself, Terry Nation was holding fast to his remaining Dalek stories ('The Chase', 'Mission to the Unknown', 'The Daleks' Master Plan', 'The Power of the Daleks' and 'The Evil of the Daleks'), and Eric Saward was unwilling to see his two Dalek stories, 'Resurrection of the Daleks' and 'Revelation of the Daleks', novelised under the terms of agreement between the publishers, BBC Worldwide and Terry Nation's agents, so this left only 19 books available to be published.

When Robinson left W H Allen in April 1987, editorship of the Target range passed to Sara Barnes for a short while before she suddenly left in June 1987 to join Collins publishers. Tim Byrne then briefly handled affairs before the range was finally taken over by Jo Thurm.

Aside from the realisation that their golden-egg-laying *Doctor Who* goose was about to dematerialise, W H Allen as a company was again having problems. 'Morale was very bad and lots of people were leaving,' Robinson recalled. 'W H Allen had nearly folded in the mid-'70s, and had been saved only by *Doctor Who* and Bob Tanner. Bob had been brought in to save the company, basically. At the time I joined, I heard that he was apparently insured by the company for one million pounds. That's how much faith they had in Bob, and he certainly turned the company round. However things still seemed to be going downhill.'

Tanner shakes his head sadly when recalling the late '80s. 'We managed to get through all the initial problems and were making money again. The company did very well for five or seven years. And then it all went wrong.'

Ian Marter at a book signing with a couple of 'friends'. Picture © Peter Williams.

PART SIX: COUNTDOWN TO DOOM

JO THURM TOOK OVER THE EDITOR-
ship of the Target range around August 1987 and continued
the publication schedule developed by Nigel Robinson. She
oversaw the novelisation both of the remaining few available
past stories and of the stories newly transmitted on television.

1988 saw the following titles published: *The Rescue* (Ian
Marter), *Terror of the Vervoids*, a novelisation of the third
story – working title 'The Ultimate Foe' – within the overall
'The Trial of a Time Lord' adventure (Pip and Jane Baker),
The Time Meddler (Nigel Robinson), *The Mysterious Planet*, a
novelisation of the first story within the overall 'The Trial of
a Time Lord' adventure (Terrance Dicks), *Time and the Rani*
(Pip and Jane Baker), *Vengeance on Varos* (Philip Martin), *The
Underwater Menace* (Nigel Robinson), *The Wheel in Space*
(Terrance Dicks), *The Ultimate Foe*, a novelisation of the
fourth story – working title 'Time Inc' – within the overall 'The

TOP: The Next Generation! A group of authors and editors comprising a new wave of *Doctor Who* writing at a Virgin Publishing gathering in the early nineties. Front: Paul Cornell, Ben Aaronovitch, Gary Russell. Middle: David J Howe, Skaroean Visitor, Paul Leonard, Peter Darvill-Evans. Back: Jim Mortimer, Gareth Roberts, Simon Messingham, Mark Gatiss, Mark Stammers, Andrew Lane, Stephen James Walker. BELOW: An example of a postmark used by W H Allen to celebrate 25 years of publishing *Doctor Who* books in 1989.

Trial of a Time Lord' adventure (Pip and Jane Baker), *The Edge of Destruction*, a
novelisation of 'Inside the Spaceship' (Nigel Robinson), *The Smugglers* (Terrance
Dicks) and *Paradise Towers* (Stephen Wyatt).

Philip Martin's *Vengeance on Varos* had been awaited for some time. Initial
discussions with Martin had commenced in March 1985 with an agreed delivery
date of 31 December 1985. The book was eventually delivered on 7 July 1987. 'We
were in an invidious position really,' comments Nigel Robinson when recalling
these delays. 'If a book did not come in on time, then we could have said that it

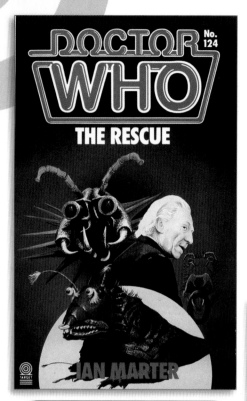

DOCTOR WHO
No. 124
THE RESCUE

IAN MARTER

PHILIP MARTIN

Philip Martin was born in Liverpool in 1938 and started his career as an actor. He made many television and stage appearances, including in the film *The Loneliness of a Long Distance Runner* (1962). In the late '60s he appeared in and wrote for *Z-Cars*.

Martin was an established television writer when he came to contribute to *Doctor Who* in the second half of the 1980s. Amongst other shows, previously he had written for *New Scotland Yard*, *Crossroads* and *Shoestring* ('Find the Lady', 1979). In 1977, Martin adapted scripts from his ground-breaking TV show *Gangsters* into two novels.

He created the character Sil for 'Vengeance on Varos' in the first full season of Colin Baker's Doctor in 1985. The character returned in the Martin-penned episodes of the following season's 'The Trial of a Time Lord'. The character would have also returned in a 1985 story called 'Mission to Magnus', however ▶

was in breach of contract and demanded the advance back. But with *Doctor Who*, we couldn't do the book at all without the scriptwriter's permission, so they had us over a barrel really.'

The Smugglers was the last novelisation to be released in hardback as well as paperback. Sales of the hardbacks had been declining and a decision was taken to stop them at this point, and to continue with paperback originals only.

The stand-out title from this year's selection appeared to be Ian Marter's *The Rescue*. 'Quite simply brilliant ... ten out of ten,' praised *Wholook*, while Ian K McLachlan in *Celestial Toyroom* wrote: 'A very descriptive book. It shows just what can be done with a *Doctor Who* story given a talented and thoughtful adapter.' The book had been completed in draft by the author before his untimely death in October 1987, and subsequently prepared for publication by Robinson. Pip and Jane Baker's *Terror of the Vervoids*, on the other hand, was perhaps the poorest received. Andrew Hair, writing in *Celestial Toyroom*, felt: 'The prose style employed is at worst, careless; at best, bland. Little or no effort is given to description ... The book isn't worth it. The undeniable tension that was woven into the first two episodes of this adventure are quite lost in the written form.'

Artwork for the covers of the 1988

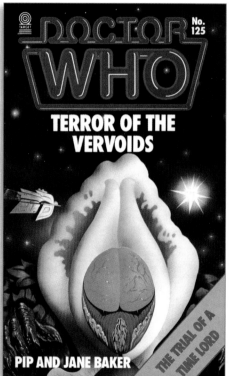

DOCTOR WHO
No. 125
TERROR OF THE VERVOIDS

PIP AND JANE BAKER

THE TRIAL OF A TIME LORD

books was handled by several artists. Regular artist Tony Masero contributed his final two covers to the range with *Terror of the Vervoids* and *The Mysterious Planet*, and other contributors included Tony Clark (*The Rescue*), Jeff Cummins (*The Time Meddler*), David McAllister (*Vengeance on Varos* – although this had actually been painted two years earlier) and Ian Burgess (*The Wheel in Space*). Clark was a well known fan illustrator, who had been contributing work to

DOCTOR WHO
No. 126
THE TIME MEDDLER

NIGEL ROBINSON

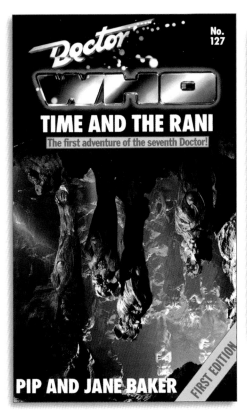

The draft cover for *Doctor Who–Time and the Rani*. This version was scrapped when it was realised that the painting by Tony Masero was upside down.

the script was not taken to production; instead it was adapted by Martin as one of *The Missing Episodes* run of Target books. Martin also wrote the *Doctor Who* adventure book *Invasion of the Ormazoids* (1986).

He went on to write scripts for *Star Cops* ('This Case to be Opened in a Million Years', 1987), *The Bill* ('Enemies', 1990), *Virtual Murder* ('Meltdown to Murder', 1992) and *Hetty Wainthropp Investigates* (four episodes, 1997-98).

He returned to *Doctor Who* when he wrote the audio adventure 'The Creed of the Kromon', released by Big Finish in January 2004. Martin has also written, produced and directed radio dramas, and his stage plays have been performed at Dukes Playhouse, Lancaster; The Royal Court, London; and Liverpool Playhouse.

Doctor Who Appreciation Society publications for several years. His initial painting for *The Rescue*, showing Koquillion standing with his power-tool device, was rejected, so he duly supplied a substitute – a more traditional collage – that was used instead. Ian Burgess was another contributor from the fan community.

Time and the Rani featured a photographic cover, the decision to do this being made quite late in the day. Tony Masero was originally commissioned to provide a painting of the bat-like Tetraps in their cave, however when he delivered the artwork, and proofs of the hardback and paperback covers were sent to the *Doctor Who* office as usual for approval, producer John Nathan-Turner noticed that the image was upside down – no-one had told the art editor at W H Allen that the creatures hung from the roof of their cave! Instead of this being corrected by a simple 180-degree rotation of the artwork, a completely new approach was taken, and a special photograph was commissioned. This involved recreating the Tetraps' cave, complete with hanging creatures. The photographer was Chris Capstick.

The remaining covers were handled by newcomer Alister Pearson. Pearson's first contribution to a W H Allen title came when one of his pencil drawings was included in the 1984 Peter Haining book *The Key to Time*. 'I'd been pestering the editor of the *Doctor Who* books, Nigel Robinson, and the art director at W H Allen, Mike Brett, every so often, writing letters, making phone calls and sending in on-spec pieces of artwork by way of demonstrating my abilities – such as they were at the time!

'I painted prospective covers for *Four to Doomsday*, *The Daleks' Master Plan* (which they somehow managed to lose), *Destiny of the Daleks*, *Vengeance on Varos*

'...it soon rose to a trumpeting shriek as though it were attempting to drown out the sound of the thundering sea...'

Nigel Robinson, 1988
Doctor Who–The Time Meddler

STEPHEN WYATT

'I have to be honest and say I regarded it as a way of making some cash.'

Stephen Wyatt, Doctor Who Magazine
(number 263), April 1998

Stephen Wyatt was born in 1948. Over a career spanning more than 30 years, he has contributed scripts to theatre, radio and television. He started out in community and children's theatre, writing over a dozen productions. Eventually he submitted a piece for television called *Claws* (broadcast in 1987). He wrote (and later novelised) two *Doctor Who* stories for producer John Nathan Turner and script editor Andrew Cartmel: 'Paradise Towers' (1987) and 'The Greatest Show in the Galaxy' (1988).

Wyatt now works largely in radio. His original radio drama includes: *Fairest Isle* (1995), which won a Sony Award; *Party Animal* (2003); *A Game of Marbles* (2004), a comedy about the Elgin Marbles; *Agnes Beaumont by Herself* (2004) and the Gilbert Harding biography *Dr Brighton and Mr Harding* (2005). He has dramatised two series of *Sketches By Boz* for Radio 4 and one series of *Tales by Thackeray*. He has written many radio adaptations, including the acclaimed *The Old Wives' Tale*, *Gilbert Without Sullivan*, *Vanity Fair* and *Tales The Countess Told*.

His other TV credits include scripts for Jean Marsh's BBC drama series *The House of Eliott* (1994) and *Casualty* (six episodes, 1990-97) and he has worked on the soap opera *Family Affairs*.

Wyatt also scripted the audio guide for an Elizabeth I exhibition at Greenwich Maritime Museum, and he has lectured in writing drama at universities throughout the UK and Europe.

and *Image of the Fendahl*.'

Pearson was more lucky with his approaches to *Doctor Who Magazine*, and by mid-1987 had seen four pieces of artwork accepted and published. This spurred him on to try W H Allen again, and now that he had published work under his belt, it seemed that Mike Brett was more willing to offer a commission.

'For my first commission, *The Underwater Menace*, Mike offered me some very poorly photocopied pages from *Doctor Who Magazine* number 78 by way of reference material,' recalls Pearson. 'I declined these, and, after a quick internal phone call to Nigel, confirmed that I would not be able

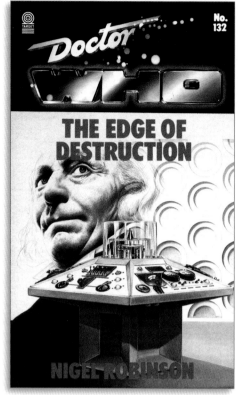

to include a portrait of Patrick Troughton. Mike seemed pleased with the final painting (the top third of which was blotted out by the new logo that came in at around the same time!) and I never really looked back for the next six years.'

Pearson's style was very photo-realistic, and his accurate collage renditions of the Doctors, characters and monsters from the series came to define the books released in the early '90s as much as Chris Achilleos's work had defined the range in the mid-'70s. Pearson went on to complete 87 covers in six years for the Target range; far more than any other artist.

Behind the scenes at W H Allen, several changes would have wide implications for the company and the Target range. Early in 1986, Robert Devereux, Managing Director of Virgin Vision Ltd, a part of Richard Branson's Virgin group, was looking for an acquisition to complement the publishing arm, Virgin Books, and wondered if W H Allen might be available. Negotiations started, and in November 1986, W H Allen bought Virgin Books as the first stage in the process. The purchase also included the changing hands of various share issues, which ultimately left the Virgin group with around 19% of W H Allen's shares. Then, on 18 September 1987, the Virgin group bought a further shareholding from Howard and Wyndham, the owners of W H Allen since 1971, and ended up with 51.6% of W H Allen's share capital. The Virgin group then made a purchase offer for all remaining shares in W H Allen. In conjunction with this, the Howard and Wyndham nominated officers, Ralph Fields and Peter Levinger, left the management board of the

The Virgin Publishing offices in St John Street–above a trendy restaurant.

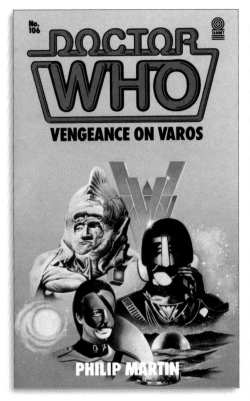

company. Finally, at the end of 1988, Bob Tanner, the Managing Director and Chairman of W H Allen, relinquished those roles and continued as consultant and non-executive director while the position of MD was taken by Tim Hailstone (who had actually started in the role in Autumn 1988) and Robert Devereux became Chairman.

Cost-cutting also occurred, and on 16 December 1988, the new Virgin-owned company, although still trading as W H Allen, departed from its lavish Mayfair residence and moved to offices above premises in St John Street, a far less salubrious area just north of the City. The main imprints for the company were consolidated as W H Allen, Virgin, Star, Mercury and Allison & Busby and rebranded with new logos. At the same time, the Target range was cut back to contain only the *Doctor Who* titles.

After about a year in the new premises, Tanner stepped down and returned full time to run his literary agency – International Scripts – whose clients included the estate of late science fiction author Robert Heinlein, anthologist Peter Haining and noted horror thriller authors Simon Clark and the late Richard Laymon. 'I look back on my time with W H Allen with a great deal of fondness. I truly do. It was a great time in my life, *Doctor Who*. There are certain periods throughout your life when you're happy about what you're doing, just as there are also periods when you are unhappy. My ten years or so at W H Allen were some of the happiest times of my life. You knew that you were producing books that people really wanted to buy and read, and you weren't worried that they were going to sit on the shelves and get forgotten. That's what publishing should all be about.'

Tanner is recognised as the saviour of W H Allen in the '80s. As *The Bookseller* noted, the company filed a loss of over

TONY CLARK

'The pose of the Space Pirate was taken from a photo of Tom Selleck in the sci-fi film *Runaway* that I spotted in *Starburst*.'
Tony Clark, interviewed by Tim Neal for
The Target Book, *March 2007*

Anthony Clark was born on 28 August 1962 in Lincolnshire and studied Graphic Design at Lincoln College of Art. He was a fan of *Doctor Who* from childhood and went on to run the art department of the Doctor Who Appreciation Society, providing many pieces of work for the Society's publications in the early '80s. In the second half of the decade he collaborated with author David Saunders on the first three parts of an *Encyclopaedia of The Worlds of Doctor Who*, published by Piccadilly Press, providing the covers and a great number of black and white illustrations.

It was around this time that he sent in several cover ideas to Mike Brett, art editor at W H Allen, which led to commissions for 'The Rescue' (1988) and 'The Space Pirates' (1990). Clark also contributed two covers to Titan Books' range of *Doctor Who* script books ('The Daleks' and 'The Tomb of the Cybermen', both 1989).

Clark contributed to *Doctor Who* on television, working behind-the-scenes on 'The Greatest Show in the Galaxy' (1988) and 'Battlefield' (1989) and on the BBC's thirtieth anniversary documentary 'Thirty Years in the Tardis' (1993). Several props and costumes designed and built by Clark have been used in *Doctor Who* related spin-offs, spoofs, sketches and adverts.

After a period as an assistant for Walt Disney films in 1987 (working on *Who Framed Roger Rabbit*), Clark moved into freelance work in the animation business, his clients including, amongst others, the award-winning Passion Pictures. He directed the animated title sequence for *The Antique Doctor Who Show* (a five-minute programme transmitted as an accompaniment to one episode of the 1993 repeat of 'Planet of the Daleks'). He has also contributed to and overseen work on hundreds of TV adverts, the films *Lost in Space* (1998) and *Miss Potter* (2006), videos for the pop group Gorillaz, model work on *Thomas the Tank Engine* and the online project Marsipan.

ALISTER PEARSON

'Once I've got photos, sketches and notes together, it's just a matter of juggling them around until something gels.'

Alister Pearson, DWB (61), December 1988

Alister Pearson was born on the Isle of Wight. His first published *Doctor Who* artwork was two pieces in Peter Haining's *Doctor Who – The Key to Time* (1984).

He left art college after one term, and for three years persistently sent artwork in to Target editor Nigel Robinson and art director Mike Brett. Eventually he was given his first commission ('The Underwater Menace') and went on to contribute more covers to the range than any other artist up until its demise in 1994. He then painted 22 covers for Virgin Publishing's ranges of original *Doctor Who* fiction.

Before being commissioned for the Target range, Pearson sold paintings to *Doctor Who Magazine* under the editorship of Sheila Cranna, John Freeman and Gary Russell. His artwork adorned over a dozen covers of the magazine, often reproduced as a free fold-out poster with the same issue. He also provided two covers for *Doctor Who Magazine*'s short-lived sister publication *Doctor Who Classic Comics* (1992-93).

From 1990 to 1993, Pearson painted 16 covers for the BBC Video releases of various *Doctor Who* stories. Much of the artwork was also used on concurrent releases of reprints of the appropriate Target novelisations.

He painted the covers for six of Titan Books' *Doctor Who – The Scripts* range (1992-94) and 12 covers for the same publisher's reprints of the *Star Trek Adventures* (1993-95). He also contributed to Titan's *Official Star Trek Fan Club Magazine* and their short-lived *Deep Space Nine* poster magazine, and he has painted CD covers for Rod Stewart ('Changing Faces'), Nik Kershaw ('Then and Now') and Stock, Aitken and Waterman ('Gold').

In 2005, he emerged from a period of quiet to provide the frontispiece for the newly relaunched *Doctor Who Annual* as well as CD covers for artists including Roy Orbison. He has since provided further illustrations for *Doctor Who*'s DVD and book releases, and also painted the cover for the book you are holding right now.

£530,000 in the 18 months to the end of 1980, but after that, and following Tanner's appointment in 1979, with the exception of 1983, made continued profits, and in 1984 went public. There was a further hiccup in 1987 when a pre-tax loss of £1.5 million was announced, due mainly to a disagreement with Australia and New Zealand distributors Gordon and Gotch, which led to the books being unavailable in those markets, and also a stock revaluation exercise to meet Virgin's different accounting procedures. Despite this, it is apparent that Tanner led the company, and the *Doctor Who* range, through its most successful period.

Shortly after the move to St John Street, editor Jo Thurm decided to move on: she left in mid-February 1989 with no replacement appointed. To try to help her eventual successor, she prepared an eight page document summarising the whole process of publishing the *Doctor Who* Target novelisations. This also detailed the current status of books in progress at the time, and covered ideas for the future.

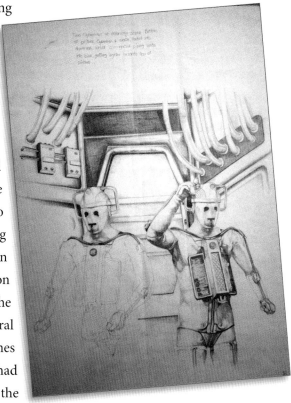

One of the ideas progressed by Thurm to maintain the publishing schedule was to novelise a so-called 'missing season'. The twenty-third season of *Doctor Who* on television had been well advanced in the planning stages, with several authors working on outlines and scripts, when the BBC had pulled the plug on it, forcing the production office to re-think, eventually resulting in the transmitted story 'The Trial of a Time Lord'. Among the scripts intended for the abandoned season were three eventually novelised by their authors: *The Nightmare Fair* (Graham Williams) and *The Ultimate Evil* (Wally K Daly) published in 1989 and *Mission to Magnus* (Philip Martin) published in 1990.

At the time Thurm left, author John Peel had successfully acted as an intermediary between Terry Nation, his agents Roger Hancock Ltd and W H Allen, and had delivered completed manuscripts for two previously-unavailable Dalek stories, *The Chase* and *The Daleks' Master Plan*. The latter, being a novelisation of a 12-episode epic TV story, W H Allen decided to publish in two volumes, including the single episode 'teaser' 'Mission to the Unknown'. Discussions were also under way with David Whitaker's widow for Peel to novelise Whitaker's two '60s Dalek stories, 'The Power of the Daleks' and 'The Evil of the Daleks'.

Other ideas mentioned in Thurm's document included talking with Eric Saward about his two Dalek stories 'Resurrection of the Daleks' and 'Revelation of the Daleks'; the possibility of Victor Pemberton novelising his non-television *Doctor Who* story 'The Pescatons'; two further 'missing episodes' books (named in the document as 'Evil of the Autons' (probably 'Yellow Fever And How To Cure It') by Robert Holmes and 'Penacasata' (probably 'Pinacotheca', a story commissioned for the 'Trial' version of the twenty-third season but not used) by Christopher H Bidmead – Graham Williams was also given the go-ahead to novelise Christopher H Bidmead's scripts for another unused story, 'In The Hollows of Time', but this

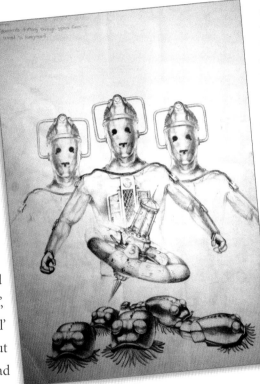

OPPOSITE AND THIS PAGE: Three concept sketches by Ian Burgess for the cover of *Doctor Who–The Wheel in Space*. The final cover is unlike all of them!

never happened); and approaching Douglas Adams' agent about trying to get 'The Pirate Planet', 'City of Death' and 'Shada' novelised. Her note stated that Adams had been approached several times before but that he was unwilling to novelise scripts or let anyone else write the books.

One of the final acts performed by Thurm was to contact Wendy Sanders of BBC Books on 6 February 1989 to ask again about the possibility of W H Allen publishing original *Doctor Who* fiction – this had previously been suggested by

WALLY K DALY

In 1975, Wally K Daly wrote the lyrics and book of the rock musical *Follow the Star*, with composer Jim Parker. The pair then wrote *Make Me A World*, based on the story of creation.

In the late 1970s, he wrote a trilogy of radio plays for the BBC about aliens endowing humans with super-powers. These were entitled *Before the Screaming Begins* (1977), *The Silent Scream* (1978) and *With a Whimper to the Grave* (1979). He has seen over 100 of his plays broadcast, many with either a religious or a science fiction slant to them. He has twice won the Giles Cooper Award for Best Radio Play of the Year (1983 and 1987).

In 1985 he was commissioned to write a script for *Doctor Who* called 'The Ultimate Evil', however this was never progressed to production. He later adapted it for Target as part of their *Missing Episodes* range of novels.

His other television work includes *There Comes a Time* (1985), *Juliet Bravo* (five episodes, 1983-85) and *Casualty* (four episodes, 1986-88). He also wrote ten episodes of the BBC TV children's soap *Byker Grove* and three novels based on the series.

He was awarded an Honorary Degree by the University of Teesside in 1993.

Daly continues to write extensively for radio, and is also writing some original books for children.

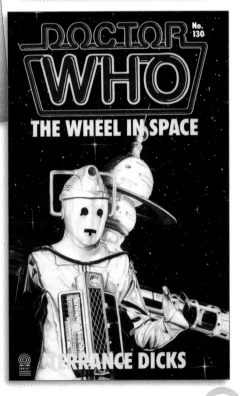

IAN BURGESS

'I wanted to paint Patrick Troughton on the cover as well, but they'd just decided that they wouldn't do that.'

Ian Burgess, interviewed by Tim Neal for **The Target Book**, *March 2007*

Ian Burgess was born in Winchester in February 1965 and went to Weston School of Art. He found work doing technical drawings and creating prototypes for a packaging design company, pursuing painting in his own time.

Burgess had just been taken on as Head of Graphic Design for a print company when Target editor Nigel Robinson engaged him to paint the cover for *Doctor Who – The Wheel in Space* (1988) on the basis of some speculative artwork he had submitted to the company some time earlier.

Burgess went on to form the company Cineffigy, which produces original photographs of actors from *Doctor Who* for their own promotional use. Clients have included Colin Baker, Sylvester McCoy, Sophie Aldred, Nicola Bryant, Nicholas Courtney, Elisabeth Sladen, Wendy Padbury and Louise Jameson.

His artwork is now almost entirely computer-based photo art. He produces the range of stamp covers for the Stamp Centre that blends photographic images from the show, and also a range of small poster prints for the same company.

As well as his *Doctor Who* pieces, he has produced artwork covering *Blake's 7, Red Dwarf, Thunderbirds, Stingray, Bagpuss* and *The Prisoner*. The images have been used on a range of items including mousemats and mugs.

In 2007 he worked for BBC Worldwide on artwork featuring David Tennant and Freema Agyeman, relating to the 2007 series of *Doctor Who*.

RIGHT: Peter Darvill-Evans and the advertisement in the *Guardian* to which he responded.

Alister Pearson's original painting for the cover of *Doctor Who– The Ultimate Foe.* This was not used due to artist clearance problems and instead a painting of Mr Popplewick used instead.

Nigel Robinson, but had been turned down by Nathan-Turner.

Thurm's replacement as editor of the *Doctor Who* books was Peter Darvill-Evans, a former general manager of Games Workshop Ltd, publishers of *White Dwarf* and other magazines in the mid-'80s, and the author of three 'Fighting Fantasy' gamebooks for Puffin. Darvill-Evans joined W H Allen around the end of February 1989 as a part-time editor to look after the *Doctor Who* range.

'I was trying at the time to make my living as a writer and so I needed to try and find a part time job,' he remembers today. 'My girlfriend saw a small advert in the *Guardian* – and it was in the wrong part of the *Guardian*, so they probably didn't get that many applicants – saying "Assistant Editor required" and going on to say that the role had responsibility for *Doctor Who* fiction. It didn't say the post was part time, but I applied for it anyway. I was interviewed by Mike Bailey, the Editorial Director, and Chelsey Fox, who was one of the senior editors. They offered me the job, which turned out to be three days a week – perfect for me.

'I was immediately attracted to the job because it mentioned *Doctor Who* in the advert. I'd watched

W H Allen
PUBLISHERS
ASSISTANT EDITOR
required to work on the mass market imprint of W. H. Allen. Duties are varied but include a particular responsibility for Dr Who fiction. Knowledge of proof reading, copy editing and blurb writing essential.
Apply in writing with c.v. to M. Bailey or C. Fox, Sekforde House, 175/9 St John Street, London EC1V 4LL.

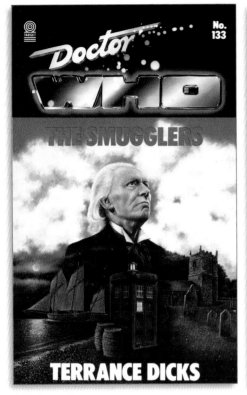

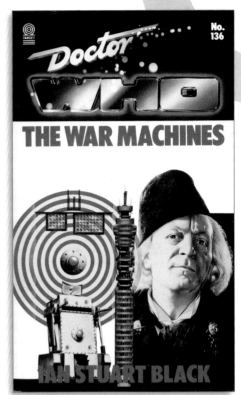

Doctor Who from the very first episode but missed out a lot of the Pertwee years as I was at university. I'd enjoyed the show and I would have described myself as a fan, and that was partly why I applied. I actually knew nothing about the Target books, I didn't even know they existed, but I went out and bought a copy of *Delta and the Bannermen* (or *Bannerman* as it said on the spine) before the interview. I think they were impressed that I had spotted this error, and thought I was therefore the best person for the job.'

'... like some kind of very old machinery...'

Ian Briggs, 1989
Doctor Who–Dragonfire

Two of Alister Pearson's concept sketches for the cover of
Doctor Who–Paradise Towers.

JOHN PEEL

'Apart from the fact that Terry's scripts were sheer joy to read, finally having written a novel about the Daleks has been something of a wish-fulfilment for me.'

John Peel, The Frame (number 8), November 1988

John Peel was born in Nottingham in the UK in 1954 and moved to America, where he still lives, in 1981.

Active in fandom, and having worked on a variety of fan publications, he struck up a friendship with writer Terry Nation. This resulted in their co-written *The Official Doctor Who & The Daleks Book*, published in America in 1988. Peel then gained agreement from Nation to novelise his *Doctor Who* stories 'The Chase' and 'The Daleks' Master Plan' (the latter over two volumes) for Target. He subsequently penned novelisations of David Whitaker's two Dalek stories, 'The Power of the Daleks' and 'The Evil of the Daleks', which were both published in 1993 at a time when the Target range was being superseded by the Doctor Who imprint.

Peel also wrote *The Gallifrey Chronicles* (1991), a large format hardback detailing the fictional history of the Doctor's homeworld and its incumbent race. He wrote the first original *Doctor Who* novel for Virgin Publishing's *New Adventures* range (*Timewyrm: Genesys*, 1991) and followed this with the *Missing Adventures* novel *Evolution* in 1994. He later contributed two books to BBC Books' *Doctor Who* range, *War of the Daleks* (1997) and *Legacy of the Daleks* (1998).

During the 1990s, he built a reputation as the author of cult TV tie-in novels, penning books based on *The Avengers* (with Dave Rogers, *Too Many Targets*, 1990), *James Bond Jr* (six books, 1992), *Star Trek: The Next Generation* (*Here There Be Dragons*, 1993; *The Death of Princes*, 1997), *Star Trek: Deep Space Nine* (three books, 1994-96), *Quantum Leap* (*Independence*, 1996), *The Outer Limits* (12 books, 1997-99) and *Eerie, Indiana* (two books, 1997-99).

He has also written many original novels, including the *Carmen Sandiego* series (nine books, 1991-94), the *Shockers* series (six books, 1992-93), the *Books of Diadem* series (ten books, 1997, 2005-06) and the *2099* series (six books, 1999). His pen-names have included J P Trent, Nicholas Adams, Rick North and John Vincent.

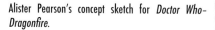

Alister Pearson's concept sketch for *Doctor Who-Dragonfire*.

When Darvill-Evans arrived, he found that there was no-one else at the company to talk to about the *Doctor Who* range, as the majority of the staff were new. He therefore used Thurm's note as a starting point and progressed from there.

'The person I really needed to know, who was crucial to the whole range, was John Nathan-Turner at the BBC. He needed to approve every element of the books as they were being novelised. My main contact there ended up being Clare Kinmont, the production secretary, and I sent everything to her for approval.

'The problem for me was mainly my own inexperience – I had come from a magazine publishing background, and the deadlines and timescales for books were unknown to me. I had a lot to learn, and there were also not many people I could ask. I could hardly go up to Mike Bailey and ask him how to publish a book as I would have looked silly, so I was very much finding my own way. I remember making lots of charts, working back from publication date to find out when the manuscript needed to be in, and when the artwork for the cover was required and so on. It actually goes back a year, assuming nothing goes wrong, and I had to work all this out for myself.'

The books published in 1989 were: *Delta and the Bannermen* (Malcolm Kohll), *The War Machines* (Ian Stuart Black), *Dragonfire* (Ian Briggs), *Attack of the Cybermen* (Eric Saward), *Mindwarp*, a novelisation of the second story within the overall 'The Trial of a Time Lord' adventure (Philip Martin), *The Chase* (John Peel), *Mission to the Unknown* and *The Mutation of Time* (John Peel), *Silver Nemesis* (Kevin Clarke) and *The Greatest Show in the Galaxy* (Stephen Wyatt). All the covers were by Alister Pearson, with the exception of that for *Attack of the Cybermen*, which was painted by Colin Howard, another fan artist who went on

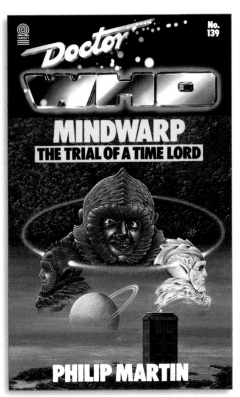

to contribute covers to the BBC's *Doctor Who* video releases. 'I was working on some stuff for Games Workshop,' remembered Howard, 'when I received a letter from W H Allen, I think it was Mike Brett who was the Art Editor there at the time. He'd liked the black and white illustrations of mine they'd published in *The Key to Time* and remembered me.' For *The War Machines*, Pearson was assisted by Graeme Wey, who airbrushed the concentric circles on the background.

Attack of the Cybermen was the Target book with perhaps the longest history. It

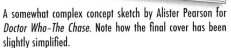
A somewhat complex concept sketch by Alister Pearson for *Doctor Who–The Chase*. Note how the final cover has been slightly simplified.

GRAHAM WILLIAMS

'It was the only way these poor old scripts would ever see the light of day!'
Graham Williams, Doctor Who Magazine *(number 151), August 1989*

Graham Williams had been working in the theatre for nearly five years when, in 1966, he decided to join the BBC in order to earn enough money to return to the theatre. He found that television was far more exciting and started working in the Script Unit. He then moved to become an assistant floor manager, and it was whilst doing this job that he gained an attachment as a script editor – a position in which he was to stay for seven years. During this time he worked on series like *Barlow at Large*, *Z Cars* and *Sutherland's Law*.

He had devised the hard-hitting series *Target* in 1977 and was involved in producing an ultimately aborted 12-part film series called *The Zodiac Factor* for the BBC when he was offered the producership of *Doctor Who*.

He left *Doctor Who* in 1979 and went on to produce *Supergran* (1986-87) for ITV. He contributed a story entitled 'The Nightmare Fair' for the series in 1985, but it was not progressed to production. He subsequently adapted the story for Target's *Missing Episodes* range.

He eventually became disillusioned with television and retired to Devon in 1987, where he ran a hotel near Tiverton.

Williams was killed in a shooting incident at his home on 17 August 1990, reportedly when a gun he was cleaning accidentally went off. He was survived by his wife Jackie and their three children.

'...a crashing noise of timbers, metals and glass...'
John Peel, 1989
Doctor Who–The Chase

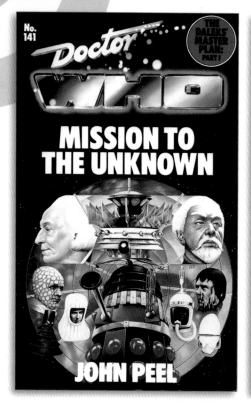

was originally discussed in June 1984 by Target editor Christine Donougher with the television story's writer Paula Moore (a pseudonym for Paula Woolsey). Moore eventually declined to write it, having spent some time working on the project, and at the end of January 1986 the book was passed over to *Doctor Who*'s former script editor Eric Saward. Saward resigned from the script editor post under acrimonious circumstances during the summer of 1986, and by the autumn of 1987 had still not delivered the manuscript, despite lengthy correspondence between himself and the publishers (respectively editors Nigel Robinson, Sarah Barnes, Tim Byrne, Jo Thurm and Peter Darvill-Evans). The book was eventually delivered to Darvill-Evans in two parts, the first 70 manuscript pages on 11 November 1987, and the remainder on 4 December.

Most anticipated amongst the year's offerings were the Dalek stories being adapted by John Peel. Thankfully, fans were pleased with what they saw. 'What on television was an often visually sloppy, overly comic romp

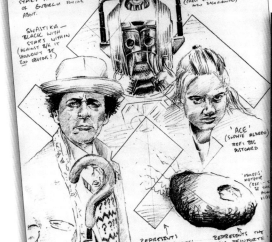

In Alister Pearson's sketch for *Doctor Who–Silver Nemesis*, the swastika logo is far more obvious than on the final cover.

with the regulars' tongues firmly in their cheeks for most of the time has been transformed into a richly descriptive and captivating adventure,' wrote James Howarth of *The Chase* in *DWB*, while the two-volume epic *The Daleks' Master Plan* received similar praise: 'Peel has transformed it,' enthused Craig Hinton in *TV Zone*. 'Extra material has been introduced to accommodate the split between the books. … Peel has taken a very complex plot and rendered it understandable. … Another worthwhile read, converting five hours of confused television into two coherent and enjoyable novels.'

ONCE UPON A TIME...

There is nothing like a great opening line to hook you into a rollicking good story. The Target novelisations had their fair share, and they can usually be divided into different types. There are those that wish to tease us with a sense of the epic that is to unfold:

'For an adventure that was to be one of the most astonishing of the Doctor's very long life, it all began very quietly.'[1]

'Events cast shadows before them, but the huger shadows creep over us unseen.'[2]

Then there are those that wish to drop us straight in on the action:

'The scream was choked off halfway through, to be followed by hoarse, panting gasps.'[3]

'The full fury of the storm hit the ship as it rounded the headland.'[4]

'The huge, furry monster reared up, as if to strike.'[5]

'Somewhere, horses' hooves were drumming the ground.'[6]

'It all began with a bang.'[7]

Some opening lines seek to remind readers that *Doctor Who* takes place on a universal stage (sometimes with a hint of irony that recognises the conflict between the ambition and the paltry finances of the television show):

'A huge crescent of brilliant pinpoints of light sliced through the unimaginable emptiness of space near the edge of a remote spiral galaxy.'[8]

'The closer one travels towards it from the cold silent darkness of infinite space, the more the planet Earth appears as a backcloth to some small theatrical performance taking place on a limited budget.'[9]

Sometimes the intention is to establish the space-operatic scale of what is unfolding (the *Doctor Who* equivalent of *'A long time ago, in a galaxy far, far away...'*):

'Centuries ago by our Earth time, a race of men on the far-distant planet of Telos sought immortality.'[10]

'In a galaxy unimaginably distant from ours, on a planet called Phaester Osiris, there arose a race so powerful that they became like gods.'[11]

Or sometimes the opening sentence merely sets out to establish a mood by conveying a dramatic sense of location:

'The full moon hung huge and heavy above the smudging, scurrying November clouds, casting baleful light on the rolling Dorset countryside; a light insufficient for the needs of the inhuman shapes populating the thicket glade.'[12]

'The electric storm clawed and tore its way across the night sky like a wild animal, flaring suddenly into ripples of lightning more eerie and majestic than the three moons of Peladon.'[13]

'It was a place of ancient evil.'[14]

'Jungle.'[15]

Once or twice we have been offered intriguing glimpses into the state of mind of opening characters:

'The woman wanted to die.'[16]

'Through the ruin of a city stalked the ruin of a man.'[17]

And on a couple of occasions, authors have been ambitious enough to try to impart a sense of action, mood, scale and alien location all in one go. Admittedly these are usually quite long sentences, but nevertheless they do do the trick of launching the reader off on a rip-roaring literary ride:

'The Random Laser Beam Emitter turned ominously on its axis, clicked, as if in irritation, then spat a searing beam of force at the lean young man chained to a wall in a corridor deep within the main Punishment Dome of the former prison planet of Varos.'[18]

'Twisting, burning metal screamed at a pitch which challenged the death-yells of the passengers and crew members throughout the massive structure of the starliner as the great space vessel hurtled, out of control, towards the shifting grey mists that enshrouded the surface of the terror planet Alzarius.'[19]

1 Terrance Dicks, *Doctor Who – The Three Doctors*
2 Christopher H Bidmead, *Doctor Who – Logopolis*
3 Graham Williams, *Doctor Who: The Missing Episodes – The Nightmare Fair*
4 Peter Grimwade, *Doctor Who – Planet of Fire*
5 Terrance Dicks, *Doctor Who and the Web of Fear*
6 Eric Pringle, *Doctor Who – The Awakening*
7 Peter Ling, *Doctor Who – The Mind Robber*
8 Ian Marter, *Doctor Who – The Dominators*
9 Kevin Clarke, *Doctor Who – Silver Nemesis*
10 Gerry Davis, *Doctor Who and The Cybermen*
11 Terrance Dicks, *Doctor Who and the Pyramids of Mars*
12 Terence Dudley, *Doctor Who – K9 and Company*
13 Brian Hayles, *Doctor Who and the Curse of Peladon*
14 Terrance Dicks, *Doctor Who – The Five Doctors*
15 Paul Erickson, *Doctor Who – The Ark*
16 Graeme Curry, *Doctor Who – The Happiness Patrol*
17 Terrance Dicks, *Doctor Who and the Dalek Invasion of Earth*
18 Philip Martin, *Doctor Who – Vengeance on Varos*
19 Andrew Smith, *Doctor Who – Full Circle*

Alister Pearson's concept sketch for *Doctor Who–The Greatest Show in the Galaxy.*

MALCOLM KOHLL

'A screenplay isn't literature, it's dialogue. You're writing a set of instructions for actors and director. Novelising the script was therefore quite a mechanical process, but you did have the luxury of putting in characters' thoughts and fleshing them out a little more.'

Malcolm Kohll, Doctor Who Magazine *(number 276), April 1999*

Malcolm Kohll was born in South Africa in 1953. He trained as a journalist before leaving the country, for political reasons, in February 1977. He gained a post-graduate diploma in Film and Television from Middlesex Polytechnic and has worked as a freelance writer and producer since 1978.

He took part in a writers' group meeting that was also attended by seventh-Doctor-script-editor-to-be Andrew Cartmel. This led to Kohll's first commissioned work, 'Delta and the Bannermen', in 1987. Shortly after, he adapted his script for Target books.

His subsequent TV work was primarily as a sketch writer and a ghost writer on several screenplays. He also worked as a reader for Roland Joffe and David Puttnam, having previously evaluated and developed screenplays alongside *Doctor Who*'s original producer Verity Lambert at Thorn EMI in 1985.

He wrote and produced the feature film *The Fourth Reich* (1990), telling the true tale of Hitler trying to install a Nazi government in South Africa during the Second World War in order to use that country's resources to fuel his war machine. This was a $10 million production shot in South Africa.

In 1995, Kohll joined Focus Films as Head of Development and in-house producer. He has brought to the screen *Secret Society* (2000), *Julie's Spirit* (2000), *The 51st State* (2001) and *The Bone Snatcher* (2003).

He is still with Focus Films, writing and developing a number of new projects.

Unfortunately, the adaptations of more recent adventures received harsher criticism. 'If the television version of "Silver Nemesis" seemed rushed, scrappy and full of holes, then these faults are as abundant in Kevin Clarke's novelisation,' observed Andrew Martin in *TV Zone*. 'Clarke's literary style consists of dropping in jazz references everywhere, but otherwise has little to commend it.' This view was echoed by Julian Knott in *DWB*: 'Unfortunately Clarke has delivered a manuscript that deviates little from the televised version in any helpful way. At best an adequate addition to the W H Allen series, but more unfulfilled potential on the *Doctor Who* book front, I'm afraid.' Stephen Wyatt's adaptation of 'The Greatest Show in the Galaxy' was also found wanting. 'There is a marked difference between the skills necessary to write a television script and those required to write a novel,' opined Peter Linford in *DWB*. 'There are worse *Who* novels than this, but what *really* grates is, having read the novelisation, I have since found myself enjoying the televised version less. And that is unforgivable.' David Richardson in *TV Zone* tended to agree: 'Without the wealth of stunning visuals to mesmerise, the whole thing falls slightly flat.'

Almost as soon as he joined the company, Darvill-Evans realised, as other editors had before him, that there were hardly any more stories left to novelise. He therefore followed up Thurm's letter of the 6 February with another on the 9 March, again asking BBC Books' Wendy Sanders about the possibility of doing original fiction. With the *Doctor Who* series apparently cancelled on television and the BBC production office closing down, Nathan-Turner finally gave the go-ahead for this in October 1989. He would continue to be involved in the development of the range, eventually to be called *The New Adventures*, as even after stepping down as *Doctor Who*'s producer in November 1989, he maintained a watching brief on *Doctor Who* merchandise at his

request and with the BBC's and BBC Worldwide's agreement.

During January 1990, rumours started to spread that W H Allen was considering selling off the *Doctor Who* list to another publisher. These rumours increased when, at the end of January, the company abruptly underwent a major upheaval and sacked half of its 60 staff. One of those who lost his job was Mike Brett, W H Allen's art director, who had worked on the *Doctor Who* titles since 1979.

The Bookseller reported that these changes were a consequence of 'the company's poor performance in a deteriorating market' and went on to quote the company chairman Robert Devereux as saying: 'The company has tried to grow quite rapidly, and organically, from a small base in a market that was

Two concepts and a detail of the first Doctor (centre) drawn by Alister Pearson for *Doctor Who-Planet of Giants*.

IAN BRIGGS

'W H Allen were unhappy with some of the violence being too gory. My point was that violence is unpleasant and it's dishonest to show it as being pretty, but I take their point that a lot of children are going to read the novel.'

Ian Briggs, Doctor Who Magazine
(number 147), April 1989

Ian Briggs studied Drama at Manchester University, graduating in 1980. He worked in the theatre on lighting and design before becoming a freelance story analyst, working on projects for BBC Television, the Royal Court Theatre and Warner Brothers.

He was part of a team of writers brought together by script editor Andrew Cartmel to shake-up *Doctor Who* in the late '80s. He contributed two stories, both pivotal in the character development of companion Ace, and novelised them shortly after transmission.

In 1990, Briggs wrote a script for *Casualty* ('Street Life', 1990) and contributed to *The Bill* ('Old Wounds'). He also worked on stroylining projects for Yorkshire Television (*Streetwise* and *All Change*) and a pilot for the BBC called *A Gull on the Roof*.

Since 1995, Briggs has worked in a variety of managerial roles within theatres, principally with the Questors Theatre, a large community theatre based in London, where he has also been an acting tutor.

'Call him showman, conjuror, great detective, mentor or tormentor, his speciality was to juggle the past, the present and the possible. No one was safe from that; anyone could be a potential skittle.'

Marc Platt, 1990
Doctor Who-Ghost Light

KEVIN CLARKE

'I hated every moment of it, even to the
point where I would do a set number of
pages each day to force myself to finish it.'
Kevin Clarke, Doctor Who Magazine
(number 244), October 1996

Kevin Clarke grew up in Birkenhead,
Merseyside. He tried his hand at being
a guitarist and an actor and went
to Leeds University to train to be a
drama teacher. He decided to become
a writer while teaching in a London
comprehensive school in the second
half of the 1970s. Eventually he became
one of seven writers selected for the
first BBC writers' scheme in the 1980s.

A meeting with *Doctor Who* script
editor Andrew Cartmel led to his being
commissioned for the twenty-fifth
anniversary serial 'Silver Nemesis',
which he then adapted for Target
books.

He has also written episodes for *The
Bill* (1988-1991), *Minder* ('The Coach
That Came in from the Cold', 1991),
Wycliffe ('On Account', 1997, 'Land's
End', 1998), *Wish Me Luck, Family
Affairs* (2003), *The Inspector Lynley
Mysteries* ('A Traitor to Memory', 2004),
The Last Detective ('Friends Reunited',
2005) and *Casualty* ('Lost in the Rough',
2007).

His first original screenplay, *Albert
and the Lion*, was networked by
Scottish Television in 1992. His first
film script, *Meek*, has been bought by
Scala Productions. It tells the true story
of early 1960s pop genius Joe Meek.

deteriorating. That has been the fundamental problem. The strategy of publishing
across the board was untenable.' *The Bookseller* translated this as meaning a 'flawed
strategic plan and a failure to meet sales targets.'

At this point, W H Allen was renamed Virgin Publishing Ltd and continued
as publisher of the Target list. Virgin eventually decided to retain the *Doctor
Who* books, but the paperback Star list was cancelled, along with the W H Allen
hardback list, the authors going elsewhere or finding themselves without publishers.
Ironically, one author of note, Dean R Koontz, was picked up by Headline Books,
and his first novel for them, *Lightning*, became an international best-seller and
launched Koontz on the road to world-wide success.

'One of the problems with this series of redundancies from the inside,' explains
Darvill-Evans, 'was that they chose to lay off almost all the editorial staff, and it's the
editorial staff who know what the books and authors are actually worth, what their
potential is and so on: you can't expect Sales or Accounts to know things like that. So
with no fiction editors to advise them, they simply set about selling off authors and
book ranges as fast as they could, with little account for their potential. I'm certain
that one of the reasons they didn't sell off the *Doctor Who* range was that they still
had me there looking after it. I was cheap, as I was working only three days a week,
and also, despite the fact that no-one there had actually experienced this, it was still
common knowledge that the *Doctor Who* books were profitable. It kind of went
without saying. Of course, the same was true of the erotic books, which I was also
looking after at the time, so I felt I was doubly safe during this shake-up.'

Darvill-Evans eventually issued a press release to assure concerned fans that
the *Doctor Who* range was safe. 'I think if someone had made a good offer, then

A very complex sketch by Alister Pearson for
Doctor Who-The Happiness Patrol which was
greatly simplified for the final cover.

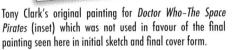

Tony Clark's original painting for *Doctor Who–The Space Pirates* (inset) which was not used in favour of the final painting seen here in initial sketch and final cover form.

COLIN HOWARD

'I was pleased with the composition of the cover itself, especially considering I wasn't allowed to use Colin Baker's face.'

Colin Howard, interviewed by Tim Neal for **The Target Book***, January 2007*

Colin Howard was born in Harleston, Norfolk, in 1965. He started out as a fan of *Doctor Who*, both the television and book series, and held down a variety of jobs while contributing artwork and comic strips to a variety of *Doctor Who* fanzines, including *Cloister Bell*, *Cosmic Masque* and *The Frame*. His first work as a paid artist came from editor John Freeman at *Doctor Who Magazine*, who commissioned him to provide black and white illustrations for a number of articles. At around the same time, he started providing illustrations for Games Workshop's role playing games and their *White Dwarf* role-playing magazine.

He contributed only one cover to the Target range of *Doctor Who* novelisations ('Attack of the Cybermen', 1990), but went on to make an extensive contribution to tie-ins with the show during the 1990s.

He provided covers for *Doctor Who Magazine* and the *Doctor Who Classic Comics* magazine, a number of the Virgin and BBC *Doctor Who* books (including the cover and internal illustrations for role-playing game book *Timelord*, 1991, and the cover for *Invasion of the Cat-People*, 1995) and 30 covers for BBC Video's *Doctor Who* releases. In 1996, examples of his *Doctor Who* artwork were released as postcards.

Howard has also painted magazine, DVD and book covers for shows such as *Red Dwarf*, *Blake's 7* and *Quantum Leap*. He has provided illustrations and artwork for, amongst other things, children's books and puzzles, CD covers (for artists such as Iron Maiden, Status Quo and Tony Christie), commemorative plates and even a set of Tarot cards.

they would have sold the *Doctor Who* books, as they didn't really fit within what the management were saying they wanted to do as a company. I don't think *any* area was truly safe. However there were three problems with trying to sell the *Doctor Who* books on. First, that the BBC's licence was with W H Allen/Virgin and would have to have been renegotiated with the BBC; second, that anyone looking into it would realise that the show was not on television, and there weren't any more books to do – it was a dead range from that point of view; and third, that I personally didn't want to sell the list, and I was in charge of preparing the details for potential buyers. I also made a strong case for retaining it internally as I believed we could make more money by doing that, than by selling the list off. I knew by this point that *The New Adventures* were going to happen, and I felt it would have been very short sighted to have sold at this point. I think my feelings matched Robert Devereux's, and so the list was ultimately retained.'

1990's novelisations reflected the increasing lack of material left to cover. The titles published were: *Planet of Giants* (Terrance Dicks), *The Happiness Patrol* (Graeme Curry), *The Space Pirates* (Terrance Dicks), *Remembrance of the Daleks* (Ben Aaronovitch), *Ghost Light* (Marc Platt), *Survival* (Rona Munro) and *The Curse of Fenric* (Ian Briggs). Of these, five were from the most recent (and final) season on television while two (both by Dicks) novelised the only available older adventures. The cover for *The Space Pirates* was by Tony Clark, while Alister Pearson handled those for all the other books.

'I learnt that I was doing the cover for *The Space Pirates* from Alister Pearson at a *Doctor Who* convention in Coventry,' explains Clark. 'At the time, there were only *Planet of Giants* and *The Space Pirates* to be scheduled (bar the Whitaker Dalek

BEN AARONOVITCH

'I'm having trouble finding new ways to describe Daleks menacingly. Answers on a postcard please – because they're very difficult to describe.'

Ben Aaronovitch, TARDIS – The Quarterly Journal of the *Doctor Who* Appreciation Society, *Summer 1989*

Ben Aaronovitch is the son of economist Dr Sam Aaronovitch and the younger brother of actor Owen Aaronovitch and journalist David Aaronovitch. He contributed two scripts to *Doctor Who* – 'Remembrance of the Daleks' (1988) and 'Battlefield' (1989). The former was adapted for Target to much acclaim by Aaronovitch himself, while the latter was adapted for the range by Marc Platt.

'Remembrance of the Daleks' was Aaronovitch's first work for television. He had been put in touch with ▶

stories and Douglas Adams scripts), and I had sent one for *The Space Pirates* in on spec. Someone asked Pearson if he was doing the cover, and he said, on stage, that he thought Tony Clark was. I phoned Peter Darvill-Evans after the weekend, and he said he would like me to do it, but that they didn't like the one I had sent, and a replacement was needed the following week!

'I spent three days faxing pencil lay-outs to him, and a couple of days painting the cover. From memory, the main pose was there from the start; it was the smaller details that changed. The pose was taken from a photo of Tom Selleck from the 1984 sci-fi film *Runaway*. To use the Doctor's face would have required artwork approval from Pat Troughton. The only person they could use without getting artwork approval was Frazer Hines, but I didn't think Jamie had a big role in the story, apart from which, there wasn't the time to paint a good likeness.'

This time, the recent adaptations found favour. Craig Hinton, writing in *TV Zone*, felt that *The Happiness Patrol* was 'an example of the best kind of *Doctor Who* book rather than the best written.' David Miller, in a review in *DWB*, commented of *Survival*: 'A somewhat inconsistent book in terms of characterisation (some characters barely "exist" at all), it has flashes of inspiration and some memorable and clever descriptive writing. It is good to see that *Doctor Who* books are now, almost consistently, science fiction novels too!' Marc Platt's *Ghost Light* was also praised by both Julian Knott in *DWB* ('Platt's book joins the top dozen or so truly

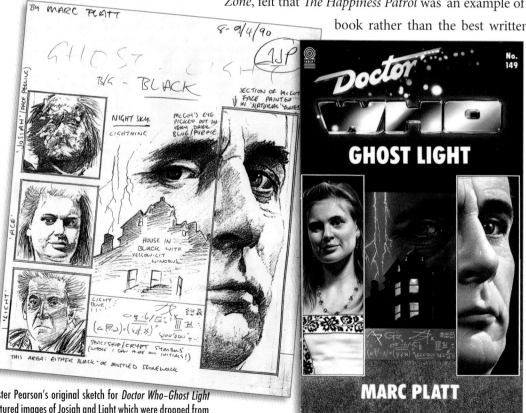

Alister Pearson's original sketch for *Doctor Who–Ghost Light* featured images of Josiah and Light which were dropped from the final artwork.

great *Doctor Who* books.') and by John Gaze in *TV Zone* ('There are some *Doctor Who* books you have to read in order to make sense, if at all possible, of the televised story. This is one of them … One of the best books of the last few years.')

However the most praise was reserved for Ben Aaronovitch's adaptation of 'Remembrance of the Daleks' and Ian Briggs' *The Curse of Fenric*, both of which took the novelisations into new territories. One of the significant shifts in this period was towards a far more 'grown-up' style. Darvill-Evans admits that he always saw the books as being written for adults rather than for children.

Alister Pearson's sketch for *Doctor Who – Survival* is almost the same as the finished art, with the omission of the face of the Master from underneath the Kitling.

'… culminating in the heavy bass-drum thud…'

Marc Platt, 1990
Doctor Who – Ghost Light

'I did this,' he explains, 'really by giving [the authors] more room. I just allowed them to write to a longer length, rather than limiting them to 110 or 120 pages. I was helped by the fact that the script editor at the BBC was Andrew Cartmel. I think Andrew's a great writer and did a lot of great work as a script editor, and the script writers that he was bringing into the show shared his vision, which I bought into as well: mainly that *Doctor Who* stories could be made more grown-up. I hesitate to use the word "adult" as that has other connotations, but just grown-up. You could cover serious themes within a *Doctor Who* story and still make it exciting and adventurous. The best example of that was Ben Aaronovitch's Dalek story, "Remembrance of the Daleks", which is all about racism. I thought that was brilliant, to cover such a serious subject and to still make it entertaining and exciting. Ian Briggs' "The Curse of Fenric" is another example: it's about growing up and sex; but very heavily disguised.

'Within Virgin, I was able to play on my inexperience in book publishing, and the fact that no-one else there knew what it was all meant to be about anyway, to get away with just about anything.'

The critics, it seemed, agreed with Darvill-Evans' policy. 'It is going to annoy you, it may even infuriate you. It will puzzle, amuse and entertain. Quite simply, *Remembrance of the Daleks* has re-written *Doctor Who* lore, breathing life, coherence and clarity into a body long dead: the *Doctor Who* novel,' enthused Julian Knott in *DWB*. 'What Ben Aaronovitch has done is carefully woven into the story that we saw on television, a network of fibres so intricate that they encompass stories from the history of the programme as far apart as 'An Unearthly Child' and

script editor Andrew Cartmel by a BBC producer, Caroline Oulton. Since *Doctor Who*, Aaronovitch has written for *Casualty* ('Results', 1990), *Jupiter Moon* (1990) and *Dark Knight* (2001).

Aaronovitch contributed to Virgin Publishing's series of original *Doctor Who* novels, writing *Transit* (1992) and *The Also People* (1995) and contributing the outline and some textual material to *So Vile a Sin* (1997), which was completed by Kate Orman.

In 2006, *Genius Loci*, Aaronovitch's first book in ten years, was published. This was the latest in a range of adventures featuring one of the Doctor's companions from the original novels, Bernice Summerfield.

In his role as script executive for B7 Media, Aaronovitch has overseen the scripts for the 2007 audio revival of cult 1970s SF show *Blake's 7*.

PAUL MARK TAMS

The cover for the novelisation of radio serial *Slipback* was the only Target range cover painted by Paul Mark Tams. He was recommended to W H Allen by writer Eric Saward, who had met Tams through his work for John Nathan Turner's annual pantomimes. He was a long time fan of the show and had previously been courted in the mid '70's by Target's original art director Dom Rodi to possibly do several covers, but due to other work commitments he was unable to work on them. *Slipback* was commissioned to be turned around in 24 hours as a cover prepared by another artist had been rejected by Nathan-Turner as it just featured the TARDIS in space. A further commission was undertaken to do a cover design for the novelisation of *Fury From The Deep*, a rough visual of which still exists. This ultimately was not used as images of earlier Doctors had been dropped from the cover designs.

Tams was commissioned for artwork for World Distributors' *Doctor Who* and Dalek annuals in the late 1970s and early 1980s. He went on to produce the covers for Keith Barnfather at Reeltime Pictures for the video releases *Where on Earth is… Katy Manning* (1998) and *Katy Manning's World Down Under* (2002).

Tams was one of the organisers behind the 1985 musical release 'Doctor in Distress'. Along with Record Shack's Jeff Weston, Tams got together a collective of people who cared to sing about the foolhardiness of Michael Grade's 'cancellation' of *Doctor Who*, and to raise money for Cancer Relief into the bargain. He stresses that although it was his idea to do it, he never heard the track until everyone turned up at the recording studio itself! He also worked as a cover designer on some of Ian Levine's record productions, including singles by Kelly Marie. Tams also performed alongside Sarah Lee (daughter of actress Lynda Baron and secretary to Nathan-Turner at the BBC) as a group called Sidewalk and they had records released in the UK and Japan. Other work included art for several annuals produced by World Distributors, including *The Dalek Annual* and *Terrahawks*.

During the 1990s, Tams worked as a record producer, with his name attached to records by former Supremes singers Scherrie Lynda & Sundray (1994), Tina Charles, Kelly Marie, Bucks Fizz featuring Mike Nolan, Damian ('The Timewarp') as well as managing chart stars Hazell Dean and Frances Nero.

Since the 1990s, Tams has been ▶

For the Target novelisation of the radio serial *Slipback*, Paul Tams created an initial sketch of the sixth Doctor, and a more detailed rendition of the same. This was then changed to an image of the main villain.

– most intriguingly – 'Ghost Light' … It expands on the televised version in every way, bringing to the fore emotions, inner thoughts and feelings that no actor could realistically expect to present.' Nicholas Briggs, writing in *TV Zone*, felt similarly: 'Ben Aaronovitch's energetic prose style engages your imagination, throws it into top gear and tumbles you headlong into some spectacular battle-action sequences, whilst plumbing the psychological depths of every single character's motivations … This is exactly what a *Doctor Who* novelisation should be. It embraces all the good points of the televised version, but adds much more.' *The Curse of Fenric* was perhaps less enthusiastically received, but at least one reviewer – John Ainsworth in *TV Zone* – picked up on the story's undercurrents: '*The Curse of Fenric* could not by any stretch of the imagination be described as a children's book. Ian Briggs touches on such subjects as lesbianism, a gay relationship and the emotional changes of a girl's transformation into a woman.'

Of the two novelisations of older adventures, *The Space Pirates* slightly disappointed Ian Garrard in *TV Zone*: 'Recently, writers have relished the chance to expand upon original works, best exemplified by Ian Briggs with *Dragonfire* or Nigel Robinson with *The Edge of Destruction*. Alas this novel seems little more than a slightly augmented camera script … The story's strengths are hampered by some lazy writing, the descriptive passages doing little to fire the memories of those halcyon black and white days of *Doctor Who*.' However Dicks seemed to hit the right nerve with *Planet of Giants*, at least as far as Jan Vincent-Rudzki, also in *TV Zone*, was concerned: 'Terrance Dicks maintains the feel of the story very well with a novelisation full of descriptions and characterisation. It's like meeting an old friend to read of the "many-sided console", and thank goodness he sets the scene by not assuming we know what the Doctor and his companions look like. For those who enjoy the *Doctor Who*s of another time, this is a must.'

Publication of *The Space Pirates* marked author Terrance Dicks' final association with the range of novelisations, which he had helped kick off in 1973 with *Doctor Who and the Auton Invasion*.

With the novelisations coming to an end, Darvill-Evans needed to find a way to bridge the gap in the publishing programme between then and the start of a range of original novels that was being set up for launch in 1991. He hit upon a scheme to re-issue some of the books with new jackets, and thus tide the range over. In addition, the BBC was increasing its programme of releasing *Doctor Who* stories on video, and so Darvill-Evans selected the titles for his initial reprints to coincide with the same stories' BBC video releases.

'I was aware that people had holes in their collections, and that when you have a numbered series of books, people want to have a complete set. It seemed obvious to

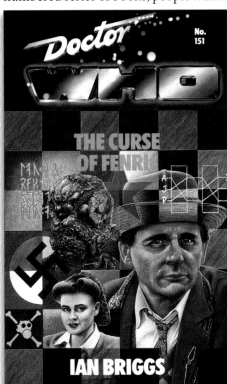

performing and acting and has appeared in TV shows such as *Mile High* (Sky TV) and movies such as *Kinky Boots* (2005) as well as working with writer Bob Baker on launching a Doctor-less K-9 spin-off series, which is currently in development with cable TV channel Jetix.

MARC PLATT

'Somehow I don't think libraries will be stocking the novel of *Ghost Light* next to copies of the Bible!'
Marc Platt, Doctor Who Magazine (number 158), March 1990

Marcus Platt was born in Wimbledon in 1953, and his family moved to Pevensey Bay near Eastbourne when he was 11. He took a catering course at technical college and found work with Trust House Forte. He then got a job at the BBC, where he spent 19 years cataloguing the BBC's radio output and then as a selector in the Sound Archives.

He was a *Doctor Who* fan from the programme's start, which led him to become a member of the Doctor Who Appreciation Society and a contributor to fanzines and *Doctor Who Magazine*. He submitted a number of ideas to the series towards the end of its initial run. One of these eventually became 'Ghost Light' (1989). He went on to adapt his own story and Ben Aaronovitch's scripts for 'Battlefield' for Target.

He wrote two original novels for Virgin (*Cat's Cradle: Time's Crucible*, 1992; *Lungbarrow*, 1997). He also penned the spin-off video *Downtime*, featuring the Brigadier, Victoria, Sarah Jane Smith, Professor Travers and the Yeti, and novelised his script for Virgin in 1996.

Platt continues to contribute to the *Doctor Who* universe with a number of acclaimed Big Finish audios (*Loups Garoux*, 2001; *Spare Parts*, 2002; *Auld Morality*, 2003; *A Storm of Angels*, 2005; *Frostfire*, 2007; *Valhalla*, 2007) and entries in a number of short-story anthologies. He has also written for the *Bernice Summerfield* range and for the 2007 audio revival of *Blake's 7*.

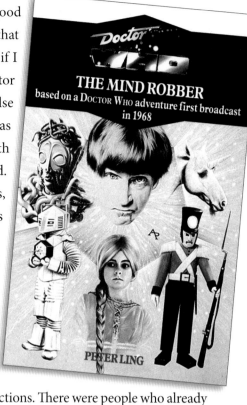

try and fill those holes. One of the good things about the publishers was that when I came up with a suggestion, if I liked it and if the Managing Director liked it, there wasn't really anyone else to say we couldn't do it. So if I was able to suggest something was worth doing, then it got the go ahead. It's also very easy to do reprints, because all you really have to do is come up with a new cover.

'Initially, the reprints were all new, but later on I realised that we could just rejacket old stock, after it became apparent that we were selling far more than could be accounted for by people just filling holes in their collections. There were people who already had these books who were buying them again because they had new covers on.

'We tried very hard to find out what the BBC's video schedules were, but they had a much shorter lead time than us, and we were always foiled in our attempts to do joint marketing. We needed to know about eight months in advance, whereas on the BBC's side, they needed only about two months' notice. They were able to give me some idea, though, which is why there was some element of tie-in present.

'The other reason for the reprints was to keep *Doctor Who* alive as far as the book trade was concerned: to continue to give them *Doctor Who* titles every month so it didn't look as though the range was fading away. We had to somehow make the book trade realise that *Doctor Who* was still a viable property to publish books around in preparation for *The New Adventures*, despite the fact that the show was no longer on television.'

The first of these 'blue spine' reprints, as they came to be known, were *The War Games*

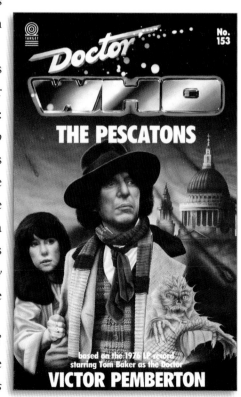

and *An Unearthly Child*, which were released in 1990, using the same artwork on the covers as on their BBC videos. These were followed later in the year by *The Dalek Invasion of Earth* and *The Mind Robber*, which also used the same artwork as the BBC videos. These tested out the market ready for further reprints the following year.

Late in 1990, another office rationalisation saw the Virgin Publishing staff based in St John Street, moving up to Ladbroke Grove, a part of West London in which many other Virgin companies were based.

1991 saw only one original television novelisation released, *Battlefield* by Marc Platt ('A damn good read,' according to Peter Linford in *DWB*), but also the publication of Victor Pemberton's novelisation in the Target range of the Argo record *Doctor Who and the Pescatons* ('It's not all bad – just 99% so,' commented David Gibbs in *DWB*, a sentiment echoed by Andrew Martin in *TV Zone*: 'After [W H Allen went] to the trouble of commissioning Victor Pemberton to flesh out "The Pescatons", the result is not only out of place in the *Doctor Who* universe, but is an execrable piece of literature by any standards.') One idea that never came to fruition was for Dicks to novelise his recent *Doctor Who* stage play *The Ultimate Adventure*.

Three final original novelisations were published in 1993 and 1994, numbered as books 154, 155 and 156 in the Target *Doctor Who* Library. These were John Peel's adaptations of 'The Power of the Daleks' and 'The Evil of the Daleks', and Barry Letts' adaptation of his

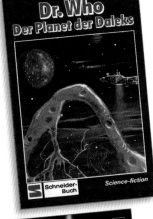

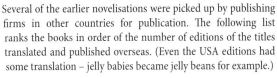

THE DOCTOR ABROAD

Several of the earlier novelisations were picked up by publishing firms in other countries for publication. The following list ranks the books in order of the number of editions of the titles translated and published overseas. (Even the USA editions had some translation – jelly babies became jelly beans for example.)

1 *Doctor Who and the Daleks* (France, Germany, Japan, The Netherlands x 2, Portugal, Turkey, USA)

1 *Doctor Who and the Day of the Daleks* (Brazil, Japan, The Netherlands, Poland, Portugal, Turkey, USA x 2)

3 *Doctor Who and the Doomsday Weapon* (Japan, The Netherlands, Portugal, Turkey, USA)

3 *Doctor Who and the Auton Invasion* (Finland, Japan, The Netherlands, Portugal, Turkey)

5 *Doctor Who and the Cave-Monsters* (Finland, Japan, The Netherlands, Portugal)

6 *Doctor Who and the Crusaders* (France, The Netherlands, Portugal)

6 *Doctor Who and the Abominable Snowmen* (France, Portugal, Turkey)

6 *Doctor Who and the Revenge of the Cybermen* (Poland, USA x 2)

6 *Doctor Who and the Dalek Invasion of Earth* (France, Germany x 2)

10 *Doctor Who and the Zarbi* (The Netherlands, Portugal)

10 *Doctor Who and the Daemons* (The Netherlands, Portugal)

10 *Doctor Who and the Loch Ness Monster* (USA x 2)

10 *Doctor Who and the Genesis of the Daleks* (USA x 2)

10 *Doctor Who and the Planet of the Daleks* (Germany x 2)

10 *Doctor Who and the Masque of Mandragora* (France, USA)

10 *Doctor Who and an Unearthly Child* (France, Germany)

17 *Doctor Who and the Sea-Devils* (Portugal)

17 *Doctor Who and the Cybermen* (Turkey)

17 *Doctor Who and the Giant Robot* (USA)

17 *Doctor Who–The Three Doctors* (Poland)

17 *Doctor Who and the Dinosaur Invasion* (USA)

17 *Doctor Who and the Seeds of Doom* (USA)

17 *Doctor Who and the Brain of Morbius* (France)

17 *Doctor Who and the Deadly Assassin* (USA)

17 *Doctor Who and the Talons of Weng-Chiang* (USA)

17 *Doctor Who and the Face of Evil* (USA)

17 *Doctor Who–Death to the Daleks* (Germany)

17 *Doctor Who and the Android Invasion* (USA)

17 *Doctor Who and the Robots of Death* (USA)

17 *Doctor Who and the Destiny of the Daleks* (Germany)

17 *Doctor Who–Meglos* (France)

GRAEME CURRY

'If you write a novel from a three-parter, you do have to find material from elsewhere to get it to the full length required.'

Graeme Curry, Doctor Who Magazine *(number 173), May 1991*

After leaving university, Graeme Curry progressed interests in journalism and writing while also working as a professional singer and actor. He won both the *Cosmopolitan* Young Journalist of the Year award in 1982 and a screenplay competition, the latter with a play about football called *Over the Moon*, which was later adapted for broadcast on Radio 4.

Over the Moon came to the attention of *Doctor Who* script editor Andrew Cartmel, who invited Curry to come up with ideas for the show. The result was Curry's first television commission, 'The Happiness Patrol', broadcast in 1988. He adapted and expanded his scripts for publication by Target.

Curry has also contributed to ITV's *The Bill* ('A Dog's Life', 1988), BBC1's *EastEnders* and the Radio 4 soap opera *Citizens*. He also wrote *PS I Love You* for Radio 4, broadcast in 1997.

In the early 1980s, Curry compiled books of poems for children with Jennifer Curry.

RONA MUNRO

'The book is virtually a transcription of my initial script, so it is closer to my original ideas.'

Rona Munro, Doctor Who Magazine *(number 189), August 1992*

Rona Munro was born in Aberdeen in 1959 and was an enthusiastic writer from the age of eight. She started writing professionally in the early 1980s, sometimes working as a cleaner to subsidise this. She attended Edinburgh University and wrote her breakthrough play *The Salesman*, which led to professional commissions.

She met *Doctor Who* script editor Andrew Cartmel at a BBC writers' training course. She wrote in 1989 what was, for 16 years, the final televised serial for the show, and later ▶

third Doctor radio serial 'The Paradise of Death'. These had mixed receptions. Matthew Cooke in *TV Zone* felt that *The Power of the Daleks* was 'enjoyable', but qualified this: 'The source material is so good that Peel would have to do something pretty appalling to spoil it.' *The Evil of the Daleks* was considered by Anthony Clark in *DWB* to be: 'A good, if at times a little workmanlike, rendition of an all time classic *Doctor Who*. For those of us who remember the original, it will help flesh out some old and faded recollections. And for those of you who have never seen anything beyond the one surviving episode, John Peel's book comes close to capturing the flavour of the original broadcasts to suggest just how good those transmissions might have been.' Matthew Cooke, however, was disappointed: 'Peel has been given it all on a plate – an inventive plot, strong characters, credible dialogue – but at times he makes it a chore to read … Some dignity is restored in later chapters set on Skaro, with its vast metal city containing "hundreds if not thousands" of Daleks. Indeed, the last half of the book is enjoyable – the early section suffers badly when the plot, which by necessity takes itself slowly, seems to grind to a halt under the weight of the author's self-indulgence.'

The Paradise of Death was liked by Darren Allen, writing in *Celestial Toyroom*: 'Barry Letts has turned in a fairly workmanlike adaptation of his original scripts and whilst the prose is unevocative it does suit the story perfectly.'

These three books were significantly different in look from the previous Target novelisations. For a start, they sported a new cover style – one that would later be adapted for Virgin's range of *Missing Adventures* (a companion range to the *New Adventures*, which started in 1994) – but perhaps more importantly, none of them featured the Target logo on the spine, and *The Evil of the Daleks* did not feature it anywhere in the book at all. The reasons for this were clear to Darvill-Evans: 'One of the things I discovered very quickly working on the books was that the fans were intelligent, articulate and of all ages, mostly adult, having grown up with the programme just as I had. There was therefore a large, well-heeled, grown-up market that we were not really addressing with Target books. I thought there was a great opportunity here, and I saw my job as moving forward *Doctor Who* publishing, but clearly Target was not the right vehicle for it. First of all, it had a history as a children's list, and secondly, we were running out of stories to novelise. I saw the Target "brand" as equalling children's novelisations, and to do something different, we needed not to use that brand. I'm a great believer in letting people know from the packaging what something is, so I thought that if we were going to publish *Doctor Who* books, we ought to publish them under the imprint "Doctor Who". Because it lets people know what it is. By the time we came to do *The Power of the Daleks* and *The Evil of the Daleks*, the "Doctor Who" imprint was well established and was doing very well. For Virgin's sales and marketing people, it was a simple decision: the books should be in the "Doctor Who" imprint and not the Target imprint as, very simply, we'd sell more copies by doing it that way.

'By 1994, we had a great range of new *Doctor Who* fiction underway, as well as a programme of superb factual books about the show, and I didn't need the "bridge" of reprint novelisations any longer. It had achieved its aim, and, in addition, the sales were dropping, so there seemed little point in continuing. We'd also reprinted a lot of the books that people wanted to complete their collections, and there was a limit to how much we could charge for them – the fact that the prices went up towards the end was a clear indication that we were selling less and that it couldn't be sustained.'

By 1994, the Target books, along with the 'Doctor Who' imprint and the erotica (which included Nexus and Black Lace), were the only ranges being published by

adapted it for Target.

Munro is now known principally as an internationally-acclaimed playwright. Her plays include the award-winning *Bold Girls* (1990), *The Maidenstone* (1996), *The House of Bernarda Alba* (1999), *Snake* (1999), *Catch a Falling Star!* (2004), *Strawberries in January* (2006) and, for the Royal Shakespeare Company, *The Indian Boy* (2006). Her women's prison drama *Iron* was one of the acclaimed hits to emerge from the 2002 Edinburgh Festival and won the John Whiting Award for new theatre writing.

Her other TV credits include *Casualty* ('Say it with Flowers', 1990), *Bumping the Odds* (1997) and *Rehab* (2003), and for the cinema she has written the Ken Loach-directed *Ladybird, Ladybird* (1994), *Aimee and Jaguar* (1999) and *Almost Adult* (2006).

Christmas 2006 saw Munro's adaptation of Richard Adams' classic *Watership Down* brought to the stage at The Lyric Hammersmith Theatre in London.

When working out the design for the new range of novels for Virgin, some trials were done using already existing artwork. The one pictured here uses artwork created for the novelisation of 'The Tenth Planet' and the fictitious author 'Jonathan Smith'.

PETE WALLBANK

'I'd had plans to make it a bit more grown-up, as I remember, but I was reminded by my editor that this was essentially a children's book. Bang went my ideas for horrific attacking Pescatons!'
*Pete Wallbank, interviewed by Tim Neal for **The Target Book**, February 2007*

Pete Wallbank was born in Staffordshire on 23 October 1968. Inspired by the work of artist Andrew Skilleter, he studied graphic design at Matthew Boulton College in Birmingham and was offered his first job with a local advertising agency while still at college. Early work included art for packaging, advertising material and album sleeves.

He was a fan of *Doctor Who* and had had artwork published in *Doctor Who Magazine* and in the fanzines *In-Vision* and *The Frame* prior to his sole commission for the Target range. He went on to provide covers for two of Virgin Books' original novels (*The Left-Handed Hummingbird*, 1993; *No Future*, 1994), two BBC Video releases ('The Visitation/Black Orchid' and 'Arc of Infinity', both 1994) and the four Encore laser disc releases of *Doctor Who* stories.

He has produced magazine, book and video artwork covering *Blake's 7*, *The Avengers*, *Planet of the Apes*, *The Hitch-hiker's Guide to the Galaxy*, *Survivors* and James Bond films, amongst many others. Commercial clients have included the RAC, Tesco and Marks & Spencer. He continues to work in commercial illustration, and through his own publishing imprint makes available limited edition fine art prints of his artwork, including pieces inspired by the ninth and tenth Doctors.

Virgin that did not feature the Virgin logo on the spine. According to Darvill-Evans, the Managing Director at the time, Rob Shreeve, strongly felt that *all* the titles they published should have the Virgin logo on, as it was a powerful symbol and a well-regarded brand. This was, for him, the most important thing. 'He didn't like the fact that I was using "Doctor Who" as an imprint. I had to fight quite hard to get the books published under other brands, as no other Virgin company produced goods or services other than under the Virgin name and logo. The Target brand was unfortunately unsalvageable. I was told by our sales people that there was a degree of hostility towards it in the trade – it had a reputation as a failed children's imprint as a result of the Virgin/W H Allen take over at the end of the '80s – and there wasn't really anything we could do with it. Crucially, its job was over, we had published every novelisation we could, and there was nothing left.'

The end of Target was in sight. The final book to feature the Target name and logo on the spine was a reprint of *The Talons of Weng-Chiang*, published on 17 March 1994.

One of the things that Darvill-Evans tried to do while he was at Virgin was to

calculate how many copies of the Target novelisations had been sold overall. 'I was working with incomplete figures for the most part,' he explains, 'and some of them were pure guesswork, but I came up with a figure of eight million books, and we started to put that on the covers. That is the true testament here. Target books were quite literally a publishing phenomenon. I don't know if they got a great deal of publicity in the '80s when they were selling 60,000 or 80,000 copies a time, but it was truly extraordinary.' Later estimations have put the total number of copies sold at nearer 13 million, taking into account all known reprint editions – a truly staggering figure.

VVOORP!
VWOORP!

'... with a raucous rattle of noises...'
John Peel, 1993
Doctor Who – The Power of the Daleks

CODA

WITH THE CANCELLATION OF THE REPRINT programme, the Target imprint ceased to exist. For 20 years, Target books had stood as a triumphant testimony to the shared vision of Richard Henwood, Brian Miles and Ralph Stokes, the Editor, Sales Director and Managing Director of the Universal Tandem Publishing Company, who, in 1972, realised that there was a gap in the market for a range of high quality, entertaining books for children of all ages. Their enthusiasm for this publishing venture, and their astute consideration that *Doctor Who* would be a prime subject for exploitation, resulted in a range of books unrivalled in its appeal and longevity. For an entire generation of pre-video readers, the Target *Doctor Who* novelisations shaped and created touchstones around *Doctor Who*'s history, offering exciting glimpses of some the Doctor's past adventures, and diligently documenting his current escapades for future generations to enjoy. Later books were more experimental, slowly growing with the audience, but always providing an entertaining and diverting read, as well as prompting memories of adventures only dimly remembered from the television.

Unused covers for reprints of *Doctor Who-The Sea Devils* and *Doctor Who-The Horror of Fang Rock.*

The distinctive Target symbol changed its look over the years, the publisher changed hands on several occasions, and the range of books was shaped by seven main editors and countless sales and marketing managers, not to mention managing, editorial and art directors. Numerous cover artists supplied their distinctive vision and interpretation of the Doctor's adventures to entice readers into buying the books, and others contributed to their success through successful distribution in the UK and overseas. Those who worked on the range have fond memories of their

THE DOCTOR OUT LOUD

The following titles have been made available as audio books (produced by BBC Audio unless otherwise indicated). Generally they have been abridged versions, read by actors involved in the series, and included appropriate atmospheric music and sound effects.

Doctor Who and the Daleks (read by William Russell)
Doctor Who and the Zarbi (William Russell)
Doctor Who and the Crusaders (William Russell)
Doctor Who and the Cave Monsters (Caroline John)
Doctor Who and the Doomsday Weapon (Geoffrey Beevers)
Doctor Who and the Curse of Peladon (Jon Pertwee)
Doctor Who–The Three Doctors (Gabriel Woolf)*
Doctor Who and the Carnival of Monsters (Gabriel Woolf)*
Doctor Who and the Space War (Geoffrey Beevers)++
Doctor Who and the Planet of the Daleks (Jon Pertwee)
Doctor Who and the Dinosaur Invasion (Martin Jarvis)+
Doctor Who and the Giant Robot (Tom Baker)+
Doctor Who and the Loch Ness Monster (Gabriel Woolf)*
Doctor Who and the Brain of Morbius (Tom Baker)++
Doctor Who and the State of Decay (Tom Baker)**
Doctor Who–Kinda (Peter Davison)
Doctor Who–Warriors of the Deep (Peter Davison)
Doctor Who–Attack of the Cybermen (Colin Baker)
Doctor Who–Vengeance on Varos (Colin Baker)

* Produced by the Royal National Institute for the Blind
** Produced by Pickwick International
\+ Available November 2007
\++ Available February 2008

time spent in the company of the Doctor. Those who read and collected the books feel likewise.

The last word goes to Terrance Dicks, who ended up contributing 64 titles to the eventual range of 156 books. Dicks was present at the start, and remained until the end, and his unflagging support contributed much to their initial success and eventual longevity.

'I'm not a fan, I'm a professional writer, and so I have a different perspective on the books,' he says today. 'The books gave me a big chunk of work at the time I most needed it, when I was leaving the BBC and going freelance. I was very happy. I would stand by the novelisations as a decent professional job.

'So much of my life has been determined by chance,' he muses. 'The whole thing goes back to when I was working as an advertising copywriter and the guy I was sharing an office with got married. He said to me that he had a couple of rooms in Hampstead and asked if I would like to stay there – I was at the time sharing a flat with some other people, one of whom got up my nose, so I wanted my own place. It was at 40 South Hill Park in Hampstead, and consisted of two rooms, which I took and moved into. I was paying five pounds a week for these rooms, and one day as I went in I saw this small, bald-headed man painting the staircase. I thought he was a handyman or something. I later learned that this was the co-owner of the house, and he'd bought the house in order to let it out, but had installed a great aunt called Winifred Boot as a permanent resident as a way of looking after her – he was very good in that way, she drove him crazy but he always looked after her. I got to know this chap – he was a writer called Malcolm Hulke – and eventually worked with him on *The Avengers*. Then, on a recommendation from Mac, I got a job on *Crossroads*. On *Crossroads* I met

The cover of a seventies Target catalogue.

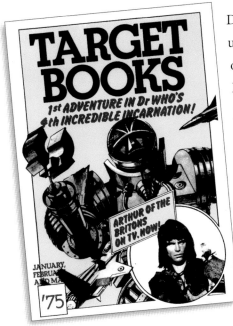

Cover for a 1975 Target catalogue.

Derrick Sherwin, and we used to travel together on the train every day. Derrick then left and joined *Doctor Who* as a story editor there, and when Derrick was offered a job elsewhere, he needed another story editor for *Doctor Who* and – I guess in some desperation – he phoned me up to ask if I was interested. I can remember to this day sitting at home and wondering where I could get some work when the phone rang …

'I couldn't have planned it out better if I'd tried. My father, who was a somewhat cynical and disappointed person in some ways, always used to say, "It's not what you know in life, it's who you know." But that's not quite right. It's what you know *and* who you know. The contacts are immensely helpful, but you can't fake it, you have to be able to *do* it.

'If, for example, that first *Doctor Who* book hadn't been any good, or they'd mismanaged the launch, or not put any effort into marketing it, then the whole thing could have stopped at that point. As it is, I have built a whole career as a writer both in television and in books, on a series of happy coincidences. I never insisted I wrote the novelisations, the publishers kept asking me; when I was short of work in one field, it increased in the other … I've been incredibly lucky over the years, and *Doctor Who* has always been something of which I'm immensely proud to have been a part.'

The Target *Doctor Who* novelisations started in Gloucester Road and ended in Ladbroke Grove, but along the way they conquered the world and added much to the myth and legend that is *Doctor Who*. It is a legacy that will never be forgotten.

COLLECTIONS

As well as being released and re-issued as individual books, and being sold as foreign editions around the world, the Target novelisations have also been released in collected states.

Doctor Who and the Daleks Omnibus (1976), Artus Publishing – collects abridged versions of *The Planet of the Daleks* and *The Genesis of the Daleks*.

The Doctor Who Omnibus (1977), Book Club Associates – collects *The Space War*, *The Web of Fear* and *The Revenge of the Cybermen*.

The Adventures of Doctor Who (1979), Nelson Doubleday Inc – collects *The Genesis of the Daleks*, *The Revenge of the Cybermen* and *The Loch Ness Monster*.

The Further Adventures of Doctor Who (1986), Nelson Doubleday Inc – collects *The Deadly Assassin*, *The Face of Evil* and *The Robots of Death*.

Doctor Who – Dalek Omnibus (1983), W H Allen – collects *The Dalek Invasion of Earth*, *The Day of the Daleks* and *The Planet of the Daleks*.

In 1988 and 1989, W H Allen issued seven paperbacks in their Star imprint, each of which collected two of the Target novelisations together. The covers were all the Target art from one of the two titles on the front, and the other on the back, in a silver border.

Doctor Who Classics – The Dalek Invasion of Earth and *The Crusaders* (1988)

Doctor Who Classics – The Myth Makers and *The Gunfighters* (1988)
Doctor Who Classics – The Dominators and *The Krotons* (1988)
Doctor Who Classics – The Daemons and *The Time Monster* (1989)
Doctor Who Classics – The Mind of Evil and *The Claws of Axos* (1989)
Doctor Who Classics – The Face of Evil and *The Sunmakers* (1989)
Doctor Who Classics – The Seeds of Doom and *The Deadly Assassin* (1989)

APPENDIX A
OTHER TARGET RANGES

ALONGSIDE THE NOVELISATIONS THAT MADE up the 'Doctor Who Library', there were a number of additional ranges of Doctor Who fiction published by Target. The first was a short run of Junior Doctor Who books, heavily illustrated versions of existing novelisations re-written in a more simplistic style.

Doctor Who and the Giant Robot (A Junior Doctor Who Book), by Terrance Dicks, cover by Harry Hants, illustrated by Peter Edwards (1980)

Doctor Who and the Brain of Morbius (A Junior Doctor Who Book), by Terrance Dicks, cover by Harry Hants, illustrated by Peter Edwards (1980)

The second range was a shortlived spin-off series that focused on the adventures of several of the Doctor's companions after they had finished travelling in the TARDIS. The final book was an adaptation of the one-off TV special *K-9 and Company*: 'A Girl's Best Friend', written by Terence Dudley and transmitted in December 1981. Additional books were considered featuring Victoria Waterfield, Tegan Jovanka, Captain Mike Yates and the further adventures of Harry Sullivan but, as range editor Peter Darvill-Evans noted at the time, 'These books have proved rather less popular than novelisations of TV scripts' and thus the range was cancelled.

The Companions of Doctor Who: Turlough and the Earthlink Dilemma by Tony Attwood, cover by David McAllister (1986)

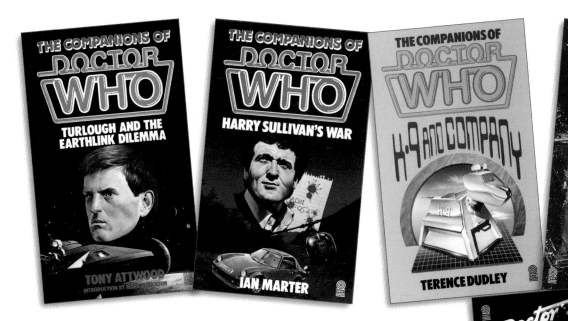

The Companions of Doctor Who: Harry Sullivan's War by Ian Marter, cover by David McAllister (1986)

The Companions of Doctor Who: K9 and Company by Terence Dudley, cover by Peter Kelly (1987)

'Slipback' was a six-part radio serial broadcast over three weeks as part of a Radio 4 programme aimed at young listeners. It was written by *Doctor Who*'s then script editor Eric Saward during a period when the television show was off the air. The writer then went on to adapt his scripts for W H Allen and Target.

Doctor Who – Slipback by Eric Saward, cover by Paul Mark Tams (1987)

In 1985, *Doctor Who* underwent a shake-up when the BBC's department heads effectively cancelled a planned season of stories. Three of these stories, all of which had made it to script format, and some of which had actually had initial production work completed on them, were picked up by W H Allen as a short range of books collectively called 'The Missing Episodes'.

Doctor Who: The Missing Episodes – The Nightmare Fair, by Graham Williams, cover by Alister Pearson (1989)

Doctor Who: The Missing Episodes – The Ultimate Evil, by Wally K Daly, cover by Alister Pearson (1989)

Doctor Who: The Missing Episodes – Mission to Magnus, by Philip Martin, cover by Alister Pearson (1990)

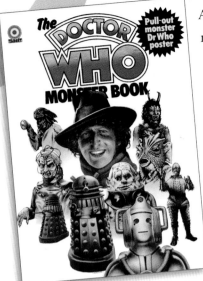

As well as the fiction and throughout the lifetime of the novelisation range, a number of non-fiction books relating to *Doctor Who* were published under the Target banner.

The Doctor Who Monster Book by Terrance Dicks, cover by Chris Achilleos (1975). A large-format, wire-bound softback book illustrated with dozens of black-and-white photographs from the history of the series and reproductions of some of the novelisation covers. The latest monster race covered was the Zygons. Included a pull-out poster reproduction of the book's cover. Was reprinted in 1985 with some changes to the photographs used but no revised text.

The Making of Doctor Who by Terrance Dicks and Malcolm Hulke, cover by Chris Achilleos (1976). An extensively overhauled 'B'-format paperback version of Pan Books' *The Making of Doctor Who* published in the Piccolo imprint in 1972.

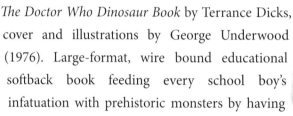

The Doctor Who Dinosaur Book by Terrance Dicks, cover and illustrations by George Underwood (1976). Large-format, wire bound educational softback book feeding every school boy's infatuation with prehistoric monsters by having the Doctor encounter a plethora of the beasties. Poster included.

The Second Doctor Who Monster Book by Terrance Dicks, cover by Chris Achilleos (1977). A5-sized, wire bound softback book with short summaries of the adventures 'Robot' to 'The Talons of Weng-Chiang', illustrated with colour and black-and-white photographs throughout.

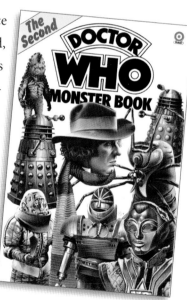

Doctor Who Discovers Early Man, edited by Fred Newman, designed by Frank Ainscough, cover artist unknown (1977). The first in a series of large-format, wire bound softback educational books. There were plans for 24 titles in the series, but in the event the range expired after just five (with three others, *The Miners*, *The Inventors* and *The Pirates*, abandoned in the planning stages). A poster of the cover was included with each book.

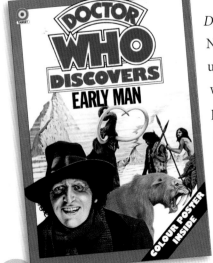

Doctor Who Discovers Prehistoric Animals, edited by Fred Newman, designed by Frank Ainscough, cover by Jeff Cummins (1977).

Doctor Who Discovers Space Travel, edited by Fred Newman, designed by Frank Ainscough, cover by Jeff Cummins (1977).

Doctor Who Discovers the Conquerors, edited by Fred Newman, designed by Frank Ainscough, cover artist unknown (1978).

Doctor Who Discovers Strange and Mysterious Creatures, edited by Fred Newman, designed by Frank Ainscough, cover by Jeff Cummins (1978).

The Adventures of K9 and Other Mechanical Creatures, by Terrance Dicks, cover and illustrations by Andrew Skilleter, puzzles devised by Andrew and Patricia Skilleter (1979). A 'B'-format paperback acting as a guide to the mechanical creatures encountered by the Doctor (illustrated with black-and-white photographs), enlivened by a number of relatively straightforward puzzles.

Terry Nation's Dalek Special, edited and compiled by Terrance Dicks, cover and illustrations by Andrew Skilleter, puzzles devised by Andrew and Patricia Skilleter (1979). A 'B'-format paperback similar to *The Adventures of K9 and Other Mechanical Creatures* but with a reprinted, Doctor-less Dalek story by Terry Nation.

The Doctor Who Programme Guide: Volume 1 – The Programmes, by Jean-Marc Lofficier, cover by Bill Donohoe (1981). Paperback containing brief plot summaries and cast lists for all the stories from '100,000 BC' to 'Logopolis'. Contained amendments and corrections to the hardback edition that had been printed earlier the same year. *The* definitive guidebook for a generation of fans.

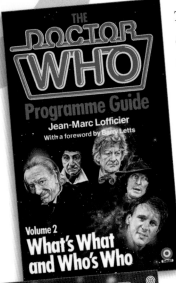

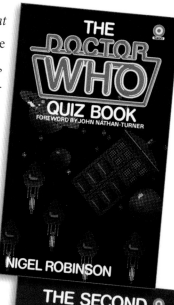

The Doctor Who Programme Guide: Volume 2 – What's What and Who's Who, by Jean-Marc Lofficier, cover by Bill Donohoe (1981). A paperback encyclopaedic view of the characters, places, monsters and other things mentioned in the *Doctor Who* TV stories.

The Doctor Who Quiz Book, by Nigel Robinson (1981). A paperback book of quiz questions and answers.

Doctor Who Crossword Book, by Nigel Robinson (1982). A paperback book of quiz questions and answers in crossword style.

The Second Doctor Who Quiz Book, by Nigel Robinson (1983). A further paperback book of quiz questions and answers.

Doctor Who – Brain Teasers and Mind Benders, by Adrian Heath (1984). A paperback book of quiz questions, puzzles and answers – set by 16 year old Heath.

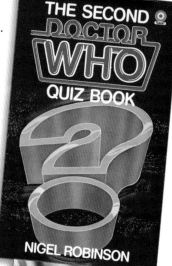

The Third Doctor Who Quiz Book, by Nigel Robinson (1985). A final paperback book of quiz questions and answers.

Doctor Who – Travel Without the TARDIS, by Jean Airey and Laurie Haldeman (1986). Lightweight and occasionally inaccurate paperback guide to the locations used on the TV show, written by two American fans.

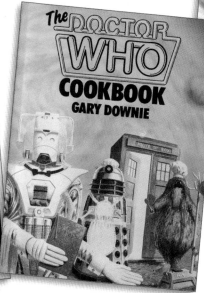

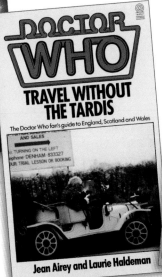

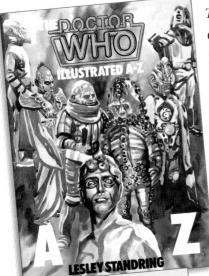

The Doctor Who Cookbook by Gary Downie, cover by Graham Potts, illustrations by Gail Bennett (1986). Large-format softback version of the hardback released 18 months earlier, bringing together recipes proffered by the stars and production crew of the TV show, compiled by production manager Downie.

The Doctor Who Illustrated A-Z by Lesley Standring, cover and illustrations by Lesley Standring (1987). Large-format softback, pretty much as described on the cover. This was the softback version of the hardback edition that was released two years earlier.

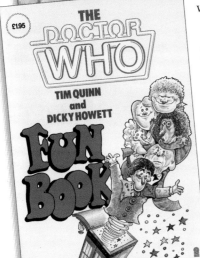

The Doctor Who Pattern Book, by Joy Gammon (1986). Large-format softback. A collection of sewing and knitting patterns themed around *Doctor Who*. This was the softback version of the hardback edition that was released two years earlier.

The Doctor Who Fun Book, by Tim Quinn and Dicky Howett (1987). Large-format, wire bound softback full of cartoons and humorous takes on the TV series.

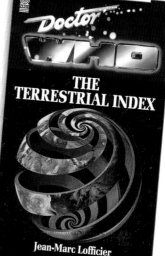

Doctor Who – Build the TARDIS, by Mark Harris (1987). Enormous wirebound softback mostly consisting of pieces to press out and assemble your very own model TARDIS. Harris also wrote *The Doctor Who Technical Manual* for Severn House in 1983. Irregularities in the time-space continuum meant this book featured a nine-inch-tall TARDIS while the *Technical Manual* featured a seven-foot-long sonic screwdriver.

Doctor Who – The Programme Guide, by Jean-Marc Lofficier, cover by Alister Pearson (1989). Expanded paperback edition of the original *Volume 1*, now covering all the stories up to and including 'Survival'. Although further updated editions followed, these were not released under the Target imprint.

Doctor Who – The Terrestrial Index, by Jean-Marc Lofficier, cover by Alister Pearson (1991). Essentially a revised and expanded paperback edition of the actor, technician and writer listings in *The Doctor Who Programme Guide Volume 2*.

APPENDIX B
THE DOCTOR WHO LIBRARY

AS DISCUSSED IN THE MAIN TEXT, IN 1983, TARGET INSTIGATED A NUMBERING SYSTEM for the books generically called the *Doctor Who* library. The following listing is in library number order and contains summary details of the titles.

DWL	Title	Author	First Published	Doctor and Companions	Aliens/Villains (as in the books)
1	Doctor Who and the Abominable Snowmen	Terrance Dicks	21-Nov-74	Dr 2, Jamie, Victoria	Great Intelligence, Yeti
2	Doctor Who and the Android Invasion	Terrance Dicks	16-Nov-78	Dr 4, Sarah, Harry, UNIT	Kraals
3	Doctor Who and the Androids of Tara	Terrance Dicks	24-Apr-80	Dr 4, Romana, K9	Count Grendel
4	Doctor Who and the Ark in Space	Ian Marter	10-May-77	Dr 4, Sarah, Harry	Wirrrn
5	Doctor Who and the Armageddon Factor	Terrance Dicks	26-Jun-80	Dr 4, Romana, K9	The Shadow, The Black Guardian
6	Doctor Who and the Auton Invasion	Terrance Dicks	17-Jan-74	Dr 3, Liz, The Brigadier, UNIT	Autons, Channing
7	Doctor Who and the Brain of Morbius	Terrance Dicks	23-Jun-77	Dr 4, Sarah	Morbius, Dr Solon, Sisterhood of Karn
8	Doctor Who and the Carnival of Monsters	Terrance Dicks	20-Jan-77	Dr 3, Jo	Drashigs, Inter Minorians
9	Doctor Who and the Cave Monsters	Malcolm Hulke	17-Jan-74	Dr 3, Liz, The Brigadier, UNIT	Reptile Men
10	Doctor Who and the Claws of Axos	Terrance Dicks	21-Apr-77	Dr 3, Jo, The Brigadier, UNIT	Axons, The Master
11	Doctor Who and the Creature from the Pit	David Fisher	15-Jan-81	Dr 4, Romana, K9	Lady Adrasta, Erato
12	Doctor Who and the Crusaders	David Whitaker	02-May-73	Dr 1, Ian, Barbara, Vicky	El Akir
13	Doctor Who and the Curse of Peladon	Brian Hayles	Jan-75	Dr 3, Jo	Ice Warriors, Arcturus, Alpha Centauri, Aggedor
14	Doctor Who and the Cybermen	Gerry Davis	20-Feb-75	Dr 2, Ben, Polly, Jamie	Cybermen
15	Doctor Who and the Dæmons	Barry Letts	17-Oct-74	Dr 3, Jo, The Brigadier, UNIT	Azal, Bok
16	Doctor Who and the Daleks	David Whitaker	02-May-73	Dr 1, Susan, Ian, Barbara	Daleks, Thals
17	Doctor Who and the Dalek Invasion of Earth	Terrance Dicks	24-Mar-77	Dr 1, Susan, Ian, Barbara	Daleks, Robomen, Slyther
18	Doctor Who and the Day of the Daleks	Terrance Dicks	Apr-74	Dr 3, Jo, The Brigadier, UNIT	Daleks, Ogrons
19	Doctor Who and the Deadly Assassin	Terrance Dicks	20-Oct-77	Dr 4	The Master, Goth
20	Doctor Who – Death to the Daleks	Terrance Dicks	20-Jul-78	Dr 3, Sarah	Daleks, Exxilons
21	Doctor Who and the Destiny of the Daleks	Terrance Dicks	20-Nov-79	Dr 4, Romana, K9	Davros, Daleks, Movellans
22	Doctor Who and the Dinosaur Invasion	Malcolm Hulke	19-Feb-76	Dr 3, Sarah, The Brigadier, UNIT	Dinosaurs, Professor Whitaker

DWL	Title	Author	First Published	Doctor and Companions	Aliens/Villains (as in the books)
23	Doctor Who and the Doomsday Weapon	Malcolm Hulke	Apr-74	Dr 3, Jo	The Master, Captain Dent, Alien Priests, Primitives
24	Doctor Who and the Enemy of the World	Ian Marter	17-Apr-81	Dr 2, Jamie, Victoria	Salamander
25	Doctor Who and the Face of Evil	Terrance Dicks	19-Jan-78	Dr 4, Leela	Xoanon, Horda
26	Doctor Who – Full Circle	Andrew Smith	16-Sep-82	Dr 4, Romana, Adric, K9	Marshmen
27	Doctor Who and the Genesis of the Daleks	Terrance Dicks	22-Jul-76	Dr 4, Sarah, Harry	Davros, Daleks
28	Doctor Who and the Giant Robot	Terrance Dicks	13-Mar-75	Dr 4, Sarah, Harry, the Brigadier, UNIT	Robot K1
29	Doctor Who and the Green Death	Malcolm Hulke	21-Aug-75	Dr 3, Jo, The Brigadier, UNIT	Giant maggots, BOSS
30	Doctor Who and the Hand of Fear	Terrance Dicks	18-Jan-79	Dr 4, Sarah	Eldrad
31	Doctor Who and the Horns of Nimon	Terrance Dicks	16-Oct-80	Dr 4, Romana, K9	Nimon
32	Doctor Who and the Horror of Fang Rock	Terrance Dicks	30-Mar-78	Dr 4, Leela	Rutan
33	Doctor Who and the Ice Warriors	Brian Hayles	18-Mar-76	Dr 2, Jamie, Victoria	Ice Warriors
34	Doctor Who and the Image of the Fendahl	Terrance Dicks	26-Jul-79	Dr 4, Leela, K9	Fendahl
35	Doctor Who and the Invasion of Time	Terrance Dicks	21-Feb-80	Dr 4, Leela, K9	Sontarans, Vardans
36	Doctor Who and the Invisible Enemy	Terrance Dicks	29-Mar-79	Dr 4, Leela, K9	The Nucleus
37	Doctor Who and the Keeper of Traken	Terrance Dicks	20-May-82	Dr 4, Adric, Nyssa	Melkur, The Master
38	Doctor Who and the Keys of Marinus	Philip Hinchcliffe	21-Aug-80	Dr 1, Susan, Ian, Barbara	Voord, Morphoton
39	Doctor Who and the Leisure Hive	David Fisher	22-Jul-82	Dr 4, Romana, K9	Foamasi, Pangol
40	Doctor Who and the Loch Ness Monster	Terrance Dicks	15-Jan-76	Dr 4, Sarah, Harry, the Brigadier, UNIT	Zygons, Skarasen
41	Doctor Who – Logopolis	Christopher H Bidmead	21-Oct-82	Dr 4, Adric, Nyssa, Tegan	The Master, Logopolitans
42	Doctor Who and the Masque of Mandragora	Philip Hinchcliffe	08-Dec-77	Dr 4, Sarah	Count Federico, Mandragora Helix, Hieronymous
43	Doctor Who and the Monster of Peladon	Terrance Dicks	04-Dec-80	Dr 3, Sarah	Ice Warriors, Alpha Centauri
44	Doctor Who and the Mutants	Terrance Dicks	29-Sep-77	Dr 3, Jo	The Marshal, Mutants
45	Doctor Who and the Nightmare of Eden	Terrance Dicks	21-Aug-80	Dr 4, Romana, K9	Mandrels
46	Doctor Who and the Planet of the Daleks	Terrance Dicks	21-Oct-76	Dr 3, Jo	Daleks, Spiridons
47	Doctor Who and the Planet of Evil	Terrance Dicks	18-Aug-77	Dr 4, Sarah	Anti-matter monster
48	Doctor Who and the Planet of the Spiders	Terrance Dicks	16-Oct-75	Dr 3, Sarah, the Brigadier, UNIT	Giant spiders, Lupton
49	Doctor Who and the Power of Kroll	Terrance Dicks	26-May-80	Dr 4, Romana, K9	Kroll, Swampies
50	Doctor Who and the Pyramids of Mars	Terrance Dicks	16-Dec-76	Dr 4, Sarah	Sutekh, robot mummies
51	Doctor Who and the Revenge of the Cybermen	Terrance Dicks	20-May-76	Dr 4, Sarah, Harry	Cybermen, Cybermats, Vogans
52	Doctor Who and the Ribos Operation	Ian Marter	11-Dec-79	Dr 4, Romana, K9	Graff Vynda Ka, Shrivenzale
53	Doctor Who and the Robots of Death	Terrance Dicks	24-May-79	Dr 4, Leela	Voc robots, Taren Capel
54	Doctor Who and the Sea-Devils	Malcolm Hulke	17-Oct-74	Dr 3, Jo	Sea-Devils, The Master
55	Doctor Who and the Seeds of Doom	Philip Hinchcliffe	17-Feb-77	Dr 4, Sarah, UNIT	Krynoid, Harrison Chase
56	Doctor Who and the Sontaran Experiment	Ian Marter	07-Dec-78	Dr 4, Sarah, Harry	Sontaran (Styre)
57	Doctor Who and the Space War	Malcolm Hulke	23-Sep-76	Dr 3, Jo	The Master, Ogrons, Daleks
58	Doctor Who and the State of Decay	Terrance Dicks	14-Jan-82	Dr 4, Romana, Adric, K9	Vampires
59	Doctor Who and the Stones of Blood	Terrance Dicks	20-Mar-80	Dr 4, Romana, K9	Ogri, Cessair of Diplos
60	Doctor Who and the Sunmakers	Terrance Dicks	18-Nov-82	Dr 1, Leela, K9	The Collector
61	Doctor Who and the Talons of Weng-Chiang	Terrance Dicks	15-Nov-77	Dr 4, Leela	Magnus Greel, Mr Sin, Li H'Sen Chang
62	Doctor Who and the Tenth Planet	Gerry Davis	19-Feb-76	Dr 1, Ben, Polly	Cybermen
63	Doctor Who and the Terror of the Autons	Terrance Dicks	15-May-75	Dr 3, Jo, the Brigadier, UNIT	Autons, The Master
64	Doctor Who – The Three Doctors	Terrance Dicks	20-Nov-75	Dr 1, Dr 2, Dr 3, Jo, the Brigadier, UNIT	Omega, Blob Men
65	Doctor Who and the Time Warrior	Terrance Dicks (& Robert Holmes)	29-Jun-78	Dr 3, Sarah	Sontaran (Linx)
66	Doctor Who and the Tomb of the Cybermen	Gerry Davis	18-May-78	Dr 2, Jamie, Victoria	Cybermen, Cybermats, Kaftan, Kleig
67	Doctor Who and the Underworld	Terrance Dicks	24-Jan-80	Dr 4, Leela, K9	The Oracle

DWL	Title	Author	First Published	Doctor and Companions	Aliens/Villains (as in the books)
68	Doctor Who and an Unearthly Child	Terrance Dicks	15-Oct-81	Dr 1, Susan, Ian, Barbara	Cavemen
69	Doctor Who and the Visitation	Eric Saward	19-Aug-82	Dr 5, Adric, Nyssa, Tegan	Terileptils
70	Doctor Who and the War Games	Malcolm Hulke	25-Sep-79	Dr 2, Jamie, Zoe	The War Lords
71	Doctor Who and Warriors' Gate	Stephen Gallagher (as John Lydecker)	15-Apr-82	Dr 4, Romana, Adric, K9	Rorvik, Tharils
72	Doctor Who and the Web of Fear	Terrance Dicks	19-Aug-76	Dr 2, Jamie, Victoria	Great Intelligence, Yeti
73	Doctor Who and the Zarbi	Bill Strutton	02-May-73	Dr 1, Ian, Barbara, Vicky	Zarbi, Menoptera
74	Doctor Who – Time-Flight	Peter Grimwade	15-Apr-83	Dr 5, Nyssa, Tegan	The Master, Plasmatons
75	Doctor Who – Meglos	Terrance Dicks	05-May-83	Dr 4, Romana, K9	Meglos, Tigellans, Gaztaks
76	Doctor Who – Castrovalva	Christopher H Bidmead	16-Jun-83	Dr 5, Adric, Nyssa, Tegan	The Master
77	Doctor Who – Four to Doomsday	Terrance Dicks	21-Jul-83	Dr 5, Adric, Nyssa, Tegan	Monarch
78	Doctor Who – Earthshock	Ian Marter	18-Aug-83	Dr 5, Adric, Nyssa, Tegan	Cybermen, Androids
79	Doctor Who – Terminus	Stephen Gallagher (as John Lydecker)	15-Sep-83	Dr 5, Nyssa, Tegan, Turlough	The Black Guardian, Vanir, the Garm
80	Doctor Who – Arc of Infinity	Terrance Dicks	20-Oct-83	Dr 5, Nyssa, Tegan	Omega, Ergon
81	Doctor Who – The Five Doctors	Terrance Dicks	24-Nov-83	Dr 1, Susan, Dr 2, the Brigadier, Dr 3, Sarah, Dr 4, Romana, Dr 5, Tegan, Turlough	The Master, Cybermen, Daleks, Yeti
82	Doctor Who – Mawdryn Undead	Peter Grimwade	12-Jan-84	Dr 5, Nyssa, Tegan, Turlough	The Black Guardian, Mawdryn
83	Doctor Who – Snakedance	Terrance Dicks	03-May-84	Dr 5, Nyssa, Tegan	The Mara
84	Doctor Who – Kinda	Terrance Dicks	15-Mar-84	Dr 5, Adric, Nyssa, Tegan	The Mara
85	Doctor Who – Enlightenment	Barbara Clegg	24-May-84	Dr 5, Tegan, Turlough	Eternals, The Black Guardian
86	Doctor Who – The Dominators	Ian Marter	19-Jul-84	Dr 2, Jamie, Zoe	Dominators, Quarks
87	Doctor Who – Warriors of the Deep	Terrance Dicks	16-Aug-84	Dr 5, Tegan, Turlough	Silurians, Sea-Devils
88	Doctor Who – The Aztecs	John Lucarotti	20-Sep-84	Dr 1, Susan, Ian, Barbara	Tlotoxl
89	Doctor Who – Inferno	Terrance Dicks	18-Oct-84	Dr 3, Liz, the Brigadier, UNIT	Infected Mutant Humans, Professor Stahlman
90	Doctor Who – The Highlanders	Gerry Davis	15-Nov-84	Dr 2, Ben, Polly, Jamie	Solicitor Grey
91	Doctor Who – Frontios	Christopher H Bidmead	10-Dec-84	Dr 5, Tegan, Turlough	Tractators
92	Doctor Who – The Caves of Androzani	Terrance Dicks	14-Mar-85	Dr 5, Peri	Sharaz Jek, Morgus
93	Doctor Who – Planet of Fire	Peter Grimwade	14-Feb-85	Dr 5, Turlough, Peri, Kamelion	The Master
94	Doctor Who – Marco Polo	John Lucarotti	11-Apr-85	Dr 1, Susan, Ian, Barbara	Tegana
95	Doctor Who – The Awakening	Eric Pringle	13-Jun-85	Dr 5, Tegan, Turlough	The Malus
96	Doctor Who – The Mind of Evil	Terrance Dicks	11-Jul-85	Dr 3, Jo, the Brigadier, UNIT	The Master, Alien Mind Parasite
97	Doctor Who – The Myth Makers	Donald Cotton	12-Sep-85	Dr 1, Vicky, Steven, Katarina	Cassandra
98	Doctor Who – The Invasion	Ian Marter	10-Oct-85	Dr 2, Jamie, Zoe, the Brigadier, UNIT	Cybermen, Tobias Vaughn
99	Doctor Who – The Krotons	Terrance Dicks	14-Nov-85	Dr 2, Jamie, Zoe	Krotons
100	Doctor Who – The Two Doctors	Robert Holmes	05-Dec-85	Dr 2, Jamie, Dr 6, Peri	Sontarans, Androgums
101	Doctor Who – The Gunfighters	Donald Cotton	09-Jan-86	Dr 1, Steven, Dodo	The Clantons
102	Doctor Who – The Time Monster	Terrance Dicks	13-Feb-86	Dr 3, Jo, the Brigadier, UNIT	The Master, Kronos
103	Doctor Who – The Twin Dilemma	Eric Saward	13-Mar-86	Dr 6, Peri	Gastropods, Jacondans
104	Doctor Who – Galaxy Four	William Emms	10-Apr-86	Dr 1, Vicky, Steven	Drahvins, Chumblies, Rills
105	Doctor Who – Timelash	Glen McCoy	15-May-86	Dr 6, Peri	The Borad
106	Doctor Who – Vengeance on Varos	Philip Martin	16-Jun-88	Dr 6, Peri	Sil
107	Doctor Who – The Mark of the Rani	Pip and Jane Baker	12-Jun-86	Dr 6, Peri	The Rani, The Master
108	Doctor Who – The King's Demons	Terence Dudley	10-Jul-86	Dr 5, Tegan, Turlough, Kamelion	The Master
109	Doctor Who – The Savages	Ian Stuart Black	11-Sep-86	Dr 1, Steven, Dodo	Elders, Savages
110	Doctor Who – Fury from the Deep	Victor Pemberton	16-Oct-86	Dr 2, Jamie, Victoria	The Weed
111	Doctor Who – The Celestial Toymaker	Gerry Davis and Alison Bingeman	20-Nov-86	Dr 1, Steven, Dodo	The Celestial Toymaker
112	Doctor Who – The Seeds of Death	Terrance Dicks	04-Dec-86	Dr 2, Jamie, Zoe	Ice Warriors

DWL	Title	Author	First Published	Doctor and Companions	Aliens/Villains (as in the books)
113	Doctor Who – Black Orchid	Terence Dudley	19-Feb-87	Dr 5, Adric, Nyssa, Tegan	George Cranleigh
114	Doctor Who – The Ark	Paul Erickson	19-Mar-87	Dr 1, Steven, Dodo	Monoids, Refusians
115	Doctor Who – The Mind Robber	Peter Ling	16-Apr-87	Dr 2, Jamie, Zoe	The Master of the Land of Fiction, White Robots, Clockwork Soldiers
116	Doctor Who – The Faceless Ones	Terrance Dicks	21-May-87	Dr 2, Ben, Polly, Jamie	Chameleons
117	Doctor Who – The Space Museum	Glyn Jones	18-Jun-87	Dr 1, Ian, Barbara, Vicky	Moroks, Xerons
118	Doctor Who – The Sensorites	Nigel Robinson	16-Jul-87	Dr 1, Susan, Ian, Barbara	Sensorites
119	Doctor Who – The Reign of Terror	Ian Marter	20-Aug-87	Dr 1, Susan, Ian, Barbara	Robespierre
120	Doctor Who – The Romans	Donald Cotton	19-Sep-87	Dr 1, Ian, Barbara, Vicky	Emperor Nero
121	Doctor Who – The Ambassadors of Death	Terrance Dicks	01-Oct-87	Dr 3, Liz, the Brigadier, UNIT	General Carrington, Alien Ambassadors
122	Doctor Who – The Massacre	John Lucarotti	19-Nov-87	Dr 1, Steven, Dodo	The Abbot of Amboise
123	Doctor Who – The Macra Terror	Ian Stuart Black	10-Dec-87	Dr 2, Ben, Polly, Jamie	Macra
124	Doctor Who – The Rescue	Ian Marter (& Nigel Robinson)	21-Jan-88	Dr 1, Ian, Barbara, Vicky	Koquillion
125	Doctor Who – Terror of the Vervoids	Pip and Jane Baker	18-Feb-88	Dr 6, Mel	Vervoids, The Valeyard
126	Doctor Who – The Time Meddler	Nigel Robinson	17-Mar-88	Dr 1, Vicky, Steven	The Meddling Monk
127	Doctor Who – The Mysterious Planet	Terrance Dicks	21-Apr-88	Dr 6, Peri	Drathro, The Valeyard
128	Doctor Who – Time and the Rani	Pip and Jane Baker	05-May-88	Dr 7, Mel	The Rani, Tetraps
129	Doctor Who – The Underwater Menace	Nigel Robinson	21-Jul-88	Dr 2, Ben, Polly, Jamie	Professor Zaroff, Fish People
130	Doctor Who – The Wheel in Space	Terrance Dicks	18-Aug-88	Dr 2, Jamie, Zoe	Cybermen, Cybermats
131	Doctor Who – The Ultimate Foe	Pip and Jane Baker	15-Sep-88	Dr 6, Mel	The Master, The Valeyard
132	Doctor Who – The Edge of Destruction	Nigel Robinson	20-Oct-88	Dr 1, Susan, Ian, Barbara	
133	Doctor Who – The Smugglers	Terrance Dicks	17-Nov-88	Dr 1, Ben, Polly	Captain Pike
134	Doctor Who – Paradise Towers	Stephen Wyatt	01-Dec-88	Dr 7, Mel	Kroagnon, Cleaning Robots
135	Doctor Who – Delta and the Bannermen	Malcolm Kohll	19-Jan-89	Dr 7, Mel	Gavrok, Bannermen, Chimeron
136	Doctor Who – The War Machines	Ian Stuart Black	16-Feb-89	Dr 1, Dodo, Ben, Polly	WOTAN
137	Doctor Who – Dragonfire	Ian Briggs	16-Mar-89	Dr 7, Mel, Ace	Kane
138	Doctor Who – Attack of the Cybermen	Eric Saward	20-Apr-89	Dr 6, Peri	Cybermen, Cryons
139	Doctor Who – Mindwarp	Philip Martin	15-Jun-89	Dr 6, Peri	Sil, The Valeyard
140	Doctor Who – The Chase	John Peel	20-Jul-89	Dr 1, Ian, Barbara, Vicky, Steven	Daleks, Aridians, Mire Beast, Mechanoids
141	Doctor Who – Mission to the Unknown	John Peel	21-Sep-89	Dr 1, Steven, Katarina, Sara	Daleks, The Meddling Monk, Mavic Chen, Varga Plants
142	Doctor Who – The Mutation of Time	John Peel	19-Oct-89	Dr 1, Steven, Sara	Daleks, Mavic Chen
143	Doctor Who – Silver Nemesis	Kevin Clarke	16-Nov-89	Dr 7, Ace	Cybermen
144	Doctor Who – The Greatest Show in the Galaxy	Stephen Wyatt	21-Dec-89	Dr 7, Ace	The Gods of Ragnarok, Chief Clown
145	Doctor Who – Planet of Giants	Terrance Dicks	18-Jan-90	Dr 1, Susan, Ian, Barbara	Forester
146	Doctor Who – The Happiness Patrol	Graeme Curry	15-Feb-90	Dr 7, Ace	Helen A, Fifi, the Kandyman
147	Doctor Who – The Space Pirates	Terrance Dicks	15-Mar-90	Dr 2, Jamie, Zoe	Caven
148	Doctor Who – Remembrance of the Daleks	Ben Aaronovitch	21-Jun-90	Dr 7, Ace	Davros, Daleks
149	Doctor Who – Ghost Light	Marc Platt	20-Sep-90	Dr 7, Ace	Light, Husks
150	Doctor Who – Survival	Rona Munro	18-Oct-90	Dr 7, Ace	The Master, Cheetah people
151	Doctor Who – The Curse of Fenric	Ian Briggs	15-Nov-90	Dr 7, Ace	Fenric, Haemovores
152	Doctor Who – Battlefield	Marc Platt	18-Jul-91	Dr 7, Ace, the Brigadier, UNIT	Morgaine, The Destroyer
153	Doctor Who – The Pescatons	Victor Pemberton	15-Sep-91	Dr 4, Sarah	Pescatons
154	Doctor Who – The Power of the Daleks	John Peel	15-Jul-93	Dr 2, Ben, Polly	Daleks
155	Doctor Who – The Evil of the Daleks	John Peel	19-Aug-93	Dr 2, Jamie, Victoria	Daleks
156	Doctor Who – The Paradise of Death	Barry Letts	21-Apr-94	Dr 3, Sarah, the Brigadier, Jeremy	Tragan

APPENDIX C
OFF TARGET

AT VARIOUS POINTS IN THE TV SHOW'S LIFELINE, *Doctor Who* has explored the idea of alternative realities – histories that could have been, or could yet be, if different decisions had been made at certain points in time. Several stories, from 1965's 'The Space Museum' through to 2006's 'Rise of the Cybermen', showed us events similar to and yet different from the version of history we are comfortable with.

The history of Target's *Doctor Who* range is littered with similar tipping points. For example, circumstance dictated that we missed out on *Doctor Who and the Time Warrior* by Robert Holmes and *Doctor Who–Battlefield* by Ben Aaronovitch.

As far back as the range's inception, titles were mentioned that did not finally appear in print until many years later. 'The Ambassadors of Death', for example, was originally scheduled for March 1974, possibly with Malcolm Hulke as the author, the writer having stepped in to finalise the majority of the scripts when credited writer David Whitaker was unable to do so. The serial was eventually adapted by Terrance Dicks and published by Target thirteen and a half years later, going from one of the earliest third Doctor stories to be discussed for adaptation to actually being the last to see print.

Producer Barry Letts may have been interested in adapting the other stories he had developed and co-written for the screen with Robert Sloman (as he did with *Doctor Who and the Dæmons* in 1974) but work and family commitments made that option an impossibility for him. Writer Robert Holmes attempted to adapt his story 'The Time Warrior' in 1978 but after three pages decided that other things had to take priority and so passed it over to Terrance Dicks to complete.

While author Douglas Adams was not willing to novelise his three *Doctor Who* stories for the Target range, much of the material which comprised his untransmitted story 'Shada' found its way into his novel *Dirk Gently's Holistic Detective Agency*, published in 1987.

148

The opening prologue of *Doctor Who and the Time Warrior* is what remains of Holmes's work on this book.

Original series script editor David Whitaker (who had written two novelisations back in the 1960s) submitted an outline for an adaptation of his own TV serial 'The Enemy of the World' in October 1979, but was prevented from completing the project by his death in February 1980.

Whitaker's wife at the time of his death, Stephanie St Clair, indicated that he would have gone on to adapt another story had he lived longer, and this may well have been the early two-parter 'Inside the Spaceship', which was eventually novelised as *Doctor Who–The Edge of Destruction* by Nigel Robinson in 1988. It has also been rumoured that David McAllister's first cover for the range (that was used on *Doctor Who and the Keys of Marinus*) was actually intended for this book. The fact that there are sketches in existence by artist Steve Kyte, using the same basic idea as McAllister's cover, although clearly marked as being for *Doctor Who and the Enemy of the World*, lends credence to this.

Two other Whitaker-penned serials were also on Target's hit-list for adaptation in the late 1970s: 'The Power of the Daleks' and 'The Evil of the Daleks'. Terrance Dicks was pencilled in to adapt them in 1979 although difficulties with clearance from Terry Nation, co-owner of the Daleks, meant that the stories finally saw the light of day only in 1993, adapted by author John Peel who had befriended Nation and managed to get the okay to write the novelisations.

All books go through an editing and approval process, and in the case of *Doctor Who* novelisations, this always included approval of all elements by the incumbent producer of the show on television. Throughout the 1980s, producer John Nathan Turner took a fierce interest in the range. This included criticism of some of the books' covers, something that had always been problematic for the production office, which then led to the replacement of artwork covers with photographic ones for many of the Davison era stories. In

an alternative universe, 1982 might have seen *Doctor Who and the Visitation* with David McAllister's artwork cover, and might also have seen a very different version of *Doctor Who and Warriors' Gate*. Author Stephen Gallagher, who used the pen name John Lydecker on the books, writing in the fanzine *Tardis* in 1988, recalled: 'The manuscript was delivered on time and was pretty well received – so much so that they were prepared to reschedule and allow a much higher page count than was

ABOVE: Douglas Adams pictured in 1979. BELOW: David McAllister's artwork for *Doctor Who and the Visitation* was not used in favour of a photographic cover. Pictured is how the cover might have looked like had the artwork been used.

usual. I was pretty happy at this stage, but then, only a week before we were due to go to press, I got a call from my editor; the show's production office felt that I'd strayed too far from the screen version and wouldn't pass it. Back in those pre-word processor days, it was a case of scissors and paste, with no time even to take a copy of the original before it got confettied and rearranged.' From the single extract of the original text that still survives, it is clear that although the basic ideas and plot structure remained the same, the sequencing of events, the interaction between Romana and Adric, some crew members' names and the dialogue would have been quite different. Gallagher has since enjoyed a career as an extremely successful novelist and director, making this glimpse of his 'lost' novelisation even more tantalising.

Some books would probably remain wishful thinking, even in an alternative universe. Range editor Nigel Robinson recalls: 'We approached Douglas Adams (via his agent Ed Victor) to novelise "The Pirate Planet". We ridiculously offered him £4,000 (or whatever was double the usual advance in those days) and not surprisingly got turned down. But to his credit, Douglas Adams (who I had never met) personally rang me to say he couldn't accept the advance and he really didn't want anyone else to do his stuff.'

It was standard for the Target range editor to approach original scriptwriters to see if they were interested in doing a novelisation. This was a policy strictly adhered to by Robinson, which led to a wave of books by the original writers in the second half of the 1980s. Only occasionally was the door left open for a novelisation to be picked up by Terrance Dicks, Ian Marter or Robinson himself, as he explained: 'I wrote to Derrick Sherwin asking him if he would like to novelise "The Invasion" (as you did to all original scriptwriters) and he had no interest in doing so.' The serial was then novelised by Ian Marter and published by Target in 1985.

Even as the range came to a natural end, there were still fluctuations between what-came-to-pass and what-might-have-been. Scriptwriter Ben Aaronovitch had penned a widely-acclaimed novelisation of his serial 'Remembrance of the Daleks', so it was only natural to expect that he would adapt his follow-up script 'Battlefield'. Fellow scriptwriter Marc Platt takes up the story: 'Ben was originally going to write the novelisation, but he had a lot of other projects lined up, so he asked me to take over. He gave me completely free rein with the text, although he had already written the first chapter, which I only adapted slightly. Ben also had several ideas for the book that I was able to incorporate: the ornithopters and flying castles in the Avallion world.'

In issue 97 of *Doctor Who Magazine*, writer Jeremy Bentham mentioned in the 'Matrix Databank' feature that an artist called Mark Bentham (no relation) would be providing the cover for *Doctor Who–The Mind of Evil*. When the book was published, the cover artwork was by Andrew Skilleter. Mark Bentham had been discussing cover art with Christine Donougher at Target for some time, and in fact saw some of his work featured in the illustrated book *Doctor Who–The Key to Time* (including one being embossed on the cover of the deluxe hardback edition). Following this, he pitched covers for both *Doctor Who–The Invasion* and *Doctor Who–The Mind of Evil*. 'The deadlines for the books were tight,' Bentham explains. 'I think I only had two weeks to do them both. For *Doctor Who–The Invasion* I decided to use the classic portrait of a Cyberman towering above Tobias Vaughn. The other cover was trouble and I didn't know what to do. I telephoned Jeremy Bentham and asked him what the Keller Machine looked like. He didn't know of any photographs of it but thought it was like a video recorder with a cylinder on top–this was before the days of video recordings of the programme were available to watch. Out of desperation I decided to base the cover on the hallucination cliff-hanger with a Dalek, Ice Lord, Cyberman and Chinese style dragon. Once finished, I sent them over to Target and was kept waiting ages only to be told that they weren't going to use them.' Reproduced on this page are Bentham's unused pieces for both covers.

THE ENEMY OF THE WORLD

David Whitaker's original outline that he submitted to Target for consideration still exists and is reproduced below. His version of the story would have differed from the televised version in a number of key ways. At this point in his adventures, the Doctor was accompanied by Jamie and Victoria, but Whitaker's synopsis makes mention only of Jamie; on television, the adventure begins with the TARDIS arriving on the shore, but in the synopsis it materialises in a beach cave; the villainous Salamander is given a first name – Ramon – that he lacks in the original; on television, scheming Giles Kent has known all along the location of Salamander's operations base, but in the synopsis he is trying to locate it in order to usurp Salamander; at the end of the story, on television, Salamander tricks his way into the TARDIS and ends up being sucked into the vortex once the ship is in flight, whereas Whitaker's novelisation would have ended with the dictator being left on Earth to face justice.

Artist Steve Kyte was commissioned to produce a cover and worked up several rough sketches along with a finished piece of artwork. Following Whitaker's death, the book eventually saw the light of day written by Ian Marter, with a cover by Bill Donohoe, published by Target in 1981.

This was originally a six-part serial, transmitted by the BBC between December 1967 and January 1968.

In essence, the serial was distinct in that it enabled the actor playing Doctor Who to play, for the first time, an additional role: that of the principal villain, the evil genius Salamander.

While this occasioned something of a tour de force *from the actor (Patrick Troughton) and allowed the producer (Innes Lloyd) to demonstrate his great abilities, what is visually surprising and effective does not always lend itself to the purely narrative form.*

As a result, I have allowed myself a free hand; keeping to the basic thrust of the story, dropping some of the sub-plots and less essential characters and planning an adventure which can be gripping and entertaining to the end of its 39,000 words.

TOP: Author David Whitaker. BOTTOM: One of Steve Kyte's unused sketches for the cover of *Doctor Who and the Enemy of the World*.

With his companion Jamie McCrimmon, Doctor Who returns to Earth

some 50 years later than our time now – the year 2030. The Tardis hides itself in a cave by the sea-shore and the Doctor proposes a pleasant day on the deserted beach before they reconnoitre. Before long, both are pursued by men in a hovercraft, determined to kill them. They are rescued by a girl named Astrid who takes them to Giles Kent, the man she works for. The reason the men tried to destroy the Doctor was because of his resemblance to Ramon Salamander, who the world believes is its saviour, who Giles Kent and Astrid insist is the enemy of the world. Assuming that the Doctor and his companion have returned from a seven-year stint on a space re-fuelling station – explaining their ignorance (which the Doctor doesn't deny) Giles Kent brings them up to date with the changes that have taken place.

The world is now vastly altered. One may travel to the other side of the globe by rocket in an hour. The videophone means one can both see and hear the caller – from whatever distance. Space travel has ferried new mineral wealth from the now accessible planets, Mars, Venus and Saturn. But the control of the world has passed from countries and the United Nations has been superseded by the World Council. Food production and the fight against the natural elements has forced the change. Some years before, extinct volcanoes began to erupt, earthquakes rent the earth, storms lashed and tempests raged. Drought was caused in some areas, vast floods in others. The man who began to isolate and warn about these natural disasters was Ramon Salamander. Encouraged by Giles Kent, Salamander rapidly became a world-wide authority. Then, with his introduction of a sun-store, Salamander provided hope for increased harvests. The world was split into zones, each one commanded by a Controller. Giles Kent was given the Australian Zone but became suspicious of Salamander. Then he was discredited and removed from office. He believes that Salamander has harnessed the natural elements, that he destroys first and then arrives as the saviour. The fortunate emergence of the Doctor, so similar in appearance, means a chance to find out where Salamander's secret base of operations is and destroy it – and he believes the answer can be found in Salamander's small research station at Kanowna.

Much as the Doctor may accept Giles Kent on face value, he prefers proof against Salamander before he moves against him.

Not only are they pitted against a man who is idolised, there is a new and aggressive Security Force headed by a clever and intelligent chief, Donald Bruce and his ruthless assistant, Benik.

In parallel, Salamander continues his secret ambition to conquer the world: warning each Zone of disaster, using threats to force into control men both loyal or subservient to him, disrupting and saving in turn, making himself indispensable while, from a secret atomic underground shelter beneath his research station, he has incarcerated a group of scientists who carry out his orders and unleash the natural forces of the world – in the belief that an atomic war is raging on the surface. To these people, Salamander is a hero who ventures into a radiation-filled atmosphere to get them their food and supplies.

Gradually the Doctor gets closer until at last he and Giles Kent penetrate Salamander's private records room, the Doctor to secure the evidence he needs, Giles Kent to find the location of Salamander's secret base of operations.

At this moment of success, the Doctor faces a different Giles Kent, a man who was once Salamander's ally in all the worst that he did and now determined merely to supplant him and take over.

The Doctor is ready for this new threat and when Kent and Salamander have fought each other and Kent is killed, the Doctor refuses to carry Salamander away in the Tardis. He leaves the enemy of the world to the justice of the people of the world.

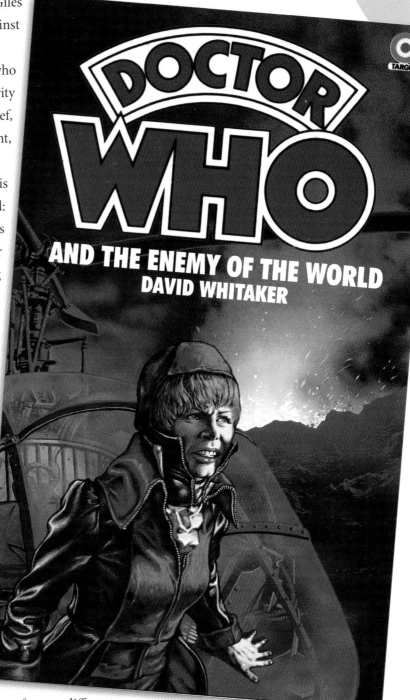

OPPOSITE PAGE: Two unused sketches by Steve Kyte for *Doctor Who and the Enemy of the World*. ABOVE: Steve Kyte completed a cover for *Doctor Who and the Enemy of the World* which was not used. Here is how it could have looked if Whitaker had written the novelisation.

Text © 1979 David Whitaker. Reproduced by kind arrangement with Soutar Accountants Pty Limited on behalf of his Estate.

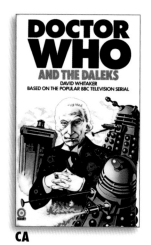

CA

CA

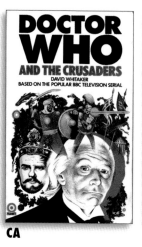

CA

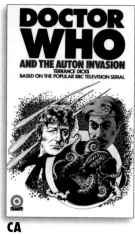

CA

CA

CA

CA

CA

CA

CA

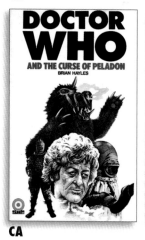

CA

CA

PB

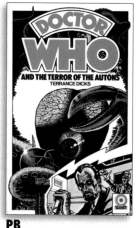

PB

PB

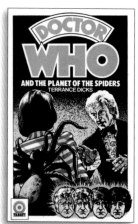

PB

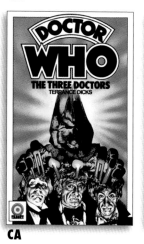

CA

CA

CA

CA

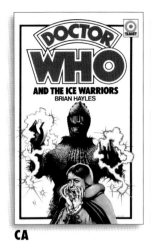

CA

CA

CA

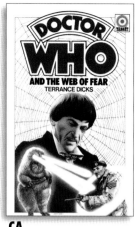

CA

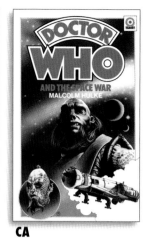

CA

CA

CA

CA

CA

CA

CA

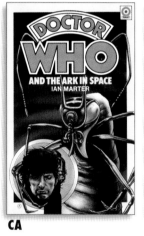

CA

ML

ML

JC

ML

JC

ML

JC

JC

DOCTOR WHO AND THE THREE DOCTORS
TERRANCE DICKS

JC

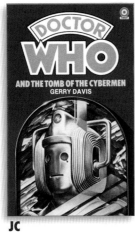
DOCTOR WHO AND THE TOMB OF THE CYBERMEN
GERRY DAVIS

JC

DOCTOR WHO AND THE DINOSAUR INVASION
MALCOLM HULKE

JC

DOCTOR WHO AND THE TIME WARRIOR
TERRANCE DICKS

RK

DOCTOR WHO DEATH TO THE DALEKS
TERRANCE DICKS

RK

DOCTOR WHO AND THE PLANET OF THE SPIDERS
TERRANCE DICKS

AH

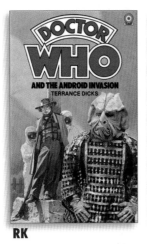
DOCTOR WHO AND THE ANDROID INVASION
TERRANCE DICKS

RK

DOCTOR WHO AND THE SONTARAN EXPERIMENT
IAN MARTER

RK

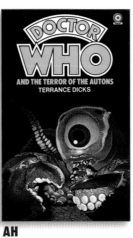
DOCTOR WHO AND THE TERROR OF THE AUTONS
TERRANCE DICKS

AH

DOCTOR WHO AND THE HAND OF FEAR
TERRANCE DICKS

RK

DOCTOR WHO AND THE GREEN DEATH
MALCOLM HULKE

AH

DOCTOR WHO AND THE INVISIBLE ENEMY
TERRANCE DICKS

RK

DOCTOR WHO AND THE SEA-DEVILS
MALCOLM HULKE

JG

DOCTOR WHO AND THE GIANT ROBOT
TERRANCE DICKS

JC

DOCTOR WHO AND THE ROBOTS OF DEATH
TERRANCE DICKS

JG

DOCTOR WHO AND THE CLAWS OF AXOS
TERRANCE DICKS

JG

DOCTOR WHO AND THE IMAGE OF THE FENDAHL
TERRANCE DICKS

JG

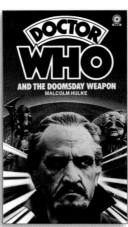
DOCTOR WHO AND THE DOOMSDAY WEAPON
MALCOLM HULKE

JC

DOCTOR WHO AND THE WAR GAMES
MALCOLM HULKE

JG

DOCTOR WHO AND THE DESTINY OF THE DALEKS
TERRANCE DICKS

AS

DOCTOR WHO AND THE RIBOS OPERATION
IAN MARTER
JG

DOCTOR WHO AND THE DÆMONS
BARRY LETTS
AS

DOCTOR WHO AND THE UNDERWORLD
TERRANCE DICKS
BD

DOCTOR WHO AND THE INVASION OF TIME
TERRANCE DICKS
AS

DOCTOR WHO AND THE STONES OF BLOOD
TERRANCE DICKS
AS

DOCTOR WHO AND THE ANDROIDS OF TARA
TERRANCE DICKS
AS

DOCTOR WHO AND THE POWER OF KROLL
TERRANCE DICKS
AS

DOCTOR WHO AND THE ARMAGEDDON FACTOR
TERRANCE DICKS
BD

DOCTOR WHO AND THE KEYS OF MARINUS
PHILIP HINCHCLIFFE
DMA

DOCTOR WHO AND THE NIGHTMARE OF EDEN
TERRANCE DICKS
AS

DOCTOR WHO AND THE HORNS OF NIMON
TERRANCE DICKS
SK

DOCTOR WHO AND THE MONSTER OF PELADON
TERRANCE DICKS
SK

DOCTOR WHO AND THE CYBERMEN
GERRY DAVIS
BD

DOCTOR WHO AND THE CREATURE FROM THE PIT
DAVID FISHER
SK

DOCTOR WHO AND THE ENEMY OF THE WORLD
IAN MARTER
BD

DOCTOR WHO AND AN UNEARTHLY CHILD
TERRANCE DICKS
First publication of the very first Doctor Who story
AS

DOCTOR WHO AND THE CRUSADERS
DAVID WHITAKER
AS

DOCTOR WHO AND THE AXTON INVASION
TERRANCE DICKS
AS

DOCTOR WHO AND THE DAY OF THE DALEKS
TERRANCE DICKS
AS

DOCTOR WHO AND THE PYRAMIDS OF MARS
TERRANCE DICKS
AS

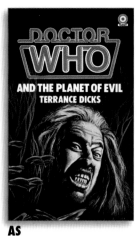
DOCTOR WHO AND THE PLANET OF EVIL
TERRANCE DICKS

AS

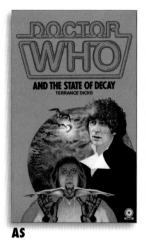
DOCTOR WHO AND THE STATE OF DECAY
TERRANCE DICKS

AS

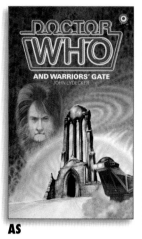
DOCTOR WHO AND WARRIORS' GATE
JOHN LYDECKER

AS

DOCTOR WHO AND THE KEEPER OF TRAKEN
TERRANCE DICKS

AS

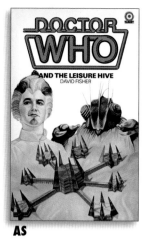
DOCTOR WHO AND THE LEISURE HIVE
DAVID FISHER

AS

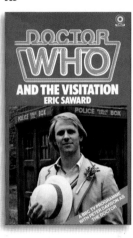
DOCTOR WHO AND THE VISITATION
ERIC SAWARD

AS

DOCTOR WHO FULL CIRCLE
ANDREW SMITH

AS

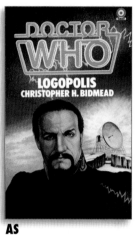
DOCTOR WHO LOGOPOLIS
CHRISTOPHER H. BIDMEAD

AS

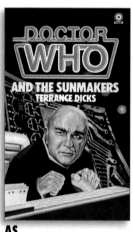
DOCTOR WHO AND THE SUNMAKERS
TERRANCE DICKS

AS

DOCTOR WHO AND THE ABOMINABLE SNOWMEN
TERRANCE DICKS

AS

DOCTOR WHO AND THE WEB OF FEAR
TERRANCE DICKS

AS

DOCTOR WHO TIME-FLIGHT
PETER GRIMWADE

DOCTOR WHO MEGLOS
TERRANCE DICKS

AS

DOCTOR WHO CASTROVALVA
CHRISTOPHER H. BIDMEAD

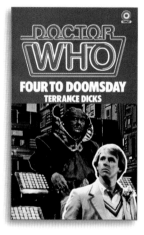
DOCTOR WHO FOUR TO DOOMSDAY
TERRANCE DICKS

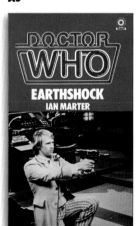
DOCTOR WHO EARTHSHOCK
IAN MARTER

DOCTOR WHO TERMINUS
JOHN LYDECKER

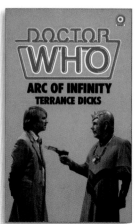
DOCTOR WHO ARC OF INFINITY
TERRANCE DICKS

DOCTOR WHO THE FIVE DOCTORS
TERRANCE DICKS

AS

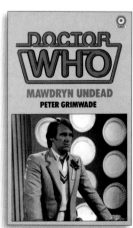
DOCTOR WHO MAWDRYN UNDEAD
PETER GRIMWADE

KINDA
TERRANCE DICKS

SNAKEDANCE
TERRANCE DICKS

AS

ENLIGHTENMENT
BARBARA CLEGG

AS

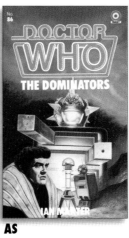

No. 86
THE DOMINATORS
IAN MARTER

AS

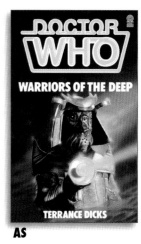

WARRIORS OF THE DEEP
TERRANCE DICKS

AS

THE AZTECS
JOHN LUCAROTTI

NS

No. 89
INFERNO
TERRANCE DICKS

NS

No. 90
THE HIGHLANDERS
GERRY DAVIS

NS

FRONTIOS
CHRISTOPHER H. BIDMEAD

AS

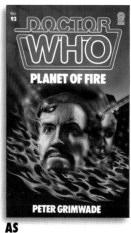

No. 93
PLANET OF FIRE
PETER GRIMWADE

AS

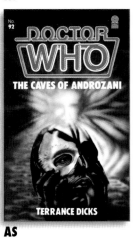

No. 92
THE CAVES OF ANDROZANI
TERRANCE DICKS

AS

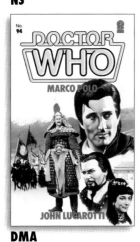

No. 94
MARCO POLO
JOHN LUCAROTTI

DMA

No. 95
THE AWAKENING
ERIC PRINGLE

AS

No. 96
THE MIND OF EVIL
TERRANCE DICKS

AS

THE MYTH MAKERS
DONALD COTTON

AS

No. 98
THE INVASION
IAN MARTER

AS

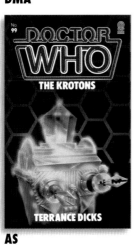

No. 99
THE KROTONS
TERRANCE DICKS

AS

THE 100TH DOCTOR WHO NOVEL!
INTRODUCTION BY JOHN NATHAN-TURNER
THE TWO DOCTORS
FIRST EDITION
ROBERT HOLMES

AS

No. 101
THE GUNFIGHTERS
DONALD COTTON

AS

No. 102
THE TIME MONSTER
TERRANCE DICKS

AS

No. 103
DOCTOR WHO
THE TWIN DILEMMA
ERIC SAWARD

AS

No. 104
DOCTOR WHO
GALAXY FOUR
WILLIAM EMMS

AS

No. 105
DOCTOR WHO
TIMELASH
GLEN McCOY

DMA

No. 107
DOCTOR WHO
THE MARK OF THE RANI
PIP AND JANE BAKER

AS

No. 108
DOCTOR WHO
THE KING'S DEMONS
TERENCE DUDLEY

DMA

No. 109
DOCTOR WHO
THE SAVAGES
IAN STUART BLACK

DMA

No. 110
DOCTOR WHO
FURY FROM THE DEEP
A CLASSIC ADVENTURE OF THE SECOND DOCTOR
NOW A BUMPER VOLUME!
VICTOR PEMBERTON

DMA

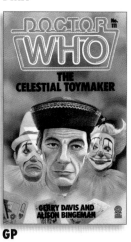
No. 111
DOCTOR WHO
THE CELESTIAL TOYMAKER
GERRY DAVIS AND ALISON BINGEMAN

GP

No. 112
DOCTOR WHO
THE SEEDS OF DEATH
TERRANCE DICKS

TM

No. 113
DOCTOR WHO
BLACK ORCHID
TERENCE DUDLEY

TM

No. 114
DOCTOR WHO
THE ARK
PAUL ERICKSON

DMA

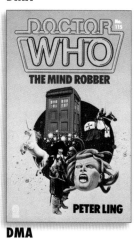
No. 115
DOCTOR WHO
THE MIND ROBBER
PETER LING

DMA

No. 116
DOCTOR WHO
THE FACELESS ONES
TERRANCE DICKS

TM

No. 117
DOCTOR WHO
THE SPACE MUSEUM
GLYN JONES

DMA

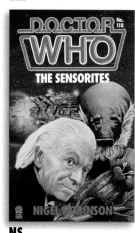
No. 118
DOCTOR WHO
THE SENSORITES
NIGEL ROBINSON

NS

No. 119
DOCTOR WHO
THE REIGN OF TERROR
IAN MARTER

TM

No. 120
DOCTOR WHO
THE ROMANS
DONALD COTTON

TM

No. 121
DOCTOR WHO
THE AMBASSADORS OF DEATH
TERRANCE DICKS

TM

No. 122
DOCTOR WHO
THE MASSACRE
JOHN LUCAROTTI

TM

No. 123
DOCTOR WHO
THE MACRA TERROR
IAN STUART BLACK

TM

DOCTOR WHO No. 124
THE RESCUE
IAN MARTER
TC

DOCTOR WHO No. 125
TERROR OF THE VERVOIDS
PIP AND JANE BAKER
THE TRIAL OF A TIME LORD
TM

DOCTOR WHO No. 126
THE TIME MEDDLER
NIGEL ROBINSON
JC

DOCTOR WHO No. 127
THE MYSTERIOUS PLANET
TERRANCE DICKS
THE TRIAL OF A TIME LORD
TM

DOCTOR WHO No. 127
TIME AND THE RANI
The first adventure of the seventh Doctor!
PIP AND JANE BAKER
FIRST EDITION
TM

DOCTOR WHO No. 132
THE EDGE OF DESTRUCTION
NIGEL ROBINSON
AP

DOCTOR WHO No. 106
VENGEANCE ON VAROS
PHILIP MARTIN
DMA

DOCTOR WHO
THE UNDERWATER MENACE
NIGEL ROBINSON
No. 129
AP

DOCTOR WHO No. 130
THE WHEEL IN SPACE
TERRANCE DICKS
IB

DOCTOR WHO No. 131
THE ULTIMATE FOE
PIP AND JANE BAKER
THE TRIAL OF A TIME LORD
AP

DOCTOR WHO No. 133
THE SMUGGLERS
TERRANCE DICKS
AP

DOCTOR WHO No. 134
PARADISE TOWERS
STEPHEN WYATT
AP

DOCTOR WHO No. 135
DELTA AND THE BANNERMEN
MALCOLM KOHLL
AP

DOCTOR WHO No. 136
THE WAR MACHINES
IAN STUART BLACK
AP & GW

DOCTOR WHO No. 137
DRAGONFIRE
IAN BRIGGS
AP

DOCTOR WHO No. 138
ATTACK OF THE CYBERMEN
ERIC SAWARD
CH

DOCTOR WHO No. 139
MINDWARP
THE TRIAL OF A TIME LORD
PHILIP MARTIN
AP

DOCTOR WHO No. 140
THE CHASE
JOHN PEEL
AP

DOCTOR WHO No. 141
MISSION TO THE UNKNOWN
THE DALEKS' MASTER PLAN PART I
JOHN PEEL
AP

DOCTOR WHO No. 142
THE MUTATION OF TIME
THE DALEKS' MASTER PLAN PART II
JOHN PEEL
AP

DOCTOR WHO No. 143
SILVER NEMESIS
JOHN CLARKE
AP

DOCTOR WHO No. 144
THE GREATEST SHOW IN THE GALAXY
STEPHEN WYATT
AP

DOCTOR WHO No. 145
PLANET OF GIANTS
TERRANCE DICKS
AP

DOCTOR WHO
THE WAR GAMES
based on a DOCTOR WHO adventure first broadcast in 1969
MALCOLM HULKE
AP

DOCTOR WHO
AN UNEARTHLY CHILD
the very first DOCTOR WHO adventure
TERRANCE DICKS
AP

DOCTOR WHO No. 146
THE HAPPINESS PATROL
GRAEME CURRY
AP

DOCTOR WHO No. 147
THE SPACE PIRATES
TERRANCE DICKS
TC

DOCTOR WHO No. 148
REMEMBRANCE OF THE DALEKS
BEN ARONOVITCH
AP

DOCTOR WHO
THE DALEK INVASION OF EARTH
based on a DOCTOR WHO adventure first broadcast in 1964
TERRANCE DICKS
AP

DOCTOR WHO
THE MIND ROBBER
based on a DOCTOR WHO adventure first broadcast in 1968
PETER LING
AP

DOCTOR WHO No. 149
GHOST LIGHT
MARC PLATT
AP

DOCTOR WHO No. 150
SURVIVAL
RONA MUNRO
AP

DOCTOR WHO No. 151
THE CURSE OF FENRIC
IAN BRIGGS
AP

DOCTOR WHO
THE WEB PLANET
based on a DOCTOR WHO adventure first broadcast in 1965
BILL STRUTTON
AP

DOCTOR WHO
THE BRAIN OF MORBIUS
based on a DOCTOR WHO adventure first broadcast in 1976
TERRANCE DICKS
AP

DOCTOR WHO
THE FIVE DOCTORS
based on a DOCTOR WHO adventure first broadcast in 1983
TERRANCE DICKS
AP

DOCTOR WHO
THE DOMINATORS
based on a DOCTOR WHO adventure first broadcast in 1968
IAN MARTER
AP

DOCTOR WHO
THE AUTON INVASION
based on a DOCTOR WHO adventure first broadcast in 1970
TERRANCE DICKS
AP

DOCTOR WHO
THE AMBASSADORS OF DEATH
based on a DOCTOR WHO adventure first broadcast in 1970
TERRANCE DICKS
AP

DOCTOR WHO
THE DAY OF THE DALEKS
based on a DOCTOR WHO adventure first broadcast in 1972
TERRANCE DICKS
AP

DOCTOR WHO

ROBOT
based on a Doctor Who adventure first broadcast in 1974
TERRANCE DICKS
AP

THE CAVES OF ANDROZANI
based on a Doctor Who adventure first broadcast in 1984
TERRANCE DICKS
AS

THE TIME MEDDLER
based on a Doctor Who adventure first broadcast in 1965
NOW BACK ON TELEVISION
NIGEL ROBINSON
JC

THE CURSE OF PELADON
based on a Doctor Who adventure first broadcast in 1972
BRIAN HAYLES
AP

THE MONSTER OF PELADON
based on a Doctor Who adventure first broadcast in 1974
TERRANCE DICKS
AP

PLANET OF THE DALEKS
based on a Doctor Who adventure first broadcast in 1973
TERRANCE DICKS
AP

DESTINY OF THE DALEKS
based on a Doctor Who adventure first broadcast in 1979
TERRANCE DICKS
AP

THE SILURIANS
based on a Doctor Who adventure first broadcast in 1974
MALCOLM HULKE
AP

WARRIORS OF THE DEEP
based on a Doctor Who adventure first broadcast in 1984
TERRANCE DICKS
AP

THE AZTECS
based on a Doctor Who adventure first broadcast in 1964
JOHN LUCAROTTI
AS

THE TOMB OF THE CYBERMEN
based on a Doctor Who adventure first broadcast in 1967
AP

THE MASSACRE
based on a Doctor Who adventure first broadcast in 1966
JOHN LUCAROTTI
AP

ATTACK OF THE CYBERMEN
based on a Doctor Who adventure first broadcast in 1985
ERIC SAWARD
AP

THE SAVAGES
based on a Doctor Who adventure first broadcast in 1966
IAN STUART BLACK
AP

THE CELESTIAL TOYMAKER
based on a Doctor Who adventure first broadcast in 1966
GERRY DAVIS AND ALISON BINGEMAN
AP

THE ARK
based on a Doctor Who adventure first broadcast in 1966
PAUL ERICKSON
AP

THE TWIN DILEMMA
based on a Doctor Who adventure first broadcast in 1984
ERIC SAWARD
AS

VENGEANCE ON VAROS
based on a Doctor Who adventure first broadcast in 1985
PHILIP MARTIN
AP

THE TENTH PLANET
based on a Doctor Who adventure first broadcast in 1966
GERRY DAVIS
AP

TERROR OF THE ZYGONS
based on a Doctor Who adventure first broadcast in 1975
TERRANCE DICKS
AP

PYRAMIDS OF MARS
based on a Doctor Who adventure first broadcast in 1975

TERRANCE DICKS

AP

THE FACE OF EVIL
based on a Doctor Who adventure first broadcast in 1977

TERRANCE DICKS

AP

MEGLOS
based on a Doctor Who adventure first broadcast in 1980

TERRANCE DICKS

AP

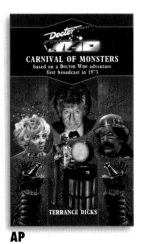

CARNIVAL OF MONSTERS
based on a Doctor Who adventure first broadcast in 1973

TERRANCE DICKS

AP

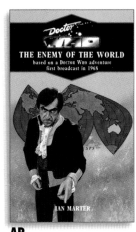

THE ENEMY OF THE WORLD
based on a Doctor Who adventure first broadcast in 1968

IAN MARTER

AP

THE TIME WARRIOR
based on a Doctor Who adventure first broadcast in 1974

TERRANCE DICKS

AP

THE KEEPER OF TRAKEN
Based on a Doctor Who adventure first broadcast in 1981

TERRANCE DICKS

AP

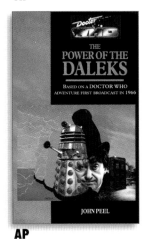

THE
POWER OF THE DALEKS
BASED ON A DOCTOR WHO ADVENTURE FIRST BROADCAST IN 1966

JOHN PEEL

AP

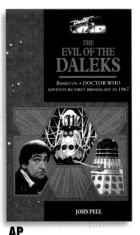

THE
EVIL OF THE DALEKS
BASED ON A DOCTOR WHO ADVENTURE FIRST BROADCAST IN 1967

JOHN PEEL

AP

THE INVASION
based on a Doctor Who adventure first broadcast in 1968

IAN MARTER

AP

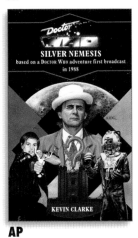

SILVER NEMESIS
based on a Doctor Who adventure first broadcast in 1988

KEVIN CLARKE

AP

THE DAEMONS
based on a Doctor Who adventure first broadcast in 1971

BARRY LETTS

AP

THE LEISURE HIVE
Based on a Doctor Who adventure first broadcast in 1980

DAVID FISHER

AP

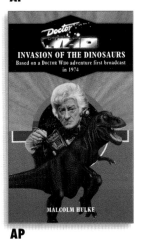

INVASION OF THE DINOSAURS
Based on a Doctor Who adventure first broadcast in 1974

MALCOLM HULKE

AP

THE WEB OF FEAR
Based on a Doctor Who adventure first broadcast in 1968

TERRANCE DICKS

AP

THE ROBOTS OF DEATH
based on a Doctor Who adventure first broadcast in 1977

TERRANCE DICKS

AP

THE TALONS OF WENG-CHIANG
based on a Doctor Who adventure first broadcast in 1977

TERRANCE DICKS

AP

ARTIST KEY:

AH	Alun Hood	JC	Jeff Cummins
AP	Alister Pearson	JG	John Geary
AS	Andrew Skilleter	ML	Mike Little
BD	Bill Donohoe	NS	Nick Spender
CA	Chris Achilleos	PB	Peter Brookes
CH	Colin Howard	RK	Roy Knipe
DMA	David McAllister	SK	Steve Kyte
GW	Graeme Way	TC	Tony Clark
GP	Graham Potts	TM	Tony Masero
IB	Ian Burgess		

INDEX

Numbers in bold indicate appearance in sidebars and captions. Titles in italics refer to tv and radio serials; all other titles are books.

100,000 BC 69, 76
Aaronovitch, Ben **109, 126-127,** 127, 128, **129,** 148, 150
Abramson, Arnold **22,** 33, 34
Abramson, Peter 34
Abramson, Robert 33, 34
Achilleos, Chris **20-21,** 20-23, **22,** 28, 29, **29,** 32, **36, 37,** 38, 46, 50, 51-52, 53, 55-56, **56,** 112, 140
Adams, Douglas 42 (no, really), 108, **108,** 115, **148, 149,** 150
Adventures of Doctor Who, The **137**
Adventures of K-9 and Other Mechanical Creatures, The 50, 54, **54,** 141
Ainscough, Frank 140, 141
Ainsworth, John 128
Airey, Jean 142
Allan Wingate 13, 34, 37
Allen, Darren 133
Ambassadors of Death, The **16,** 20
Android Invasion, The **33**
Androids of Tara, The **68**
Ark, The **82, 101**
Attack of the Cybermen **69**
Attwood, Tony **90-91,** 94, 96, 138
Awakening, The **84**
Bailey, Mike 116, 118
Baker, Bob **129**
Baker, Colin 89, 90, **91, 136**
Baker, Pip and Jane **21, 95,** 97, 109, 110
Baker, Tom 43, **44, 58, 136**
Banks, David 99
Banks Stewart, Robert **73**
Barnes, Sara 94, 108, 120
Battlefield **113**
BBC 18, 20, 21, 23, 29, 48, 50, 56, 59, 64, 66, 73, 77, 79, 84, 88-89, 93, 94, 105, 106, 115, 122, 123, 125, 129, 130
Beevers, Geoffrey **136**
Bellamy, Frank 22

Bennett, Francis 57
Bennett, Gail 143
Benoy, Mark 86, 87
Bentham, Jeremy 105, **150**
Bentham, Mark **150**
Beynon, Alison 96
Bidmead, Christopher H **21, 69, 72-73,** 73, **74,** 77, 79, 85, 87, 115, **121**
Bingeman, Alison (pseudonym for Alison Beynon) **21,** 96, 97
Black, Ian Stuart **21,** 97, 106, 119
Blythe, Daniel 85
Boa, Stephen P 72, 74, 75
Bok, John 75
Borland, Martin 52
Boyle, Brian 14, 16, **20,** 21, 25, 28, 51
Bray, Leslie 87
Bresman, Ian 91
Brett, Mike 53, **60,** 65, 93, 98-99, **98,** 101, 102, 111, 112, 113, **114,** 119, 123
Briggs, Ian **117,** 119, **123,** 125, 127, 128, 129
Briggs, Nicholas 128
Brookes, Peter **27,** 28-29, **29,** 32, **32, 33,** 34, **36,** 53
Bull, Howard 78
Burdon, Mattie 61, 94
Burgess, Ian 110, 111, **116**
Byrne, Tim 108, 120
Capstick, Chris 111
Cartmel, Andrew **123, 124,** 127, **127, 132, 133**
Charles, Alec 78
Chase, The 108, 115, **118**
Christmas, Matthew 86
City of Death, The **68,** 108, 115
Clark, Anthony 132
Clark, Tony **36,** 110-111, **113,** 125-126, **125**
Clarke, Kevin 119, **121,** 122, **124**
Claws of Axos, The 20
Clegg, Barbara **82,** 85, 86
Colony in Space **18,** 20, 30

Companions of Doctor Who, The **60, 90,** 93-94, 96, 138-139
Cooke, Matthew 132
Cornell, Paul **109**
Cotton, Donald **21, 45, 83, 88,** 90, 95, 97, 98, 105, 106, 107
Creature from the Pit, The **68**
Crusade, The **16**
Cummins, Jeff **36, 37, 45,** 46-47, 52-53, 110, 140, 141
Cusick, Ray 106
Curse of the Daleks, The **16**
Curry, Graeme **121,** 125, **132**
Dæmons, The 21, **32**
Daleks' Master Plan, The 108, 111, 115, 119, 120
Daly, Wally K 115, **115,** 139
Darvill-Evans, Peter **109,** 116-118, **116,** 120, 122, 124-125, 126, 127, 129-130, 133, 134, 138
Davis, Gerry **21,** 30, 38, **38-39,** 39, **43,** 47, 49, 50, 85, **88,** 94, 96, 97, **121**
Davison, Peter 74, **136**
Day, Martin 86-87
Devereux, Robert 112, 113, 123, 124
Dicks, Terrance **14-16, 17,** 19-20, 21, **21,** 22, 25-27, **25, 26, 27, 30,** 30, **33,** 37, 38, 39, 40, 42, 43, 44, 45, **45,** 46, 47, 48-49, 50, 51, 54-55, **55,** 58, 63-64, 65, 67-68, **68,** 70-71, **70,** 72, 75, 77, **77,** 78-79, **81,** 83, 84-85, 86, 88, 90, 91, 94, 97, 98, 100, 104, 106, 107, 109, **121,** 125, 129, 131, 136-137, 138, 140, 141, 148, 149, 150
Doctor Who: A Celebration 80, **99**
Doctor Who: The Early Years 105
Doctor Who: The Missing Episodes 73, 115, **119,** 139
Doctor Who: The Missing Episodes – Evil of the Autons 115
Doctor Who: The Missing Episodes – Mission to Magnus 115, 139
Doctor Who: The Missing Episodes – Penacasata 115
Doctor Who: The Missing Episodes – The Nightmare

Fair 115, **119, 121,** 139

Doctor Who: The Missing Episodes – The Ultimate Evil 115, **115,** 139

Doctor Who – Arc of Infinity **71,** 77, 79

Doctor Who – Attack of the Cybermen 119, 120, **125, 136**

Doctor Who – Battlefield **126, 129,** 131, 148, 150

Doctor Who – Black Orchid **71,** 106-107, 108

Doctor Who – Brain Teasers and Mind Benders 142

Doctor Who – Build the TARDIS 143

Doctor Who – Castrovalva 77, 79

Doctor Who – Dalek Omnibus **137**

Doctor Who – Death to the Daleks 44, 47, **49, 71, 103, 131**

Doctor Who – Delta and the Bannermen 117, 119

Doctor Who – Dragonfire **117, 118,** 119, 129

Doctor Who – Earthshock **71,** 77, 78, **79**

Doctor Who – Enlightenment 85, 86-87

Doctor Who – Four to Doomsday 77, 111

Doctor Who – Frontios **71,** 85

Doctor Who – Full Circle 72, 73, 75, **121**

Doctor Who – Fury from the Deep 82, 94-95, 97, 98, **128**

Doctor Who – Galaxy Four **91, 92,** 97

Doctor Who – Ghost Light **123,** 125, 126-127, **126, 127, 129**

Doctor Who – Inferno 30, **71,** 83, 85, 86, 91, 94, 100

Doctor Who – Kinda **71,** 82, 85, 86, **136**

Doctor Who – Logopolis 72, 73, **74,** 75, **121**

Doctor Who – Marco Polo **71,** 90, 91-92, 93

Doctor Who – Mawdryn Undead **83,** 85, 88

Doctor Who – Meglos **71, 73,** 77, 78-79, 108, **131**

Doctor Who – Mindwarp 119

Doctor Who – Mission to the Unknown **71,** 115, **118,** 119, 120

Doctor Who – Paradise Towers **71,** 109, **117**

Doctor Who – Planet of Fire 90, 91, **121**

Doctor Who – Planet of Giants **123,** 125, 129

Doctor Who – Remembrance of the Daleks 125, **126,** 127, 150

Doctor Who – Silver Nemesis 119, **120, 121,** 122, **124**

Doctor Who – Slipback **128,** 139

Doctor Who – Snakedance **71,** 82, 85, 86

Doctor Who – Survival 125, 126, **127**

Doctor Who – Terminus **37,** 77-78, 79, 86

Doctor Who – Travel Without the TARDIS 142

Doctor Who – Terror of the Vervoids **71,** 109, 110

Doctor Who – The Ambassadors of Death 102, 106, 107, 108, 148

Doctor Who – The Ark **71, 101,** 106, 107, **121**

Doctor Who – The Awakening 84, 90, 92, **121**

Doctor Who – The Aztecs 83, 85, 87-88, 100

Doctor Who – The Caves of Androzani **71,** 77, 86, 90, 91

Doctor Who – The Celestial Toymaker **71,** 96, 97, **99,** 100

Doctor Who – The Chase **71,** 115, **118,** 119, **119,** 120

Doctor Who – The Curse of Fenric **71,** 125, 127, 128

Doctor Who – The Dominators **71,** 83, 85, 87, **121, 137**

Doctor Who – The Edge of Destruction **71,** 104, 109, 129, 149

Doctor Who – The Evil of the Daleks 115, **118,** 131, 132, 133, 149

Doctor Who – The Faceless Ones **26, 71,** 106

Doctor Who – The Five Doctors 70, **71,** 76-77, 79, **121**

Doctor Who – The Ghosts of N-Space **33**

Doctor Who – The Greatest Show in the Galaxy 119, 122

Doctor Who – The Gunfighters **88,** 97-98, **137**

Doctor Who – The Happiness Patrol **121, 124,** 125, 126, **132**

Doctor Who – The Highlanders 85, 100

Doctor Who – The Invasion 90, 91, 150, **150**

Doctor Who – The Key to Time **54,** 88, 111, **114,** 119, **150**

Doctor Who – The King's Demons **93,** 97, 98, 107

Doctor Who – The Krotons **71, 88,** 90, 91, **137**

Doctor Who – The Macra Terror **71,** 102, 106

Doctor Who – The Mark of the Rani **54, 71,** 90, **93,** 97, 98, 99

Doctor Who – The Massacre **71,** 106,

Doctor Who – The Mind of Evil **71,** 90, 91, **137, 150**

Doctor Who – The Mind Robber **71,** 96, **105,** 106, 107, **121,** 131

Doctor Who – The Missing Adventures 93, **118,** 133

Doctor Who – The Missing Adventures – Evolution 118

Doctor Who – The Mutation of Time **71,** 115, **118,** 119, 120

Doctor Who – The Mysterious Planet **71, 81,** 109, 110

Doctor Who – The Myth Makers **71,** 83, **88,** 90, 92, 93, 98, **137**

Doctor Who – The New Adventures **118,** 122, 125, 130, 133

Doctor Who – The New Adventures – Timewyrm: Genesys **118**

Doctor Who – The Paradise of Death **33, 132,** 133

Doctor Who – The Pescatons **71,** 115, 131

Doctor Who – The Power of the Daleks 115, **118,** 131-132, 133, **134,** 149

Doctor Who – The Programme Guide 143

Doctor Who – The Reign of Terror **71, 100, 101,** 106

Doctor Who – The Rescue **83,** 109, 110, 111, **113**

Doctor Who – The Romans **88,** 95, **101,** 102, 106, 107-108

Doctor Who – The Savages 97, 106

Doctor Who – The Seeds of Death **71,** 97, 102

Doctor Who – The Sensorites **71,** 100, 104, 106, 107

Doctor Who – The Smugglers **71,** 109, 110

Doctor Who – The Space Museum **71, 105,** 106

Doctor Who – The Space Pirates **25, 71,** 113, 125, **125,** 126, 128-129

Doctor Who – The Terrestrial Index 143

Doctor Who – The Three Doctors 29, **29,** 30, **34,** 53, **71, 121, 131, 136**

Doctor Who – The Time Meddler **47, 71,** 110, **111**

Doctor Who – The Time Monster **71,** 97, 98, 109, **137**

Doctor Who – The Twin Dilemma 89-90, **91,** 97

Doctor Who – The Two Doctors 82, **89,** 90, 92-93

Doctor Who – The Ultimate Foe 109

Doctor Who – The Underwater Menace 109, 112, **114**

Doctor Who – The War Machines 119

Doctor Who – The Wheel in Space **71,** 109, 110

Doctor Who – Time and the Rani **71, 98,** 109, 111, **111**

Doctor Who – Time-Flight **37,** 77-78, 79-80

Doctor Who – Timelash **94,** 97

Doctor Who – Vengeance on Varos **71,** 80, 109, 110, 111, **121, 136**

Doctor Who – Warriors of the Deep **71,** 85-86, **136**

Doctor Who and an Unearthly Child **17,** 68, 69, 70, 71, 72, 76, 131, **131**

Doctor Who and the Abominable Snowmen 30, 32, **71, 131**

Doctor Who and the Android Invasion 44, **71, 131**

Doctor Who and the Androids of Tara **61,** 64

Doctor Who and the Ark in Space 32, 43, 44, **44,** 51, **71**

Doctor Who and the Armageddon Factor 64, 66

Doctor Who and the Auton Invasion **18,** 19, 20, 25, 26-27, 53, **71,** 86, 129, **131**

Doctor Who and the Brain of Morbius 44, 46, **71,** 72, **131, 136**

Doctor Who and the Carnival of Monsters 44-45, **71, 136**

Doctor Who and the Cave Monsters **18,** 20, 22, 25, 26-27, **71, 131, 136**

Doctor Who and the Claws of Axos 44, 50, **71, 137**

Doctor Who and the Creature from the Pit **65,** 68, **68,** 71

Doctor Who and the Crusaders 23, 24, 103, **131, 136, 137**

Doctor Who and the Curse of Peladon 30, 32, **37, 61, 67, 71, 121, 136**

Doctor Who and the Cybermen **18,** 30, **61, 103, 121, 131**

Doctor Who and the Dæmons 20, 30, **59, 71,** 72, **131, 137,** 148

Doctor Who and the Dalek Invasion of Earth 44, 46, **71, 121,** 131, **131, 137**

Doctor Who and the Daleks 23-24, **71,** 103, **131, 136**

Doctor Who and the Day of the Daleks 20, 21, 30, 46, **71, 131, 137**

Doctor Who and the Deadly Assassin 44, 46, **44, 52, 71, 131, 137**

Doctor Who and the Destiny of the Daleks 54, **54,** 71, **71,** 111, **131**

Doctor Who and the Dinosaur Invasion **18,** 38, **71, 131, 136**

Doctor Who and the Doomsday Weapon **18,** 20, **21,** 30, **71, 131, 136**

Doctor Who and the Enemy of the World 62, 64, 65, **67,** 68, 71, 83, 149, 151-153, **151, 153**

Doctor Who and the Face of Evil 44, **71, 131, 137**

Doctor Who and the Genesis of the Daleks 38, 39, **71, 131, 137**

Doctor Who and the Giant Robot **18,** 28, **29,** 30, 32, 53, **131, 136**

Doctor Who and the Green Death **26,** 28, **29,** 30, **32,** 53, **71**

Doctor Who and the Hand of Fear 54, **71**

Doctor Who and the Horns of Nimon 64, **64,** 72, 87

Doctor Who and the Horror of Fang Rock 44, 50, **71, 135**

Doctor Who and the Ice Warriors 38, **71**

Doctor Who and the Image of the Fendahl 54, 112

Doctor Who and the Invasion of Time 64, **71,** 86

Doctor Who and the Invisible Enemy 54, **55, 71**

Doctor Who and the Keeper of Traken **71,** 72

Doctor Who and the Keys of Marinus 64, 65, 66, 67, **71,** 149

Doctor Who and the Leisure Hive **68, 71,** 72, 74-75

Doctor Who and the Loch Ness Monster **18,** 38, **71, 131, 136, 137**

Doctor Who and the Masque of Mandragora 44, **53, 71, 131**

Doctor Who and the Monster of Peladon 64, **71**

Doctor Who and the Mutants 40, **43,** 44, 50, 52, **71**

Doctor Who and the Nightmare of Eden 64, **71**

Doctor Who and the Pescatons **100,** 115, 131

Doctor Who and the Planet of Evil 44, 46

Doctor Who and the Planet of the Daleks 38, **71, 131, 136, 137**

Doctor Who and the Planet of the Spiders 28, 29, **29,** 30, **34,** 37, 53, **71**

Doctor Who and the Power of Kroll 64, 66, **71**

Doctor Who and the Pyramids of Mars 38, 39, **121**

Doctor Who and the Revenge of the Cybermen 38, 39, **71, 131, 137**

Doctor Who and the Ribos Operation 54

Doctor Who and the Robots of Death 54, 55, **71, 131, 137**

Doctor Who and the Sea-Devils 20, 30, **31,** 53, **71, 131, 135**

Doctor Who and the Seeds of Doom 44, 45, **71, 131, 137**

Doctor Who and the Silurians **18,** 20

Doctor Who and the Sontaran Experiment 43, 44, 47, **71**

Doctor Who and the Space War **18,** 38, 39, 50, **71, 136, 137**

Doctor Who and the State of Decay 68, **71,** 72, **136**

Doctor Who and the Stones of Blood 64, **71**

Doctor Who and the Sunmakers **71,** 73, 75, **137**

Doctor Who and the Talons of Weng-Chiang 44, 46, 52, **71, 131,** 134

Doctor Who and the Tenth Planet 29, **29,** 38, 49, **133**

Doctor Who and the Terror of the Autons 28, **29,** 30, 32, **33, 71**

Doctor Who and the Time Warrior 44, 47, 50, **71, 89,** 148-149

Doctor Who and the Tomb of the Cybermen 43, 44, 47-48, **47,** 50, 52, **71, 71**

Doctor Who and the Underworld 64, **71**

Doctor Who and the Visitation **60,** 72, 74, 75, 88, 149, **149**

Doctor Who and the War Games 54, 55, **71,** 130

Doctor Who and Warriors' Gate **60,** 74, 149-150

Doctor Who and the Zarbi 23, 24, **71,** 103, **131, 136**

Doctor Who Classics **137**

Doctor Who Cookbook, The **99,** 143

Doctor Who Crossword Book, The 77, **83**

Doctor Who Dinosaur Book, The 140, 142

Doctor Who Discovers ... **37, 47,** 50, 53, 140, 141

Doctor Who Discovers Early Man 140

Doctor Who Discovers Prehistoric Animals **47,** 140

Doctor Who Discovers Space Travel 47

Doctor Who Discovers Strange and Mysterious Creatures **47, 141**

Doctor Who Discovers the Conquerors 141

Doctor Who File, The **98**

Doctor Who Fun Book, The 143

Doctor Who Gift Set **61, 99**

Doctor Who Illustrated A-Z, The 143

Doctor Who Meets Scratchman 44

Doctor Who Monster Book, The 37, 55, **55, 107,** 140

Doctor Who Omnibus, The **137**

Doctor Who Pattern Book, The 143

Doctor Who Programme Guide, The (see also Doctor Who – The Programme Guide) **37, 61,** 77, 141-142

Doctor Who Programme Guide, The: Volume 1 – The Programmes (see also Doctor Who – The Programme Guide) 141

Doctor Who Programme Guide, The: Volume 2 – What's What and Who's Who (see also Doctor Who – The Terrestrial Index) 142

Doctor Who Quiz Book, The 81, **83,** 142

Doctor Who Technical Manual, The 143

Don, Ian (pseudonym for Ian Marter) **44, 45,** 103

Donaldson, Stuart 74

Donohoe, Bill **36, 37, 45, 61, 62,** 64, 67, **103,** 141, 142, 151

Donougher, Christine 58, 63, 64, 69, 76, 81, 82, 83, 94, 105, 120, **150**

Downie, Gary **99,** 143

Dudgeon, Piers 34

Dudley, Terence **21, 39, 93,** 94, 97, 106, 107, **121,** 138, 139

Duncan, Michael 98

Dunk, Chris 47-48

Earthshock **69**

Edmond, Carola **22,** 36

Edwards, Peter 51, 138

Ellis, David **26**

Emms, William **91,** 97

Englander, M R 92

Englefield, Andrew 107

Erickson, Paul 82, **101,** 106, **121**

Enemy of the World, The **16, 17,** 32

Evil of the Autons – see Doctor Who: The Missing Episodes – Evil of the Autons

Evil of the Daleks, The **16,** 108, 115, **118**

Faceless Ones, The **26**

Fielding, Janet 88, 94

Fields, Ralph 33, 57, 61, 62, 94, 112

Fisher, David 68, **68,** 72, 87

Fisher, Margery 26

Five Doctors, The **20**

Flint, Robert 86

Fox, Chelsey 116

Fox, Henry 23

Franks, Robert 78

Frederick Muller 17, **17,** 19, **19,** 23

Frontier in Space **18,** 38

Full Circle **72**

Further Adventures of Doctor Who, The **137**

Fury from the Deep **100**

Gaze, John 127

Gallagher, Stephen **37, 60, 66-67,** 70, 72, 77, 78, 149-150

Gallifrey Chronicles, The **118**

Galaxy 4 **91**

Gammon, Joy 143

Gardner, Brenda 39, 41-42, 49, 50-51, 56-58, 59, 100

Garrard, Ian 129

Gatiss, Mark **109**

Gearing, Brian 77

Geary, John **36, 52,** 53

Ghosts of N-Space, The **33**

Gibbs, Anthony 13, 14

Gibbs, David 131

Glover, Michael 27-28, 37

Godfray, Elizabeth 25, **25,** 28, 37-38, 39, 48

Greatest Show in the Galaxy, The **112, 113**

Green, Gillian 107, 108

Green Death, The **26**

Grimwade, Peter **21,** 77, 78, **80,** 85, 90, 91, 96-97, **97, 121**

Gunfighters, The **88**

Hailstone, Tim 113

Haining, Peter 54, 80, 88, **98, 99,** 102, 111, **114**

Hair, Andrew 110

Haldeman, Laurie 142

Hamlyn, Paul 13

Hancock, Roger 50-51, 115

Hants, Harry 138

Harding, John C 46, 55

Harris, Mark 143

Harrison, Denis 87

Harry Sullivan's War **71,** 94, 139

Hayles, Brian 20, **22,** 30, 32, 38, **40, 121**

Heath, Adrian 142

Henwood, Richard **14,** 15-19, **15,** 16-19, 20, 21, **22,** 23, 24, 25, **25,** 27, 28, 37, 38, 135

Herdsmen of Aquarius, The **88**

Highlanders, The **38**

Hinchcliffe, Philip **21,** 29-30, **34,** 42, 43-44, 45, **46, 53,** 64, 66, 87, **89**

Hinton, Craig 120, 126

Hollowood, Jane 16

Holmes, Robert **21, 27,** 46, 50, 82, **89,** 90, 92, **95,** 115, 148-149

Hood, Alun **36, 52,** 53

Hopkins, Gary 46

Houghton, Don 20

Howard, Colin 119, **125**

Howard and Wyndham 33-36, 112

Howarth, James 120

Howett, Dicky 143

Hulke, Malcolm **14,** 20, 21, **21,** 23, 25-27, **26-27,** 27, 30, **31,** 38, 39, 54, 55, 67, 136, 140, 148

Imps, The **91**

In the Hollows of Time 115

Inferno 20

Inside the Spaceship **16,** 109, 149

Invasion of the Dinosaurs **18,** 38

Invasion of the Ormazoids **111**

Jarvis, Martin **136**

John, Caroline **136**

Jones, Elwyn **39**

Jones, Glyn **105,** 106, 107

Jordan, Tony 107, 108

Junior Doctor Who: Doctor Who and the Brain of Morbius 51, 138

Junior Doctor Who: Doctor Who and the Giant Robot 51, 138

K-9 and Company 94, **121,** 138, 139

Kelly, Peter 139

Key to Time, The – see Doctor Who – The Key to Time

Kinmont, Clare 118

Kitchen, Henry 34

Knipe, Roy **36, 44, 48-49,** 52, 53, **103**

Knott, Julian 107, 122, 126, 127-128

Kohll, Malcolm 119

Krotons, The **89**

Kyte, Steve **36, 62-63,** 64-65, **64, 65,** 67, 149, 151, **151, 153**

Lane, Andrew **109**

Leisure Hive, The **68**

Leonard, Paul **109**

Leopold, Guy (pseudonym for Barry Letts and Robert Sloman) 21

Lessiter, Sandy 38

Letts, Barry **14,** 19, 21, **25, 27,** 30, **32-33,** 43, **46,** 131-132, 133, 148

Levinger, Peter 112

Linford, Peter 122, 131

Ling, Peter **27,** 96, **104-105,** 106, 107, **121**

Little, Mike **36, 49,** 53

Lofficier, Jean-Marc 141, 142, 143

Logan, John 85-86

Lonnan, Gareth 87

Lucarotti, John **21, 84-85,** 85, 87, 90, 92, 106, 107

Lydecker, John – see Gallagher, Stephen

Lydiard, Simon 46

Mahoney, John 74

Make Your Own Adventure with Doctor Who **91, 95, 111**

Making of Doctor Who, The **26, 37,** 140

Manning, John 72

Marks, Louis 21, 46 (footnote)

Marter, Ian **21,** 42, 43, 44, **44, 45,** 46, 47, 49, 54, 64, 68, 77, 78, **79, 83,** 84, 85, 87, 90, 91, 94, **101,** 103, 106, **108,** 109, 110, **121,** 139, 150, 151

Martin, Andrew 75, 122, 131

Martin, Philip **21,** 80, 109, **110-111,** 115, 119, **121,** 139

Marton, Chris 47, 71

Masero, Tony **36, 98-99,** 100-103, **100-102,** 110, 111, **111**

May, Dominic 92, 107

McAllister, David **36, 60,** 64, 65, 74, 100, 110, 138, 139, 149, **149**

McCoy, Glen 84, **94,** 97

McDonald, Graeme 50

McLachlan, Ian K 66, 87, 107, 110

Menzies, John 60

Mercer, Steve 78-79

Messingham, Simon **109**

Miles, Brian 13, 14-15, 16, 17-19, 21, **22,** 24, 33-36, 60, 135

Miller, David 126

Miller, Keith 26-27, 30, 32, 39, 44-45

Mind of Evil, The 20

Mind Robber, The **104**

Missing Episodes, The – *see* Doctor Who: The Missing Episodes

Mission to Magnus **110,** 115

Mission to Magnus – *see* Doctor Who: The Missing Episodes – Mission to Magnus

Mission to the Unknown 108, 115, **118**

Mission to Venus 91

Moonbase, The **18,** 30, **100**

Moore, Paula 120

Morris, Mark 104

Mortimer, Jim **109**

Mould, Russ 75, 77, 79

Mount, Paul 55

Mulkern, Patrick 97

Munro, Rona 125, **132-133**

Munro, Tim 55

Myth-Makers, The **88**

Nathan-Turner, John **33, 54,** 58, 66, 69, **72,** 73-74, 76-77, 83, 84, 93, 94, 105, 106, 111, 116, 118, 122-123, **128,** 149

Nation, Terry 23, **39,** 50, **90,** 108, 115, 118, 141, 149

New Adventures, The – *see* Doctor Who – The New Adventures

Newell, Peter 47

Newman, Fred 140, 141

Nightmare Fair, The 115, **119**

Nightmare Fair, The – *see* Doctor Who: The Missing Episodes – The Nightmare Fair

O'Day, Andrew 91

O'Mara, Kate 90

Owen, David 75

Paradise of Death, The **33,** 132

Paradise Towers **112**

Pearson, Alister **36, 37,** 111-112, **114, 117, 118,** 119, **119, 120, 123, 124,** 125, 126, **126, 127,** 139, 143

Pedler, Kit **39**

Peel, John **21,** 87-88, 115, **118,** 119, **119,** 120, 131, 132, **134,** 149

Pemberton, Victor 95, 97, 98, **100,** 115, 131

Penacasata – *see* Doctor Who: The Missing Episodes – Penacasata

Pertwee, Jon 21, 102, **102, 136**

Picadilly Press 54, 57-58, 100, **113**

Pinacotheca **73,** 115

Pirate Planet, The 108, 115, 150

Platt, Marc **123,** 125, 126, **126, 127, 129,** 131, 150

Potts, Graham **99,** 100, 143

Power of the Daleks, The **16,** 108, 115, **118**

Pringle, Eric **84,** 90, 92, **121**

Quinn, Tim 143

Race Against Time 95

Read, Anthony **68**

Redford, Steven 75

Rescue, The **16**

Resurrection of the Daleks **69,** 108, 115

Revelation of the Daleks **69,** 108, 115

Revenge of the Cybermen **39,** 39

Richardson, David 122

Rigelsford, Adrian 94, 99

Roberts, Gareth **109**

Robinson, Nigel **21, 44,** 81-84, **83,** 90, 93, 94-96, **103,** 103-106, **104,** 107, 108, 109-110, 111, **111,** 112, **114,** 116, **116,** 120, 129, 142, 149, 150

Robot **18,** 30

Rodi, Dom 51-52, 53, **128**

Romans, The **88**

Roxburgh, Gordon 92, 106

Russell, Gary 66, 71, **109**

Russell, William **136**

Sanders, Wendy 115, 122

Saunders, David 58, 113

Saward, Eric **21, 69,** 72, 75, 78, **82,** 84, **95,** 97, 108, 115, 119,120, **128,** 139

Schwartzman, Arnold 23

Scott, Lesley **82, 101**

Second Doctor Who Monster Book, The **37,** 140

Second Doctor Who Quiz Book, The 142

Shada 115, **148**

Sherwin, Derrick 137, 150

Short, Darren 86

Short Trips: The Centenarian **94**

Shreeve, Rob 134

Skilleter, Andrew **36,** 53-54, **54-55,** 58, **59, 61,** 64, 65, 70, **73, 88, 89,** 90, **92,** 93, **93,** 98-100, 141, **150**

Skilleter, Patricia 141

Slipback **69, 128**

Sloman, Robert 21, **26,** 148

Smith, Andrew 72, **72,** 73, 75, **121**

Smith, Cecil **98,** 101, 106

Sontaran Experiment, The **105**

Space Museum, The **105**

Spearhead from Space **18,** 19, 20, 21, 26

Spender, Nick **36, 99,** 100

Spooner, Dennis **88,** 95, **105**

St Clair, Stephanie 149

Stammers, Mark **109**

Standring, Lesley 143

Stokes, Ralph 13, **13,** 14, 15, 16, 21, **22,** 25, 34, 36, 60, 63, 135

Stones of Blood, The **68**

Strickson, Mark 94

Strutton, Bill **19,** 23, 24

Stuart, Lyle 55, 76

Tams, Paul Mark **128-129,** 139

Tandem Publishing Ltd 34

Tanner, Bob 57, 59-64, 68, 69, 73-74, 76, 77, 80, 90, 93, 94, 104, 105, 106, 108

TARDIS Inside Out, The **54**

Tenth Planet, The 49

Terminus **66**

Terror of the Autons 20

Terror of the Zygons **18,** 38

Terry Nation's Dalek Special 50, 54, **54,** 141

Third Doctor Who Quiz Book, The 142

Thompson, Andrew 91

Thurm, Jo 108, 109, 114, 118, 120, 122

Time Travellers' Guide, The **98,** 102

Time Inc 109

Timelash **94**

Tomb of the Cybermen, The **100**

Topping, Keith 98

Torrance, Fanny 39

Tosh, Donald **88**

Trial of a Time Lord, The **95,** 108, 109, **110,** 115, 119

Turlough and the Earthlink Dilemma **90,** 94, 96, 138

Ultimate Adventure, The 131

Ultimate Evil, The 115, **115**

Ultimate Evil, The – *see* Doctor Who: The Missing Episodes – The Ultimate Evil

Ultimate Foe, The 109

Unearthly Child, An 69

Underwood, George 140

Universal-Tandem Publishing Company 13-15, **13,** 24, 27, 32-33, 34, 37, 135

Vanezis, Paul 79

Vengeance on Varos **110**

Victor, Ed 150

Vincent-Rudzki, Jan 38-39, 49, 129

Virgin Publishing 33, 81, **83,** 112-114, **114,** 124, **129,** 131, 134

Visitation, The **69**

W H Allen 33, 34, 36, 37-38, 39, 55-56, 56-57, 61-64, 66, 68, 73, 76, 77, 82-83, 84, 88, 94, 99, 104, 106, 108, 112-114, 115, 123-124, 134

Wales, Gary

Walker, Stephen James 104, **109**

Wallbank, Pete **134**

War Games, The **26**

Ware, Peter 98

Warriors' Gate 66

Web Planet, The **19**

Webb, Kaye 17

Webb, Nick 64

Wey, Graeme 119

Wheel in Space, The **16, 116**

Whitaker, David **16-17,** 23-24, 64, **105,** 115, **118,** 148, 149, 151-153, **151**

Williams, Graham 51, 54, 58, 66, **89,** 115, **119, 121,** 139

Williams, Paul 66

Wilson, Donald **16,** 38

Witch Lords, The 50

Woolsey, Paula – *see* Moore, Paula

Wood, Graeme 54-55

Wood, John 23

Woolf, Gabriel **136**

Wyatt, Stephen 109, **112,** 119, 122

Wyman, Mark 91

Wyndham Publications Ltd 34

Yellow Fever and How to Cure It 115

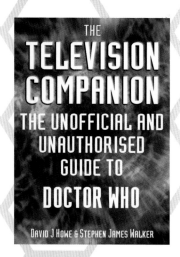

THE TELEVISION COMPANION: THE UNOFFICIAL AND UNAUTHORISED GUIDE TO DOCTOR WHO by DAVID J HOWE & STEPHEN JAMES WALKER
Complete episode guide (1963–1996) to the popular TV show.
£14.99 (+ £4.75 UK p&p) Standard p/b
ISBN: 1-903889-51-0

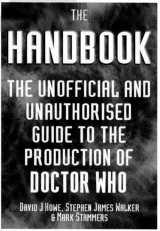

THE HANDBOOK: THE UNOFFICIAL AND UNAUTHORISED GUIDE TO THE PRODUCTION OF DOCTOR WHO by DAVID J HOWE, STEPHEN JAMES WALKER and MARK STAMMERS
Complete guide to the making of *Doctor Who* (1963 – 1996).
£14.99 (+ £4.75 UK p&p) Standard p/b
ISBN: 1-903889-59-6
£30.00 (+ £4.75 UK p&p) Deluxe h/b
ISBN: 1-903889-96-0

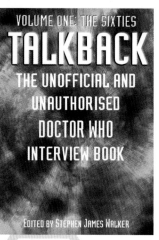

TALKBACK: THE UNOFFICIAL AND UNAUTHORISED DOCTOR WHO INTERVIEW BOOK: VOLUME 1: THE SIXTIES edited by STEPHEN JAMES WALKER
Interviews with cast and behind the scenes crew who worked on *Doctor Who* in the sixties.
£12.99 (+ £2.50 UK p&p) Standard p/b
ISBN: 1-84583-006-7
£30.00 (+ £2.50 UK p&p) Deluxe h/b
ISBN: 1-84583-007-5

TALKBACK: THE UNOFFICIAL AND UNAUTHORISED DOCTOR WHO INTERVIEW BOOK: VOLUME 2: THE SEVENTIES edited by STEPHEN JAMES WALKER
Interviews with cast and behind the scenes crew who worked on *Doctor Who* in the seventies.
£12.99 (+ £2.50 UK p&p) Standard p/b
ISBN: 1-84583-010-5
£30.00 (+ £2.50 UK p&p) Deluxe h/b
ISBN: 1-84583-011-3

All Telos Publishing's acclaimed film and television guides can be ordered online by credit card or Paypal.
Visit **www.telos.co.uk** for full details.

TALKBACK: THE UNOFFICIAL AND UNAUTHORISED DOCTOR WHO INTERVIEW BOOK: VOLUME 3: THE EIGHTIES edited by STEPHEN JAMES WALKER
Interviews with cast and behind the scenes crew who worked on *Doctor Who* in the eighties.
£12.99 (+ £2.50 UK p&p) Standard p/b
ISBN: 978-1-84583-014-4
£30.00 (+ £2.50 UK p&p) Deluxe h/b
ISBN: 978-1-84583-015-1

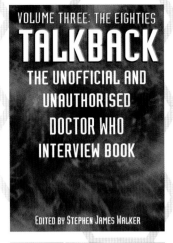

BACK TO THE VORTEX: THE UNOFFICIAL AND UNAUTHORISED GUIDE TO DOCTOR WHO 2005 by J SHAUN LYON
Complete guide to the 2005 series of *Doctor Who* starring Christopher Eccleston as the Doctor.
£12.99 (+ £2.50 UK p&p) Standard p/b
ISBN: 1-903889-78-2
£30.00 (+ £2.50 UK p&p) Deluxe h/b
ISBN: 1-903889-79-0

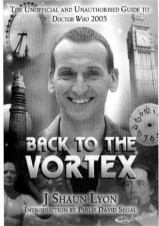

SECOND FLIGHT: THE UNOFFICIAL AND UNAUTHORISED GUIDE TO DOCTOR WHO 2006 by J SHAUN LYON
Complete guide to the 2006 series of *Doctor Who* starring David Tennant as the Doctor.
£12.99 (+ £2.50 UK p&p) Standard p/b
ISBN: 1-84583-008-3
£30.00 (+ £2.50 UK p&p) Deluxe h/b
ISBN: 1-84583-009-1

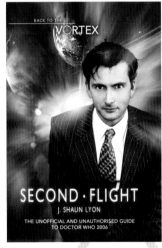

THIRD DIMENSION: THE UNOFFICIAL AND UNAUTHORISED GUIDE TO DOCTOR WHO 2007 by STEPHEN JAMES WALKER
Complete guide to the 2007 series of *Doctor Who* starring David Tennant as the Doctor.
£12.99 (+ £2.50 UK p&p) Standard p/b
ISBN: 978-1-84583-016-8
£30.00 (+ £2.50 UK p&p) Deluxe h/b
ISBN: 978-1-84583-017-5

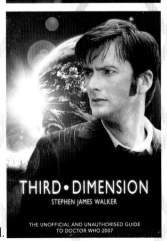

All Telos Publishing's acclaimed film and television guides can be ordered online by credit card or Paypal. Visit **www.telos.co.uk** for full details.

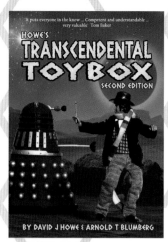

HOWE'S TRANSCENDENTAL TOYBOX: SECOND
EDITION by DAVID J HOWE & ARNOLD T BLUMBERG
Complete guide to *Doctor Who* Merchandise 1963-2002.
£25.00 (+ £4.75 UK p&p) Standard p/b
ISBN: 1-903889-56-1

HOWE'S TRANSCENDENTAL TOYBOX: UPDATE NO. 1:
2003 by DAVID J HOWE & ARNOLD T BLUMBERG
Complete guide to *Doctor Who* Merchandise released in
2003.
£7.99 (+ £1.50 UK p&p) Standard p/b
ISBN: 1-903889-57-X

HOWE'S TRANSCENDENTAL TOYBOX: UPDATE NO. 2:
2004-2005 by DAVID J HOWE & ARNOLD T BLUMBERG
Complete guide to *Doctor Who* Merchandise released in
2004 and 2005.
£7.99 (+ £1.50 UK p&p) Standard p/b
ISBN: 1-84583-012-1

INSIDE THE HUB: THE UNOFFICIAL AND
UNAUTHORISED GUIDE TO TORCHWOOD by
STEPHEN JAMES WALKER
Complete guide to the 2006 series of *Torchwood*, starring
John Barrowman as Captain Jack Harkness.
£12.99 (+ £2.50 UK p&p) Standard p/b
ISBN: 978-1-84583-013-7
£25.00 (+ £2.50 p&p) Deluxe hardback
ISBN: 978-1-84583-022-9

All Telos Publishing's acclaimed film and television guides can be ordered online by credit card or Paypal.
Visit **www.telos.co.uk** for full details.

BEYOND THE GATE: THE UNOFFICIAL AND
UNAUTHORISED GUIDE TO STARGATE SG1:
VOLUME 1 by KEITH TOPPING
Complete episode guide to the first five seasons of the
popular TV show.
£9.99 (+ £2.50 p&p) Standard p/b
ISBN: 1-903889-50-2

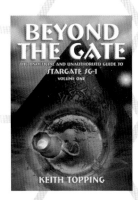

A DAY IN THE LIFE: THE UNOFFICIAL AND
UNAUTHORISED GUIDE TO 24 by KEITH TOPPING
Complete episode guide to the first season of the popular TV
show.
£9.99 (+ £2.50 p&p) Standard p/b
ISBN: 1-903889-53-7

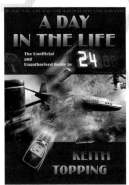

LIBERATION: THE UNOFFICIAL AND UNAUTHORISED
GUIDE TO BLAKE'S 7 by ALAN STEVENS & FIONA
MOORE
Complete episode guide to the popular TV show.
Featuring a foreword by David Maloney
£12.99 (+ £2.50 UK p&p) Standard p/b
ISBN: 1-903889-54-5

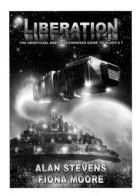

TRIQUETRA: THE UNOFFICIAL AND UNAUTHORISED
GUIDE TO CHARMED by KEITH TOPPING
Complete guide to *Charmed*.
£12.99 (+ £2.50 UK p&p) Standard p/b
ISBN: 1-84583-002-4

THE END OF THE WORLD?: THE UNOFFICIAL AND
UNAUTHORISED GUIDE TO SURVIVORS by ANDY
PRIESTNER & RICH CROSS
Complete guide to Terry Nation's *Survivors*.
£12.99 (+ £2.50 UK p&p) Standard p/b
ISBN: 1-84583-001-6

All Telos Publishing's acclaimed film and television guides can be ordered online by credit card or Paypal.
Visit **www.telos.co.uk** for full details.

FALL OUT: THE UNOFFICIAL AND UNAUTHORISED
GUIDE TO THE PRISONER by ALAN STEVENS & FIONA
MOORE
Complete guide to *The Prisoner*.
Featuring a foreword by Ian Rakoff.
£12.99 (+ £2.50 p&p) Standard paperback
ISBN: 978-1-84583-018-2
£30.00 (+ £2.50 p&p) Deluxe hardback
ISBN: 978-1-84583-019-9

A VAULT OF HORROR by KEITH TOPPING
A guide to 80 classic (and not so classic) British Horror
Films.
£12.99 (+ £4.75 UK p&p) Standard p/b
ISBN: 1-903889-58-8

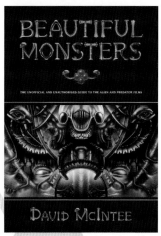

BEAUTIFUL MONSTERS: THE UNOFFICIAL AND
UNAUTHORISED GUIDE TO THE ALIEN AND
PREDATOR FILMS by DAVID McINTEE
A guide to the *Alien* and *Predator* films.
£9.99 (+ £2.50 UK p&p) Standard p/b
ISBN: 1-903889-94-4

ZOMBIEMANIA: 80 MOVIES TO DIE FOR by DR
ARNOLD T BLUMBERG & ANDREW HERSHBERGER
A guide to 80 classic zombie films, along with an extensive
filmography of over 550 additional titles.
£12.99 (+ £2.50 UK p&p) Standard p/b
ISBN: 1-84583-003-2

All Telos Publishing's acclaimed film and television guides can be ordered online by credit card or Paypal.
Visit **www.telos.co.uk** for full details.

BBC AUDIO

INTRODUCING...

EXCITING AUDIO VERSIONS OF CLASSIC DOCTOR WHO BOOKS
– COMPLETE AND UNABRIDGED ON CD AND DOWNLOAD

WITH MUSIC AND SOUND EFFECTS!

DOCTOR WHO AND THE CAVE MONSTERS

DOCTOR WHO AND THE DOOMSDAY WEAPON

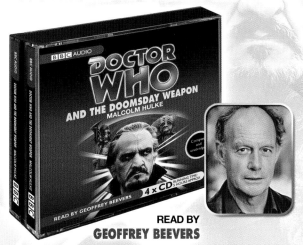

**READ BY
GEOFFREY BEEVERS**

**READ BY
CAROLINE JOHN**

DOCTOR WHO AND THE DINOSAUR INVASION

DOCTOR WHO AND THE GIANT ROBOT

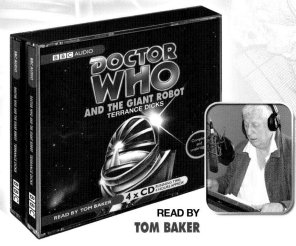

**READ BY
TOM BAKER**

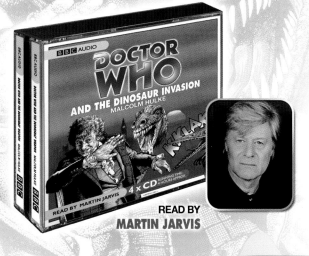

**READ BY
MARTIN JARVIS**

ALL DETAILS CORRECT AT TIME OF GOING TO PRESS, CHANGES MAY OCCUR

Available at bbcshop.com and all other good high street, online and download audio retailers

AVAILABLE FEBRUARY 08

**DOCTOR WHO
AND THE SPACE WAR**
READ BY GEOFFREY BEEVERS

**DOCTOR WHO
AND THE BRAIN OF MORBIUS**
READ BY TOM BAKER

...others in preparation

If you enjoyed this book and would like to have information sent you about other TELOS titles, write to the address below enclosing an A5-sized stamped, self addressed envelope (if you are outside the UK, then please include two IRCs with your request).

You will also receive:
A FREE TELOS BADGE!
Based on the cover of this book, this attractive colour badge, pinned to your blazer lapel, or jumper, will excite the interest and comment of all your friends!

SEVEN TO COLLECT!

Please specify which actor you would like, Hartnell, Troughton, Pertwee, Tom Baker, Davison, Colin Baker or McCoy.

Write to: TELOS PUBLISHING
61 Elgar Avenue
Tolworth
Surrey KT5 9JP
ENGLAND